Promises Made to the Fathers

PUBLICATIONS IN MORMON STUDIES • VOLUME FIVE

PROMISES MADE TO THE FATHERS
Mormon Covenant Organization

Rex Eugene Cooper

University of Utah Press
Salt Lake City
1990

Publications in Mormon Studies
Linda King Newell, editor

The series, Publications in Mormon Studies, was established to encourage
the creation and submission of work on Mormon-related topics that would
be of interest to scholars and to the general public. The initiation of the
series represents an acknowledgment by the press and the editor of the
region's rich historical and literary heritage and recognizes the quality of
work being done in various areas of Mormon studies today.

ISSN 0893-4916

Library of Congress Cataloging-in-Publication Data

Cooper, Rex Eugene, 1945-
    Promises made to the fathers : Mormon covenant organization
/ by Rex Eugene Cooper.
    p. cm. — (Publications in Mormon studies : v. 5)
    Includes index.
    Bibliography: p.
    ISBN 0-87480-324-1
    1. Church of Jesus Christ of Latter-Day Saints—Membership.
2. Mormon Church—Membership. 3. Church of Jesus Christ of
Latter-Day Saints—Government. 4. Mormon Church—Government.
5. Covenants (Theology) 6. Patriarchs (Mormon theology) I.
Title. II. Series.
BX8635.2.C66   1989   89-4827
262'.093—dc20   CIP

Contents

List of Abbreviations

BM	Book of Mormon	
	T Pg.	Title page
	1 Ne.	First Nephi
	2 Ne.	Second Nephi
	Jac.	Jacob
	Enos	
	Jarom	
	Omni	
	W of M	Words of Mormon
	Mosiah	
	Alma	
	Hel.	Helaman
	3 Ne.	Third Nephi
	4 Ne.	Fourth Nephi
	Morm.	Mormon
	Moro.	Moroni
D&C	Doctrine and Covenants	
EJ	*Elders' Journal*	
EMS	*Evening and Morning Star*	
HC	*History of the Church of Jesus Christ of Latter-day Saints*	
JH	"Journal History of the Church"	
JD	*Journal of Discourses*	
MA	*Latter Day Saints' Messenger and Advocate*	
MS	*Latter-day Saints' Millennial Star*	
PGP	Pearl of Great Price	
	Moses	
	Abr.	Abraham
	JS—H	Joseph Smith—History
	A of F	Articles of Faith
TS	*Times and Seasons*	
WA	[Westminster Assembly of Divines], *The Confession of Faith*	
WE	*Women's Exponent*	

Preface

Group cohesiveness has long been regarded as one of Mormonism's most notable features. In the following pages, I examine this issue from a different perspective than that of previous treatments. I argue that Mormon identity and solidarity grow from Mormon covenant organization, which integrates a complex of beliefs and practices. I illuminate the Mormon system by comparing it with the similar covenant organization of New England Puritanism.

Although the book deals with historical issues, it is not a conventional history. It first identifies the basic features shared by Mormon and Puritan covenant organization, presents a general overview of Puritan covenant organization and its consequences for social cohesion in seventeenth-century New England, then analyzes Mormon covenant organization in detail. I treat Mormon covenant organization as an adaptive system of beliefs and practices which simultaneously provides a basis for Mormon group identity and solidarity, a framework by which the Mormon group conceptualizes its relationship to larger society, and a mechanism which facilitates the continuity of Mormonism.

I have divided Mormonism into a number of historical periods, briefly described the historical circumstances of each period, and then analyzed how covenant organization contributes to Mormon group cohesion within that specific context. Juxtaposing the various periods clarifies how Mormonism has adapted to changing circumstances.

My academic training is in sociocultural anthropology with particular emphasis in British social anthropology. I have, however, preferred an eclectic approach to analyze Mormon covenant organization rather than using Mormonism to demonstrate a particular social model or theory. I introduce several anthropological and sociological concepts in detail, not assuming that the reader has a background in anthropology or sociology.

I appreciate the efforts of several people in the development of this book. Merlin G. Myers, professor of anthropology at Brigham Young University, introduced me to the fascinations of anthropology. George W. Stocking, Raymond T. Smith, and Bernard S. Cohn, of the University of Chicago, supervised the dissertation upon which it is based. The stimulating conversations that I have had over the years with my good friends and fellow anthropologists John Hawkins, Steven Olsen, and David Beer have clarified the applications of anthropology to Mormon group development. The staff of the historical library of the Church of Jesus Christ of Latter-day Saints (Salt Lake City, Utah) helped me locate many of the primary documents cited in the text. The Mormon History Association gave my dissertation the 1986 Reese History Award, giving me the courage to begin the rewriting process. David Catron, director of the University of Utah Press, has been extremely helpful as I have attempted to prepare the work for publication.

While I have benefited from the help of others, I take responsibility for the book's limitations and conclusions. I regard those conclusions as logical outcomes of my analysis of the data; but they are not necessarily the same conclusions I would draw if I used my own religious framework as an active participant in the Mormon Church. What I say in this book should in no way be understood as representing the position of the Church of Jesus Christ of Latter-day Saints or any of its agencies.

Behold, I will reveal unto you the Priesthood, by the hand of Elijah the prophet, before the coming of the great and dreadful day of the Lord.

And he shall plant in the hearts of the children the promises made to the fathers, and the hearts of the children shall turn to their fathers.

If it were not so, the whole earth would be utterly wasted at his coming.

—Doctrine and Covenants 2:1-3

1

Introduction

I . . . would perhaps begin a look at Mormonism . . . with
the example of Puritan New England in mind.
Robert N. Bellah (1978:3)

The year 1844 began bleakly for the Mormons of Nauvoo, Illinois. According to the official history of the church, "A cold blustering rainstorm ushered in the new year" (*HC* 6:155). Chilling turmoil
was also sweeping through their thriving community. Blustering
around them were forces almost identical to those which, six years
before, had climaxed in the governor of Missouri's ordering them
to be expelled from the state or "exterminated." And even while the
Mormons saw themselves as pitted against a hostile world, they were
racked by internal dissension which threatened to divide and weaken
the church through schism and apostasy.

Three weeks later, on Sunday, January 21, thirty-eight-year-old
Joseph Smith, the movement's prophet-founder, "preached at the
southeast corner of the temple to several thousand people, although
the weather was somewhat unpleasant. My subject was the sealing
of the hearts of the fathers to the children and the hearts of the children to the fathers" (*HC* 6:183). As he spoke, his followers huddled
before him, wrapped in blankets. Behind him rose the walls of the
partially completed temple. Almost exactly three years earlier, he had
pronounced the revelation which commanded the building of the
temple. The revelation had contained an ominous contingency: "I
grant unto you a sufficient time to build a house unto me; . . . and
if you do not these things at the end of the appointment ye shall be
rejected as a church, with your dead, saith the Lord your God" (D&C
124:31-32).

Now in the early weeks of 1844, the time did not seem "sufficient." Joseph talked urgently, stressing that both the continued existence of the church and their individual salvation depended on

finishing the temple. There they must perform sealing ordinances that would establish eternal ties between children and parents, thus assuring their mutual salvation:

> . . . I would to God that this temple was now done, that we might go into it, and go to work to improve our time, and make use of the seals while they are on earth.
>
> The Saints have not too much time to save and redeem their dead, and gather together their living relatives that they may be saved also, before the earth will be smitten.
>
> . . . My only trouble at the present time is . . . that the Saints *will be divided, broken up, and scattered* before we get our salvation secure. (*HC* 6:184)

It's a strange scene: a religious group perceives imminent persecution, mobbings, and potential annihilation. In the dead of winter, they gather in a large outdoor assembly before a partially completed temple where their leader tells them that their salvation depends on completing the temple so that they can perform certain rituals for themselves and their deceased ancestors. Surely they should be concerned about fortification or flight instead?

However, the threat of the situation underscores as nothing else could the importance of these rituals. They are central to the beliefs and practices which shape Mormon group identity and solidarity. The substances of this particular sermon had become a favorite theme of Joseph Smith's during the winter of 1843-44; and its purpose was to enhance group cohesion—an important attempt given the situation then confronting the Mormons of Nauvoo.

Competent observers have long noted the Mormons' unusually high degree of group identity and solidarity. Sociologist Talcott Parsons (1961:250), for example, in describing a religious sect, characterizes it as committed "to make its religion the unequivocally dominant consideration in its members' lives" and cites as examples "the Anabaptists in the Reformation period in Europe, and the Mormons in nineteenth-century America." Writing fifty-eight years earlier, economist Richard Ely (1903:667) observed: "We find in Mormonism, to a larger degree than I have ever seen in any other body of people, an illustration of the individual who is willing to sacrifice himself to the whole." Two decades later, sociologists Robert Park and Ernest Burgess (1924:872-73) suggested that Mormonism had developed from a sect to a near "nationality." During the early 1950s, participants in the Harvard "Comparative Study of Values in Five Cultures Project" were struck by the contrast between Mormon cooperation and Texan individualism among two groups living near each other in northern New Mexico (Bellah 1978:8-11; C. Kluckhohn 1956; 1961; F. Kluckhohn and Strodtbeck 1961:259-83; Vogt and Albert 1966; Vogt and O'Dea 1953). Sociologist of Religion A. Leland Jamison (1961:212) has stated: "One may reasonably maintain that no other sizable religious group in this country, not even Roman Catholicism or Orthodox Judaism, has so effectively blended religious and secular elements of life into a coherent ethos." Martin Marty (1970:124), a historian of religions, has suggested that the Mormon church has perpetuated an "imperial idea" among its membership. And Thomas O'Dea (1954:292-93; 1957:115-16; 1966a:xii-iv; 1966b:70; 1968:133; 1972:140-42), who subjected Mormonism to more careful sociological analysis than perhaps any other single individual, concluded that the LDS people might best be characterized as a quasi-ethnic group with a religious organization at its core.

Much of that social cohesion can be best explained by a complex of beliefs and practices that Joseph Smith preached about in his January 1844 sermon—a system I call Mormon covenant organization. This book will examine Mormon covenant organization and investigate its impact on Mormon group identity and solidarity.

My analysis will begin not with the founding of Nauvoo in 1839 nor with the organization of the church in 1830, but rather with the development of Puritanism, a most illuminating parallel group for comparison. The Puritans had earlier developed a covenant organization resembling that of the Mormons in many important respects.

Although Mormonism clearly emerged within a post-Puritan milieu, my purpose is not to establish any direct historical influences of Puritanism on Mormonism. Instead, I will use the approach of British social anthropology, which deals more in analogy than in genealogy.

British social anthropology developed as a way to study social structure and process without being locked into theories of cultural and social evolution.[1] These anthropologists reason that beliefs and practices must be analyzed within their specific social contexts; if social conditions change, so will beliefs and practices, even though radical

---

[1] For an overview of the development, scope, and methods of social anthropology, see Beattie 1964:3-90; Burrow 1970; Evans-Pritchard 1962: 1-191; Firth 1961; Fortes 1969; 1970:127-46, 160-78; Kuper 1983; Leach 1971:1-27; Lienhardt 1964; Mair 1965:1-47; Malinowski 1944; Nadel 1951; Radcliffe-Brown 1965: 1-15, 178-204; Stocking 1984; 1986; 1987.

discontinuity is not likely. Furthermore, they permit the possibility that similar beliefs and practices may emerge independently in different geographic locations or in the same location at different times. In short, they teach a healthy wariness about assuming influence in the presence of similarity.

British social anthropology makes creative use of comparative analysis—again, more to understand the underlying structures and processes of social and cultural phenomena than to demonstrate historical connection. Many would agree with Raymond Grew's (1980:769) statement that ''only comparison establishes that there is something to be explained.''

And finally British social anthropologists attempt to adhere to the concept of cultural relativism. This does not mean that they lack individual values. They take the position, however, that (as far as is humanly possible) social and cultural systems should be analyzed and described in terms of their own internal logic independent of the observer's personal values and beliefs. I have strong opinions and beliefs about many of the issues that I discuss in the following pages. I have made a consistent effort, however, not to be influenced by those opinions and beliefs in the selection, analysis, and presentation of material. I will thus be speaking essentially in a neutral voice.

ENGLISH PRELUDE

Our analysis of American Puritanism must begin even a step earlier by understanding English Puritanism and some of its most important features.

Puritanism is the child of the English Reformation. Unlike Protestantism on the Continent, Anglican Protestantism from its inception was directed by royal decrees and state policy. When the 1534 Act of Supremacy established Henry VIII as ''the only supreme head on earth of the Church of England,'' no significant popular movement in his realm called for religious reform. Henry VIII's struggle with Rome stemmed from no doctrinal disputes but rather represented a contest between church and state in regulating England's internal affairs. The Act of Supremacy clearly subordinated church to state; ironically, Henry thus became head of a church for whose doctrine and organization he had no clear agenda.

In subsequent years, the Church of England was molded and reshaped by vacillations in the governmental policies which regulated it. During Henry's reign, the church remained essentially Catholic in doctrine and practice though ecclesiastically and politically separate from Rome. Henry's son, Edward VI, moved it in the direction of Continental Protestantism. Daughter Mary reincorporated it into the Roman Catholic church. Daughter Elizabeth again disassociated it from Rome. These "generations" of change all occurred between the Act of Supremacy in 1534 and Elizabeth's ascension in 1558—twenty-four years.

The clearest concept during these years of turmoil was that the church was a creature of the state. The state directed and regulated its organization, doctrine, and practice. The crown appointed its bishops and other ecclesiastical leaders. Acts of Uniformity dictated that all public worship adhere to the Parliament-approved Book of Common Prayer. Citizens were required by law to attend church services. Nonconformists were subject to various legal penalties.

Elizabeth's religious policies over her long reign were basically pragmatic attempts to achieve religious consensus through compromise, defusing the divisions and hostilities between Catholic and Calvinist extremes by finding a middle course in worship and doctrine.

Historically, English Puritanism was a by-product of Elizabeth's pragmatic policy, though it was never a unified movement. *Puritan* became the name for those who felt that the church was inadequately reformed; and while most prominent Puritan leaders regarded themselves as Calvinists, their single shared perspective was that the Church of England was not a completely adequate expression of organized Christianity. Disagreements within the movement centered on how to bring about the desired purification and what, exactly, the nature of that purity would be.

A useful way to understand the relationship of English Puritanism to its larger society is through the paired concepts of centrality and distinctiveness—both important elements in my analysis of New England Puritanism and Mormonism as well.

CENTER AND PERIPHERY

American sociologist Edward Shils (1975) characterizes the basic aspects of social cohesion with a model of interaction between a society's center and periphery. *Center* refers to a society's central values, its most prominent institutional arrangements, and the elite personnel who occupy its key institutional roles and most clearly espouse its central values. Others become attached to the center by espousing the central values, identifying with the elite personnel, and becoming involved in its centralizing institutional structure. The more they do, the more cohesive the society is. The stronger his or her attachment to the center, the closer an individual is to that center; the weaker the attachment, the closer he or she is to its periphery.

Members of peripheral groups, in contrast, have weak attachments to the center because of their involvement in their own groups. The most cohesive of these groups have their own well-developed centers, complete with distinctive values, unique elite personnel, and particularistic institutions.

It is possible for individuals in such groups to have dual attachments: in some aspects of their lives, they may strongly identify with the localized center but identify in other aspects with their larger societal center. Over time the relative intensity of their dual identifications may change. Furthermore, various political and economic pressures from the larger society may affect the subgroup's internal dynamics (Bronfenbrenner 1979:3-105; Scott 1981:109-11; Wolf 1959).

If the peripheral group is to survive, it must often make pragmatic adjustments to the central values, personnel, and institutions of the larger society.[2] There is no way *a priori* to determine what those adjustments will be nor their consequences for the group. The group may become more integrated into the larger society, or it may remove itself still farther from the center.

Puritanism as Periphery

Many of the Puritan sects and religious groups that emerged during the sixteenth and early seventeenth centuries were such peripheral groups involved in this condition of dynamic flux. The larger society had no clear consensus about what the central religious values should

---

[2] I have adopted the term "pragmatic adjustments" from linguistics, where pragmatic categories (as opposed to grammatical categories) are those which are context specific. They include such things as person, place, and tense. Without them, there could be no way to relate the speech act to concrete reality. As a component of social action, a pragmatic mechanism is a way to relate a cultural paradigm to a concrete social context. Like pragmatic categories, these pragmatic mechanisms must change as social situations are modified in order for the paradigm to continue to inform social action.

be or what institutional form the church should have. Both values and institutional arrangements were imposed by elite individuals who occupied central positions within the political system. Naturally, those who agreed with the elites' values, beliefs, and institutional arrangements established attachments to this elite. Those who did not were pushed to a peripheral position within the social-political order.

During Elizabeth's reign, most Puritans were neither completely central nor completely peripheral. While the religious situation was not wholly to their liking, Puritans had some voice in government, sat in Parliament, and were included among Elizabeth's advisors. Furthermore, because official church doctrine was vague and its policies loosely enforced, it was fairly easy for men and women of conscience to remain nominally Anglican while espousing Puritan views. Consequently, most Puritans could be fully participating members of the English societal order, anticipating a time of greater political power in which to work out their own religious agenda. As a result, only a small number of groups attempted to establish peripheral religious systems independent of the state church.

The same condition, to a lesser extent, characterized the reign of Elizabeth's successor, James I. However, after James's son, Charles I, came to the throne in 1625, the situation changed significantly. Charles and his archbishop, William Laud, attempted to impose more religious conformity on the English populace than their predecessors had, enunciating policies that were fundamentally inconsistent with the values of most Puritans. Charles simultaneously attempted to rule without Parliament, thus denying the whole people, including the large Puritan minority, any effective voice in establishing state policy. The result was a lack of social cohesion, a proliferation of religious sects, and finally civil war and regicide.

Prior to the outbreak of that war in 1642, a sizable number of Puritans migrated to New England and there established a social order like the one they would have attempted to institute in England if they had been able to achieve political control. The result was a remarkably cohesive society centered on localized values, elite individuals, and institutions (Breen and Foster 1977; Gura 1984:11-15, 156-57; Rutman 1970:88; Ziff 1973:155-56).

This system, dominant within New England, operated for a number of years nearly autonomous of the larger English social system, but it gradually became politically and religiously less peripheral as the seventeenth century drew to a close (Ziff 1973:183-313). Simultaneously, other changes reoriented its members increasingly away from England and toward their local center until what finally emerged was essentially a new society whose members no longer defined themselves as part of the original English social order (Ziff 1973:99). This new society, in time, would contribute significantly to the American independence movement and to a subsequent new social order.

Mormons as Peripherals

Two hundred years after the Puritan migration to New England, a somewhat analogous situation was to occur. Amid the social and religious flux of the Second Great Awakening, the Mormon church would emerge as a cohesive group centered on distinctive values, institutions, and individuals. In important respects it was peripheral to the larger American society. In the isolation of the Great Basin, like New England Puritanism, it achieved a degree of autonomy.

It also continued to adapt socially and politically to the larger society. Partly as a result of these pressures, it underwent various internal modifications in practice and policy, becoming less peripheral in important aspects of its values and institutional structure. Despite this increasing orientation toward the general American societal center, it has preserved a strong localized center, still characterized by unique beliefs, an identifiable elite, its particularistic values, and distinctive institutional arrangements. Professional investigators are increasingly referring to it as a ''new religion'' (e.g., Shipps 1985). Its adherents in the United States are certainly American in their economic and political orientation; but at the same time, they remain Mormon. Part of their identity is seeing themselves as a unique people with a particularistic covenant relationship with God.

DISTINCTIVENESS, CHARISMA, AND RELIGIOUS SECTS

The clearest way to understand cohesion within peripheral groups is to understand their beliefs about their uniqueness and distinctiveness—what distinguishes them from individuals in the larger society. When this uniqueness involves spiritual ''specialness,'' special access to God, or a preferred status with God, the sociological label for such a group is a religious sect.

The Forms of Charisma

A useful sociological method for examining a group's sense of specialness is provided by the categories and processes Max Weber

(1864-1920) developed in his analysis of charisma. In adopting the term from Koine Greek (where it means "gift"), Weber had in mind its New Testament connotations (see Paul's discussion of the "gifts of the Spirit," 1 Cor. 12). In Weber's sociological model, charisma refers to an extraordinary power or quality, usually of divine origin or linked to the supernatural, that is understood to rest upon an individual, object, or institutional structure (1968:241, 1120, 1136, 1147).

Weber describes three types of religiously grounded charisma associated with individuals: personal, office, and hereditary. An individual with "personal charisma" is understood to possess unusual qualities by virtue of his or her personal or individual receptiveness to supernatural influence. "Office charisma" resides in the individual's position and is independent of his or her personal qualities or qualifications. "Hereditary charisma" results from the understanding that extraordinary and supernatural capabilities can be biologically transmitted (1968:241-54, 439-51, 1135-41, 1163-66).

Sectarian Solidarity

Weber regarded a sect as "a community of personally charismatic individuals" that derives identity and solidarity from its members' belief that they are personally endowed with supernatural power; this characteristic is a boundary, separating the charismatic group from the rest of humanity (Weber 1968:1164, 1204).

Contemporary sociologists agree that this sense of distinctiveness is basic to sectarian organization. Bryan Wilson (1959:4), for example, describes a sect's self-concept as that "of an elect, a gathered remnant, possessing special enlightenment."

When a well-developed sense of group distinctiveness based on shared charisma joins with members' strong attachment to the group's central values, elite personnel, and institutions, the result can be a very cohesive and inner-directed religious system. Participants' world views and their relationships to the larger society can be almost totally informed by the sect's central values, beliefs, and regulations.

The issue of religious distinctiveness lay at the center of the controversy between Puritans and Anglicans. In saying that the church was not sufficiently pure, Puritans were also saying that it was not sufficiently distinctive. Because the church nominally included the entire English population, no boundary separated the religiously qualified within the church from the disqualified without.

While early seventeenth-century English Puritanism united in opposing some features of the Anglican church, it generally remained
fragmented and disorganized. This lack of cohesion resulted in part
from the emphasis many Puritans placed on individual religious experience (Gura 1984). When a person feels in personal contact with
the divine, his or her interpretation of this experience may contradict
the established order and beliefs of the group. Thus, any religious
group that lets its members follow personal revelation can be in danger of fragmentation and institutional collapse. A religious system,
to survive through time, must develop mechanisms to contain its members' charisma (Weber 1968:1111-57).

A second source of instability in English Puritanism was the
peripheral status of its adherents within general English society. The
power to establish charisma-restraining structures above the congregational level resided in the state. In the early seventeenth century, Puritans did not have access to state power for religious ends. Instead,
English Puritanism was essentially a reactionary movement, consisting of a number of sectlike groupings whose members' main common ground was their rejection of the Church of England.

In seventeenth-century New England, in contrast, Puritanism
found a way to keep its emphasis on personal religion but to control
such charisma within distinctive authority structures. The "holy" colonies of Plymouth, Massachusetts, Connecticut, and New Haven each
had elites who built their religious beliefs and values into the key political institutions. Puritan beliefs became the central social values of
these colonies, ordering their political, religious, and domestic institutions. Many of these beliefs, values, and practices were associated
with the concept of covenant. Since basic to the Puritan covenant concept was the notion of voluntary engagement, it provided a mechanism for containing individualism within a social framework which
stressed voluntary conformity and subordination. The covenantal
ideology and the process of covenant making simultaneously linked
individuals to one another and oriented them to the colony's central
values, personnel, and institutions. This covenantal system allowed
personal religious expression but contained it in accordance with
prescribed rules and conventions.

A somewhat similar phenomenon would also occur in nineteenth-
century Mormonism. During the Second Great Awakening, religion
in America was generally fragmented and lacked a centralizing institutional focus; but the early Mormon church developed its social

structures through Joseph Smith's religious regulations. Converts who remained active participants either shared or adopted this religious orientation. It became central to Mormonism, embedded in its beliefs and practices. As in New England Puritanism, a significant complex of Mormon beliefs and practices centered on covenant making, forming an integrated system by which practicing Mormons related both to their fellow Saints and to their church's central values, personnel, and institutions. Furthermore, while Mormonism stressed the importance of personal religious experience, the mechanisms of the Mormon covenant order provided channels for containing and regulating this charisma.

COVENANT ORGANIZATION AS PARADIGM

Although my study will concentrate on the central values and beliefs of seventeenth-century New England Puritanism and nineteenth-century Mormonism, both societies experienced serious disagreements and conflicts. Darrett Rutman (1970; 1972), Philip Gura (1984) and Larzer Ziff (1973) have amply demonstrated the pluralism of Puritan New England, while Mormonism during its formative years was replete with dissension and schisms. Many of the disruptions in both systems resulted when personal charisma broke out of the containing forms.

A society's central value and belief system is not central because it is universally understood and accepted but because it is espoused by that society's elite, because it informs the society's key institutions, and because a sizable proportion of the people accept or at least acquiesce to it. In both early seventeenth-century Puritan New England and nineteenth-century Mormonism, covenant organization was such a system—basic to social cohesion of both groups.

American anthropologist David Schneider, whose landmark study (1968) of American kinship is a model of intricate cultural analysis, makes a useful analytical distinction between norms (patterns or rules for action) and culture (the system of symbols and meanings by which a group defines reality, itself, and the universe). Culture provides a way of relating norms for many aspects of the society to each other and providing continuity over time through a framework of shared understandings (D. Schneider 1976:198-205).

Puritan and Mormon covenant organizations provided a matrix of culture to integrate disparate rules, conventions, and understandings on religious salvation, family life, and political control. As changes occurred in the rules and understandings associated with both Puritan and Mormon covenant organization, the covenant system itself accommodated them in continuity.

Underlying the varying manifestations of these covenant organizations is a "paradigm," which British social anthropologist Victor Turner defines as a set "of 'rules' from which many kinds of sequences of social action may be generated but which further specify what sequences must be excluded" (1974:17; see also Levi-Strauss 1960: 50-54). In this book, I analyze sequences of social action that may be performed according to the Mormon covenantal paradigm and how Mormons pragmatically adjusted these sequences to various historical contexts. I use the Puritan covenant paradigm primarily for comparative purposes, and it receives less attention as the book progresses.

In chapter 2, I will summarize five basic aspects of the seventeenth-century New England Puritan covenant organization: (1) its mythological underpinnings; (2) the bases of covenantal relationships; (3) the ordering of covenantal relationships; (4) the pattern of subsumption by which one covenantal subsystem is incorporated into a more embracing subsystem; and (5) the distribution of power by which covenantal relationships are established and regulated. I will focus on conditions within Massachusetts Bay Colony for the sake of simplicity; the variations that occurred in the other three colonies are not significant for my purposes.

In chapter 3, I will briefly discuss the social milieu in which Mormonism emerged and its possible consequences on the formation of Mormon covenant organization. The remaining chapters will analyze the nature and development of nineteenth-century Mormon covenant organization, using the same five aspects employed in the Puritan system, with some observations about twentieth-century developments. Chapter 4 will discuss the development of Mormon covenant organization prior to the 1838-39 expulsion from Missouri. Chapter 5 will present an overview of the system of covenant organization that emerged during the Nauvoo period and has continued to develop thereafter. I call this system the patriarchal order to distinguish it from the earlier Mormon covenant system. This chapter, essentially ahistorical, examines the patriarchal order as an integrated system. Chapters 6 through 7 will be concerned with the historical development of the patriarchal order from the early 1840s to the present.

Although such an investigation is exploratory, I feel that it provides useful insights into Mormon group cohesion and supplies a new way to view structural similarities between Mormonism and New England Puritanism.

2

The Holy Commonwealth:
The Covenant System
of New England Puritanism

The Believing Gentiles are now the Children of God, the Surrogate Israel.   Cotton Mather (1705:22)

And it came to pass that I beheld the Spirit of God, that it wrought upon other Gentiles; and they went forth out of captivity, upon the many waters . . . , and they did prosper and obtain the land for their inheritance.
                        Book of Mormon, 1 Nephi 13:13, 15

Confronted with Charles I's religious policies, some Puritans in the mid-1620s began seriously considering the possibility of establishing a Puritan colony in British North America. They had as a model Plymouth Plantation on Cape Cod Bay, settled by a small group of Separatists in 1620.

In 1629 a group of prominent Puritans applied for and received a royal charter to organize a trading company for the development of the Massachusetts Bay area. The powers granted to the Massachusetts Bay Company, as it became known, were not unusual: the crown granted broad powers to colonize, govern, and economically develop the region from three miles south of the Charles River to three miles north of the Merrimack River. Unlike the charters of other companies, however, this one failed to specify the city in which the company was to hold its meetings, probably assuming that company headquarters would be in an English city.

The members of the company, however, took advantage of this oversight to choose the colony as the meeting place. Thus, they could avoid the direct surveillance of the king and his ministers and use the broad provisions of the charter to establish a societal order according to their principles.

They faced, of course, the risk that the crown would simply revoke the charter and impose another form of government on the colony; but until the charter was revoked in 1684 as a consequence of Massachusett's unwillingness to comply with royal decrees and regulations, the Puritans essentially had a free hand in regulating the internal affairs of Massachusetts Bay Colony (Johnson 1981:3-70; Morgan 1958:18-53).

Two related ideas guided the establishment and organization of the colony. First, those who conformed their lives to the will of God would there find refuge while the judgments of God were poured out upon the wicked of England (Bercovitch 1975:50-53; 1978:38-40, 86-88; Gura 1984:13, 126-53; Maclear 1975; Toon 1970). As John Winthrop (1588-1649) explained his reasons for migrating to Massachusetts: "All other Churches of Europe are brought to desolation . . . and it cannot be, but the like Judgment is comminge upon us: And who knows, but that God hath provided this place, to be a refuge for manye, whom he meanes to save out of the general destruction" (in Morgan 1958:40). Second, it was to be a model society, organized and managed according to divine principles (Gura 1984:189-90). Thus, Winthrop (1964:203-4) explained to his fellow passengers en route to Massachusetts Bay:

Wee must Consider that wee shall be as a Citty upon a Hill, the eies of all people are uppon us; soe that if wee shall deale falsely with our god in this worke wee have undertaken and soe cause him to withdrawe his present help from us, wee shall be made a story and a by-word through the world. . . . We are Commaunded this day to love the Lord our God, and to love one another to walke in his wayes and to keepe his Commaundements and his Ordinance, and his lawes, and the Articles of our Covenant with him that wee may live and be multiplyed, and that the Lord our God may blesse us in the land whether we goe to possesse it.

INTELLECTUAL FOUNDATIONS OF THE COVENANT SYSTEM

John Winthrop and his fellows who were most influential in establishing and governing Massachusetts Bay Colony during its formative years shared similar beliefs and values about religion and social order. Such beliefs became the central belief and value system of the fledgling colony; and the developing familial, religious, and political institutional arrangements reflected them. As Perry Miller (1961 esp. 374) has convincingly demonstrated, these beliefs and values were grounded in three intellectual concepts: federal theology, Ramist logic, and congregationalism.

Federal Theology

Federal (from the Latin *foeder*, meaning compact or covenant) was an attempt to address Arminian and Antinomian challenges to orthodox Calvinism (Bercovitch 1975:25-26; W. A. Brown 1914; Gura 1984:49-92; P. Miller 1961:365-97; 1964:48-98; Rutman 1970:15-16; Ziff 1973:49-67). At issue was the old question of faith vs. works— the relationship between divine and human endeavor in salvation. John Calvin's (1509-64) theology insisted on the sovereignty of God. The Calvinist God was an all-powerful and absolute monarch who saved or damned his subjects according to his arbitrary will. Human beings lacked not only the ability but also the will to do good (Calvin 1957; Orr 1913).

From the perspective of Orthodox Calvinism, Arminianism overvalued the religious significance of human behavior while radical Antinomians undervalued it. Taking their name from Dutch theologian Jacobus Arminius (1560-1609), Arminians held that individuals can both act independently of God and also initiate behavior that can affect their salvation (Platt 1913). Radical Antinomians, on the other hand, agreed with Calvinists that salvation is not a consequence of human endeavor. They took the implications of this concept, however, much further. Unlike orthodox Calvinists, they affirmed that since the elect are saved by the grace of God, they are under no moral obligation to comply with social or religious rules and regulations. They held that such individuals have a union with the Holy Ghost which cannot be weakened by human imperfection and that their one consuming goal in life should be to follow that divine light within regardless of what it might direct them to do.

Federal theologians considered themselves orthodox Calvinists. As they attempted to respond adequately to the positions of Arminians and Antinomians, however, they evolved a religious system which deviated in significant ways from the theology of John Calvin. "Federal" captures their basic theological position. Calvin dealt with the concept of covenant only incidentally, but it was fundamentally significant to the federal theologians.

As historian Darrett Rutman (1970:25) has observed, federal theology was a logical development for that time and milieu: "That the preachers should seize upon the covenant in any fashion was only natural. The notion of covenant underlay the social fabric of the time. Men gathered in guilds, in companies, in communities, and in their allegiance to the monarch under the explicit terms of covenants, contracting to give faithful support to the whole in return for the protection and fulfillment of the part.''

Federal theologians regarded a covenant as ''a mutual agreement between parties upon Articles or Propositions on both sides, so that each party is tied and bound to performe his own conditions.'' One of the most prominent federal theologians, William Ames (1576-1633), further defined the most basic element of any covenant to be voluntary engagement (P. Miller 1961:375; Zaret 1985:128-98).

According to federal theologians, God was indeed all-powerful, completely free to exercise his will in any fashion that he desired. He condescended, however, to deal with human beings on the basis of covenants. If individuals kept their part of such a divinely established covenant, then God bound himself to kept his part. Basic to salvation was having ''saving faith.'' By covenant, God agreed to save all who possessed such faith. However—and here they approached the Arminian position—one aspect of saving faith was a desire to obey the moral law. Consequently, although a person was not saved by works, no one would be saved who was not trying to obey God's commandments (Bercovitch 1975:22-23, 80).

The belief that God always interacted with individuals on the basis of covenant led logically to the position that ideal human associations should likewise be based on covenants. According to Thomas Hooker (1586?-1647), the Puritan founder of Connecticut, ''the mutual consenting involved in a covenant . . . is the 'sement' which solders together all societies, political or ecclesiastical; for there is no man constrained to enter into such a condition unlesse he will; and he that will enter, must also willingly binde and ingage himself to each member of that society to promote the good of the whole, or else a member actually he is not' '' (in P. Miller 1964:90).

Ramist Logic

Much of the logic federal theologians used came from the system of Pierre La Ramèe, anglicized as Petrus Ramus (1515-72). Ramus was a French Huguenot who attempted to develop an alternative to the Aristotelian logic taught in the universities of his day (P. Miller 1961:110-80; Morgan 1966:21-28; Ong 1967; Richardson 1629; Wotton 1626). He held that relationships among concepts and beings in the universe could be explained with a finite set of formal principles which explicated the actual structure of the universe and, consequently, the pattern of divine order. Thus, in the preface to his *Art of Logick*, he states that the methods it outlines will "make clear the mysteries and celestial secrets of the sacred and divine doctrine" (in P. Miller 1961:117). As such, it was a variety of Platonism.

As Perry Miller's pioneering work on Puritan intellectual strains has shown, Ramus's logic had a decisive influence on the covenantal philosophy of early New England. The Puritan fathers believed that it could lead them to understand the nature of God, the world of nature, and human nature. Drawing from Ramus, William Ames, the English federal theologian who exerted perhaps the most decisive influence on the development of New England covenant organization) taught that there were three basic manifestations of the divine order. The first, or "archetypal," was God's pattern or "preexistent platform" which existed before the creation of the universe. The second, or "entypal," was that same pattern manifest in visible creation. The third, or "ectypal," corresponded to the human mind. It was thus possible, using Ramus's principles, to move from understanding one's own logical processes to comprehending the pattern of relationships within the universe and finally to apprehending God's directing power in the universe (P. Miller 1961:164-71).

Congregationalism

The questions of what organizational form a properly ordered church should have, what relationship should exist between church and state, and who should be members of the church were divisive questions for English Protestantism (S. Foster 1984; Gura 1984: 157-58; P. Miller 1961:432-62; Morgan 1965; Zaret 1985; Ziff 1973: 30-33). The founders of Massachusetts Bay Colony were nonseparatist independents or nonseparating congregationalists. As such, they affirmed that the Church of England was a true church and that (unlike the settlers of Plymouth) they were not seeking to separate themselves from it. They did believe, however, that it was improperly organized. They desired to establish in Massachusetts the organization they felt the Church of England should have.

They held that each local congregation should be free to regulate its internal affairs and appoint its own pastor. Each congregation could set its own qualifications for membership, allow the entry only of individuals who qualified, and excommunicate those who violated the covenant. Although independent of one another, the church congregations were still regulated by the state, which determined the orthodoxy of the congregations, disallowed the unorthodox groups, and punished or expelled disobedient individuals.

The members of each local congregation organized themselves and established unity through a church covenant. Such covenants had appeared in England at least as early as Mary's persecutions when Reformation leaders and their sympathizers "separated from the reste of the Lande, as from the world and ioyned in couenaunt, by voluntarie profession . . . to obey the trueth of Christ and to witness against the abominations of Antichrist" (in Burrage 1967:70).

The typical covenant briefly stated the rules of conduct and doctrine of a congregation, thus providing a way for a religious congregation to establish an existence independent of the state religion. In short, a peripheral group could thus establish an identity separate from the center and build the solidarity of its subgroup. In New England, a covenant acted more as a device for separating the religiously qualified from the unqualified. Only the individuals within each congregation who subscribed to the covenant were regarded as fully religiously qualified; they determined which individuals seeking entry to their group could subscribe to the covenant, thus becoming members.

THE BASIC STRUCTURE OF THE NEW ENGLAND COVENANT ORDER

One of the most fascinating aspects of New England Puritanism was how federal theology, Ramist logic, and congregationalism combined to produce an integrated and highly cohesive social system. In the words of Sacvan Bercovitch (1978:44), this system created a "community at once purer and more political than its Old World counterparts, effecting a social cohesion more profound than that of national groupings and, simultaneously, raising the church's spiritual authority beyond the limits of the most militant English congregation."

Its most fundamental aspect was the manner in which it linked sanctity, covenant, and social organization. Perry Miller (1961:447) observed:

> That which made New Englanders unique in all seventeenth-century Christendom, which cut them off from all reformed churches and constituted them in truth a peculiar people was their axiom: "The Covenant of Grace is clothed with Church-Covenant in a Politicall visible

Church-way." They held that the love of God reached not merely into their souls, but that it pervaded their community. "God delights in us, when we are in his Covenant, his Covenant reacheth to his Church, and wee being members of that Church: Hence it comes to passe that we partake of all the pleasant springs of God's love."

In this chapter, I will examine that covenant system by analyzing five of its basic aspects: (1) mythological underpinnings; (2) bases of covenantal relationships; (3) ordering of covenantal relationships; (4) subsumption; and (5) loci and distribution of power.

MYTHOLOGICAL UNDERPINNINGS

According to Bronislaw Malinowski (1926), one of the pivotal figures in the development of anthropology, a myth is a sacred narrative that links a social institution or practice with a primordial or other-worldly existence. It thus bestows significance upon the social institution and justifies current social forms and activities. Employing the terminology of the American anthropologist, Clifford Geertz (1972:123), myths are simultaneously models for and models of the significant beliefs and practices of social groups.

From this anthropological perspective, Christian scriptural texts have mythic properties. Authors of the New Testament identified various events and statements from the Old Testament as "types" which found their fulfillment (or antitypes) in the life of Jesus Christ. They regarded both type and antitype as objectively and historically true. Later historians and theologians used the same basic exegetical method in explaining the history of the Christian church, the lives of prominent individuals, and the attributes of believers (T. Davis 1972).

This method of biblical interpretation meant that (1) "redemptive history" became the framework for interpreting particular events and (2) Old Testament events became the map that individuals seeking religious salvation must follow. Of all the leading reformers, Calvin most comprehensively used Old Testament events to interpret both the sweep of history and the events of individual lives (T. Davis 1972:38), and the New England Puritans followed him. Other groups like Antinomians and Quakers also read scriptures allegorically, but the Puritans outstripped them in how thoroughly they used this system to establish their group identity and redemption: "The single most important factor in the evolution of the New England Puritan's corporate identity lay in their typological reading of history, and, in particular, in their strong identification with the covenanted people

of Israel'' (Gura 1984:216). Gura continues: ''The majority of the New England Puritans assumed a biblical literalism that provided from the Old Testament's typological relation to the New a basis for belief in the progressive unfolding of the history of redemption *in this world*, a history that involved not only individual souls but an entire people in outward covenant with their God'' (Gura 1984:216).

Devout Puritans conceptualized the distinctive circumstances associated with the colonization of New England—the exodus from a wayward society, the journey to a new land, the establishment of a social order in North America—as antitypes for which the biblical narrative provided ample and well-developed types. They viewed themselves as active participants in the divinely established pattern of redemptive history and the embodiment of biblical prophecy (T. Davis 1972:44-45).

Like the Puritans before them, Mormons interpreted historical events using a general model of redemptive history; scriptural incidents were landmarks on the map of how to gain individual salvation and exaltation. Since I am most concerned with the consequences of such conceptions for both groups, I will not draw distinctions between mythology and typology but simply refer to both as covenantal myth.

The covenantal myth of Puritan New England sprang from Calvin's interpretations of biblical narrative, which federal theologians then amplified using Ramist logic. The result was an integrated sacred history which justified and gave significance to much of their social life and practice.

The ''Preexistent Platform''

The Puritan covenant myth begins before the creation. God established an archetypal pattern or ''preexistent platform'' that would govern the shaping of the physical universe and all things in it. As Samuel Willard (1640-1707) explained:

> God contrives in his Mind an *Eternal Idea* of all things that are to be. God having a Work to do, in the Creation and Gubernation of the World; lays out the *Whole Scheme* of it in his Infinite Understanding, in which he hath a Pattern of the Whole World, and everything in it. . . .
> There was a consultation in heaven, how that the Godhead might bee manifest, might bee observed, else were there none to apprehend it. (in P. Miller 1961:167-68)

The universe was then created as an entypal manifestation of this divine archetype.

Adam and the Covenant of Works

God created Adam with properties similar to His own divine essence (Calvin 1957 I:159-70; WA 136), then placed him in the Garden of Eden as lord over the earth and as the intermediary between God and the rest of the physical order (Morgan 1966:12-13). Adam's position was established and maintained by a relationship referred to as "the covenant of works" (W. Brown 1914:42, 138; Forell 1975:263), which essentially confirmed that God would preserve Adam in his current position in return for Adam's absolute obedience. When Adam ate the forbidden fruit, he broke the covenant, he lost his favored relationship with God, and his essence became changed and corrupted. Among the divine attributes that he lost were the intellect and will to do good. In this depraved condition, he was alienated from God and a fit subject for eternal damnation (Calvin 1957 I:209-47; WA 137-41).

Adam's action also affected his posterity, for he had entered the covenant of works as an agent for the human race. He was a "federal" or "parliamentary" man. As Adam's posterity could have received his special privileges in the pre-Fall state, so they suffered with him the consequences of breaking that covenant. All human beings are consequently born corrupt, lacking the ability to do good. Not only individuals but the entire social order suffers. Hence, human relationships fall short of the perfection of their archetypal counterparts in the preexisting platform (Calvin 1957 I:209-20; H. S. Smith 1955:1-9; P. Miller 1961:400-402; WA 42, 139).

Abraham and the Covenant of Grace

God next instituted the covenant of grace. Its operations and implications to the Puritans were most clearly revealed in the biblical narrative of Abraham, which they interpreted with a heavy reliance on contemporary legal concepts and vocabulary.

In part as a response to Abraham's "saving faith," God "elected" Abraham to be saved and unilaterally established a covenant relationship with him. Circumcision was the "seal" or visible and legally binding sign of this covenant (Calvin 1957 II:528-32; Holifield 1974:5-26).

As a result, Abraham became an adopted child of God and was declared "just." By the legal terms of seventeenth-century England, this meant that he was no longer liable for the penalties of his transgressions. Now, having been justified, he began to undergo "sanctification," the depraved nature he had inherited from Adam being slowly transformed into an essence more similar to that of God, his adopted father. In other words, his reasoning and will gradually approximated those of Adam before the Fall. As this occurred he became "regenerated." As a result of the whole process—adoption, justification, and sanctification—Abraham was assured of salvation, an eternal and heavenly relationship with God in the next life (W. Brown 1914; Calvin 1957 II:1-276; Morgan 1965:103; Rutman 1970:100-101; WA 53-100, 161-73; Ziff 1973:28, 58-59).

Abraham was also a "federal man," and God's covenant of grace with him also included Abraham's posterity. Puritan theologians placed considerable weight on God's declaration: "I will establish my covenant between me and thee and thy seed after thee in their generations for an everlasting covenant" (Genesis 17:7). The Israelites, as the seed of Abraham, were "born in the covenant" and had legal rights to the promises made to Abraham. The circumcision of infant males was a "seal" or "outward witness" that they were included in the group with which the Lord had established a special covenant relationship (Calvin 1957 II:532; Ziff 1973:138).

The New England Puritans and Redemptive History

Although the essential provisions of the covenant of grace never changed, the internal relationships among those included in the covenant could be modified. Thus, at the time of Abraham, the covenant community was familial in form; when Israel was camped at Sinai, it became "national"; and with the coming of Christ, it became "congregational" (Walker 1960:205). Furthermore, during Christ's time, baptism replaced circumcision as the "seal of the covenant" (Calvin 1957 II:530-32).

The Puritan founders of the Holy Commonwealth believed that they also were heirs to the covenant of grace and identified strongly with ancient Israel (Bercovitch 1975:92; 1978:73-78). They saw themselves as the "spiritual" children of Abraham and as a new or "surrogate" Israel (e.g., Mather 1705). This view was not a Puritan preserve; years before, Calvin (1957 II:536-38) had identified Protestants with ancient Israel:

The children of Abraham, under the old dispensation, were those who derived their origin from his seed, but that appellation is now given to those who imitate his faith. [Thus] we are called his sons, though we have no natural relationship with him. [And] we, in comparison of them are termed posthumous, or abortive children of Abraham, and that not by nature, but by adoption, just as if a twig were broken from its tree, and ingrafted on another stock.

Puritans, however, conceptualized their identification with Israel differently from continental Protestants. European Protestants identified with ancient Israel as individuals: through his or her individual election by God, each person destined for salvation became part of the spiritual house of Israel. In contrast, early in the development of English Puritanism, the tendency had developed to view this relationship on a national as well as an individual level. Partly as a result of the typological approach of John Foxe's (1516-87) highly influential *The Book of Martyrs*, many English Puritans came to regard the English collectively as the "New Israel" with a special covenantal relationship with God (Bercovitch 1975:72-86; 1978:33-38; Rutman 1970:23; Ziff 1973:5, 9-10).

New England Puritans molded this national identification with Israel to model more precisely the distinctive circumstances associated with their colonizing endeavors. The founders of New England first saw themselves as providing a pattern by which backsliding England could be led back to God. As Winthrop (1964:203) told his fellow saints aboard the *Arbella*, "Wee must Consider that wee shall be as a Citty upon a Hill." But when England refused to follow this lead, the American Saints gradually came to regard themselves as the New Israel in the New Canaan and England as the Egypt or Babylon from which they had fled. Thus, New England became a holy land, distinctive from all others. As Sacvan Bercovitch (1975:125-85; 1978:68-73, esp. 69; see also Gura 1984:180, 215-34) has shown, the boundaries of this New Canaan in time included all of America and became "God's chosen land" with a divine mission (Gura 1984: 215-16, 227-28).

What was this mission? During the Holy Commonwealth's early years, many New England Puritans believed they were preparing a society and a people for Christ's second coming and millennial reign (Gura 1984:126-52). This concept was sometimes called "establishing the New Jerusalem," a term with several meanings: the New Canaan, the existent social order of the Holy Commonwealth, the ideal and "pure" social order toward which they were working, and the millennial order that Christ would establish. Thus, in 1635 William Twisse held that "when New Jerusalem should come down from Heaven *America* would be the seat of it" (in Bercovitch 1978:72).

Another important aspect of New England Puritans' identification with Israel was their special interest in Jews (Bercovitch 1978:73-83; Gura 1984:133-36, 256), who, they anticipated, would be converted as a nation before the Second Coming. "The ministers discussed and prayed for the event. At times they undertook themselves to convert the Jews; [and they were excited over reports] about an influx of Jews to the Holy Land" (Bercovitch 1978:75).

This interest in the conversion of the Jews most probably led to the speculation that the American Indians were descendants of the biblical Hebrews. Such speculations were fueled by Thomas Thorowgood's 1650 *Jewes in America* reporting the supposed discovery of a South American tribe which practiced Jewish rites and claimed descent from Abraham. "In New England such strong 'proof' of the Indians' relationship gave further impetus to the translation of Scripture into the Indian tongues, and with every new Indian convert the Puritans found more evidence that the Jews were indeed being 'called in' to the fold" (Gura 1984:134; see also Bercovitch 1978:75).

This, in outline, is the New England Puritan covenantal myth. This myth can be regarded as a model for and a model of the system of social relationships that developed in Massachusetts Bay Colony between 1630 and 1660.

These social relationships can be visualized as three interrelated covenantal subsystems: the household, the church, and the state. I will next analyze the bases of each's covenantal relationships and how those relationships were ordered. Then I will explore how household, church, and state are unified by means of subsumption and, last, how power is distributed.

THE HOUSEHOLD

The Puritan domestic model conjoined economic and legal procedures with religious understandings. Its legal and economic aspects were, in large measure, patterned upon the form of domestic organization to which William Ames and other English federal theologians had been introduced while in Holland, where the household had many of the attributes of a small firm (Ziff 1973:16). Its religious aspects were grounded in Puritan covenantal myth and in large measure were amplifications of Puritan understandings regarding the Abrahamic covenant.

Bases of Relationships

In using the term "bases of relationship," I have in mind the attributes shared by individuals linked within a social system. Anthropologists for many years have attempted to determine the fundamental concepts underlying human associations. In the 1880s, William Robertson Smith (1882; 1885), one of the most influential precursors of British social anthropology, identified two basic aspects of semitic society: "natural" relationships based on blood ties and "covenant" relationships established through legally defined rights and duties. He demonstrated how much of the unity within semitic society was grounded in the interplay between these two types of relationships.

In recent years, American anthropologist David Schneider (1968; 1969; 1972; 1979) has analyzed American kinship in much the same way. He argues that there are two general categories in American culture: the order of nature (things as they exist in nature) and the order of law (human regulations and conditions and relationships resulting from their implementation). Patterns of American kinship follow this division: "natural" relatives are those who share "genetic substance," and legal relatives are those whose relationships are created by law. The most cohesive kinship relationships are simultaneously grounded in both law and nature. For example, the bond between a woman and child born to her in wedlock is perceived as more cohesive than the bond between a woman and her illegitimate child or between a woman and her legally adopted child. When a relationship is simultaneously grounded in law and nature, either element can be emphasized according to the needs of a particular situation. The dual concepts of nature and law underlie both Puritanism and Mormonism, as we will see.

In Puritan thought, relationships had to be established in one of three ways: natural law, force, and covenant or mutual agreement (Morgan 1966:26). Natural law was the directing power within objects or beings that had been established by God in the creation. By means of natural law, that harmony was maintained between the archetypes of the "preexistent platform" and their earthly counterparts. As John Preston (1587-1628), one of the chief architects of federal theology, declared: "Nature, it cannot be altered againe, for that is the property of Nature, it stickes by us and will not be changed" (in P. Miller 1964:67). John Davenport (1597-1670), one of the founders of New Haven, affirmed, "The Law of Nature is God's Law" (in P. Miller 1964:150). Manifestations of natural law could be seen in what we today might call instinct and the laws of physics. However, as a consequence of the Fall, important aspects of the created world lost their ability to be regulated by primeval, God-established natural law (Calvin 1957 I:159-70, 209-20; P. Miller 1961:239-79; Miller and Johnson 1963 I:195-207). The Puritans regarded human conduct in particular as removed from the governing power of divine law. With the single exception of the parent-child relationship, they conceptualized all human relationships as being, of necessity, maintained either by force or by covenant.

Of the two, covenant was by far the preferred basis for human association. Thomas Hooker declared: "Amongst such who by no impression of nature, no rule of providence, or appointment from God, or reason, have power each over other, there must of necessity be a mutuall ingagement, each of the other by their free consent, before by any rule of God they have any right or power, or can exercise, each towards the other" (in Morgan 1966:26).

According to Puritan thought, humankind had "appointment from God" to apply force only as a punishment for misdeeds (such as committing crimes or being involved in unlawful warfare). In such cases relationships of force could be established through imprisonment or the imposition of involuntary servitude (Morgan 1966: 110-12). Such situations were seen as exceptional and theoretically would not be part of a perfected societal order. Thus, as in David Schneider's American kinship model, there were two basic types of relationships in the ideal Puritan social system: the restricted field of relationships in nature which included only the parent-child bond, and the much broader field of relationships based on covenant.

Associated with both types of relationships was an equally ideal pattern of behavior or code of conduct based on Christian love as explained in the New Testament (Bercovitch 1975:91-92). As John Winthrop (1964:196, 201) expressed it:

> Love [is] the bond of perfection. . . . There is noe body but consistes of partes and that which knitts these partes together gives the body its perfection, because it makes eache parte soe contiguous to other as thereby they doe mutually participate with eache other. . . . Wee ought to account our selves knitt together by this bond of love, and live in the exercise of it, if wee would have comforte of our being in Christ.

Marriage was the preeminent covenantal relationship within the household, based in law, and imbued with religious and mythical significance. Puritans believed that God, in joining Adam and Eve, had "Solemnized the First Marriage that ever was" (in Morgan 1966:29). The New England marriage ceremony, however, was a state function that established a covenantal compact. A man and a woman first agreed to abide by the rules and obligations which God had declared to be appropriate to the marital union, then were declared husband and wife by a civil magistrate, and finally sealed both covenant and contract by sexual intercourse. Unless and until it was consummated in this way, no marriage was valid or complete (Morgan 1966:34).

A central part of the marriage covenant was the obligation to love. Wrote Benjamin Wadsworth (1670-1737) in his *Well Ordered Family*, a 1712 New England publication on marital ethics: "This duty of love is mutual, it should be performed by each, to each of them. They should endeavour to have their affections really, cordially and closely knit, to each other. . . . The plain Command of the Great God, required Husbands and Wives, to have and manifest very great affection, love and kindness to one another" (in Morgan 1966:47-48).

As Wadsworth's words suggest, Puritans did not anticipate that marriage and the resulting association of a husband and wife would naturally generate such love. Rather, it was a covenantal "duty [which] God required." And New England courts granted divorce when it could be proved that either husband or wife had violated or neglected one of the fundamental duties of the marriage covenant (Morgan 1966:34).

In contrast to this law-based relationship was the parent-child relationship. The Puritans saw the parent-child tie as the only human relationship that was still preserved by the directing power of natural law (Morgan 1966:25) and that operated as an instinctual solidarity or love in both human and animal parents (Morgan 1966:65). They believed that the parent-child relationship was so strong that it might even interfere with the strongest covenantal obligation—that of an individual's duty toward God (Morgan 1966:77; Ziff 1973:44).

Although the parent-child relationship was predominantly based in the order of nature, it also involved the order of law. For example, only the offspring of legally married parents were legitimate and both parents and children were expected to have certain obligations and meet certain standards of behavior.

Still, the natural love between parents and child was different from the covenantal obligation to love between husband and wife and the legally specified rights and duties that were part of marriage. We might say that the definition and regulations of marital love were attempts to employ legal means to engender between husband and wife the relationship that occurred naturally between parent and child.

Puritan households quite routinely had a third relationship, that of the master-servant. Covenants from the order of law were used to attach indentured servants, hired servants, and indentured apprentices to the household. There was no obligation to love, but the reciprocal rights and duties that these covenants established resembled the legal aspects of the parent-child relationship (Morgan 1966:109-32; Ziff 1973:43, 85). For example, the household head was responsible for the spiritual needs of the servants. If he was a covenant member of a church, they had the right to join if they could demonstrate that they were otherwise religiously qualified.

Thus, relationships within the Puritan household match David Schneider's American kinship categories in several ways: (1) There are two basic orders: nature and law. (2) Natural relationships exist independently of human conventions and social forms. (3) They are created by shared genetic substance—or "blood," as the Puritans would have called it. (4) The order of law consists of socially established rules and regulations. Schneider calls them "codes of conduct"; the Puritans called them "covenants." (5) Individuals who are not naturally related can adopt the behavior of those linked by natural bonds. (6) Solidarity based on law is more tenuous and difficult to preserve than that based on nature.

The Ordering of Covenantal Relationships

When using the term "ordering of relationships," I have in mind the positioning of individuals linked together within a social system. The ordering of most covenant relationships within both Puritanism and Mormonism share two characteristics: inequality (one person is always superordinate and the other is subordinate) and affirmative opposition. I have adapted this second term from Ramus's "affirmative contrary." Basically it means that the superordinate and the subordinate individuals derive the significance of their position within the system from each other.

Puritans accepted the medieval view that inequality was basic to order (Rutman 1970:65, 71-73). The preexistent platform was hierarchical, with the archetypical categories arranged according to their relative superordinate and subordinate positions. Although the current social order was not fully consistent with the preexistent platform, social inequality per se was not evidence of this inconsistency. As John Winthrop (1964:190-91) explained: "God Almightie . . . hath soe disposed of the Condicion of mankinde, as in all times some must be rich some poore, some highe and eminent in power and dignitie, others meane and in subjeccion . . . that every man might have need of [the] other, and from hence they might be all knitt more nearly together in the Bond of brotherly affeccion."

This view received strong reinforcement from Ramus's logical category called "relatives" or "relates." Two entities were "relates" if they stood in relation to one another as "affirmative contraries"— meaning that they mutually caused each other. Common examples would be husband/wife, minister/congregation, and parent/child, the existence of one involving the existence of the other (Morgan 1966:23).

This concept manifested itself in the Puritan belief that the ideal social order was bound together through interdependency; Emile Durkheim (1858-1917) (1964:111-99), arguably the pivotal figure in the development of British social anthropology, would use "organic solidarity" to define this condition. As I have already noted, Puritans believed that Ramus's logic revealed actual relationships among existent entities in a Platonic sense. This system did not have the intellectual category to identify an individual separately from the individuals to whom he or she stood in affirmative opposition. Consistent with this logic, Puritans viewed personhood as emerging from the relationship itself, not as residing in an individual. John Winthrop (1964:196) was explaining this organic conception of the social order when he declared: "There is noe body but consists of partes and that which knitts these partes together gives the body its perfeccion, because it makes eache parte soe contiguous to [the] other as they doe mutually participate with eache other both in strengthe and infirmity in pleasure and paine."

In the Puritan household, these concepts had obvious consequences. First, inequality was assumed to be inevitable, and desirable. The husband was superordinate to the wife, the parent to the child, and the master to the servant. However, such hierarchies were not sheer power-based units, for individuals within the household were organically united as affirmative opposites and should ideally base their interactions on the principles of Christian love.

Within the marital bond, the husband was clearly superordinate and the wife subordinate. He was her director, and she was expected to obey and reverence him. ''He stood before her in the place of God: he exercised the authority of God over her, and he furnished her with the fruits of the earth that God had provided. To her and to the rest of the family he was 'the Conduit Pipe of the variety of blessings that God suplyeth them with.' '' But the wife was not a slave. The husband was obligated to provide for her economic needs, and his authority was strictly limited. ''He could not lawfully strike her, nor could he command her anything contrary to the laws of God, laws which were explicitly defined in the civil codes'' (Morgan 1966:44-45).

In dealing with their children and servants, the husband and wife were on a more equal footing. Despite the husband's superordinate position in the marriage, within the context of the household as a whole, each was a parent or master and, as such, was superordinate to the children and servants (Morgan 1966:45-46).

This domestic pattern of inequality and interdependence was maintained by legal regulations and sanctions. Civil law supported the head of household's authority; and when he seemed to be failing in his responsibilities to other household members, tithingmen came to see that he reformed his ways (Ziff 1973:244). If he refused to reform, his household might be broken up and its members distributed among other households (Morgan 1966:147-48).

Another important consequence of such organic philosophy was that for any individual to be regarded as a socially complete person, he or she had to belong to a properly ordered household. If for some reason an individual was not attached to a household, the civil authorities took action to remedy this situation. Before a number of unattached indentured servants arrived in the fledgling colony in 1629, they were organized into domestic units by the company heads who wrote to John Endicott, the acting governor: ''For the better accommodation of businesses, wee have devyded the servants belonging to the Company into severall famylies, as wee desire and intend they should live together'' (in Morgan 1966:144). And in 1638, each town in the colony received orders ''to dispose of all single persons and inmates to servise or otherwise'' (in Morgan 1966:145).

THE CHURCH

The founders of Massachusetts Bay Colony maintained that the established Church of England was not a false church but that it was in grave error by not allowing local congregations sufficient autonomy in regulating their internal affairs and determining who was or was not qualified to be regarded as members. Before leaving England they had come to the conclusion that the only proper and adequate way to overcome this error was through the employment of church covenants (Burrage 1967:289-90; Knappen 1966:332-33; P. Miller 1961:412-13; Morgan 1965:64-65; Rutman 1970:24-25; Zaret 1985; Ziff 1973:50).

By creating their own religious polity in Massachusetts, they were endeavoring to correct the flaws they saw in the English church policy. They did not see themselves as creating a schism by taking this action: the king, his bishops, and Parliament regulated the church polity in England, while Massachusetts magistrates regulated the religious polity in New England. Since the Acts of Uniformity applied only to England and Wales, they technically had the right to establish any religious system which was not inconsistent with the provisions of the charter that had been granted them.

Paralleling the situation in England at the time, the religious polity the American Puritans developed tolerated only one form of ecclesiastical organization within Massachusetts Bay Colony. And, also as in England, all inhabitants of the colony were required to attend the religious services of the established church and were forbidden by law from any form of religious association that did not conform with government-sanctioned procedures and doctrine.

One of the most important deviations from the policies of the Church of England was church membership. No one was required by law to be a member of the church or to formally subscribe to any religious doctrine or creed. Indeed, full church membership remained restricted to a minority who could prove themselves qualified.

Each congregation was established by an explicit covenant, appointed its own minister, determined when an individual could become a member, and excommunicated backsliders. And no formal level of ecclesiastical jurisdiction higher than the individual congregation existed.

Full membership required subscribing to a church covenant; but New England Puritans required, as a prerequisite, that an individual must have received the covenant of grace. The practical difficulty of this position was that God established this covenant unilaterally, independently of human ritual. Although God might be expected to establish his covenant with individuals possessed of saving faith, there was no way to determine directly just when an individual had received the covenant of grace.

Puritans avoided that difficulty to some extent by looking for the effects of sanctification in an applicant's life, since they believed that sanctification began after an individual received the covenant of grace. Puritan policy, therefore, required prospective covenant members to examine their lives for demonstrable evidence of sanctification which they would then present to the covenant members of the congregation (Cohen 1986:137-61; Gura 1984:161-64; Moran 1974; Morgan 1965:67-89; Rutman 1970:99-101; Ziff 1973:28). If, after careful scrutiny, the congregation agreed that candidates were indeed experiencing the effects of sanctification, they concluded that God had probably established a covenant of grace with them.

Such individuals would then be permitted to attest formally to that congregation's particular church covenant and would thus become covenant members. They would be designated as "visible saints" with the right to partake of communion and have the rights and duties associated with covenant church membership. Although Puritans acknowledged that mistakes were possible, they believed that such procedures by and large limited covenant membership to the elect and sanctified.

Children, however, were in an ambiguous position. By analogy with Abraham, whose offspring were included in the covenant with God, it was reasoned that the offspring of covenant church members also participated with them in the covenant of grace and were thus "born in the covenant" (Holifield 1974:43). As a result, they received baptism as a seal of the covenant and were regarded as members of the church. They were not deemed fully participating members of the congregation, however, until they could present evidence of sanctification. When and if this happened, they were then allowed to subscribe to the church covenant and become fully functioning members of the congregation.

The founders of the Holy Commonwealth seem to have assumed that most if not all of the children of covenant members would have saving faith and eventually receive full covenant membership (Bercovitch 1978:63-64). If they were born in the covenant of grace, it would be reasonable that the consequences of that covenant should operate in their lives. John Cotton (1584-1652), the most influential minister in early Massachusetts, declared: "The children of believers doe come on themselves to believe, by reason of the Covenant of grace which God hath made with believers and their seed, for by that Covenant hee hath promised to write the law of faith (as of all other saving graces) in their hearts, that they also may come in Gods time and way to enjoy all the other saving privileges of the Covenant, as did their Fathers before them'' (in Holifield 1974:157).

However, many of the children of original covenant members failed to become fully qualified covenant members of the church. What, theologically, was their status? In 1662 the Massachusetts General Court called a synod of ministers who resolved this issue with the "half-way covenant" (Bercovitch 1975:94; 1978:63-64; Bushman 1967:147-79; Morgan 1965:125-32; Pope 1969:43-74; H. Schneider 1958:86-87; Sweet 1952:58-59; Walker 1960:238-339; Ziff 1973: 128-33).

The half-way covenant allowed the "unregenerate" child of a covenant member to have his or her own child baptized if he or she would publicly "own" the covenant into which he or she had been born and which had been sealed upon him or her by baptism. This public declaration essentially meant that such members would place themselves under the discipline of the church, attempt to govern their lives according to its regulations, and instruct their children in proper conduct. But they would still not be regarded as "visible saints," be allowed to partake of communion, nor receive the rights and duties of full covenant membership.

Most congregations accepted the recommendation of the synod, and the half-way covenant became a regular feature of most New England Congregational churches. Sacvan Bercovitch (1978:62-65) refers to the ideas that shaped the half-way covenant as "the genetics of salvation" and sees this logic as a way to blend "the heterogeneous covenants of community and grace." Through the "genetics of salvation," kinship and familial concepts and symbols were employed to define religious and political associations and boundaries. In this way, kinship identity and solidarity were merged with that of religious and national identity and solidarity. The result was a conceptually integrated and highly cohesive social system.

The Bases of Relationships

A useful way to clarify the consequence that familial concepts had for solidarity within the church polity is to examine the "genetics of salvation" in understandings regarding the half-way covenant.

Like the solidarity of Puritan households, the solidarity of Puritan congregations resulted from both nature and law. After the Great

Migration (which ended in the early 1640s when the English civil war broke out) it became almost impossible for an individual to be admitted to church membership unless he or she descended from visible saints. If the covenant of grace could be transmitted by descent, then it seemed logical to assume that such transmission was generally restricted to a few select families. Increase Mather explained: "God hath seen meet to cast the line of election so, as that generally elect Children are cast upon elect Parents. . . . There are some Families in the world, that God hath designed to shew mercy to them from generation to generation" (in Morgan 1966:183; see also Bercovitch 1974:94-95; Pope 1969:3-42).

The fact that not all children manifested signs of sanctification and regeneration required a theological explanation. For a number of years there was no consensus regarding the proper explanation for this phenomenon. The debate over the half-way covenant, however, generated the need to resolve the issue. In an effort to provide support for the provisions of the half-way covenant, in 1663 Thomas Shepard, Jr., published a manuscript which his father had written shortly before his death in 1649 (Morgan 1965:134). In this work the elder Shepard had developed the explanation that God's covenant with Abraham actually included the promise of two forms of holiness: "inward reall holyness" that was Abraham's own as a consequence of his personal sanctification, and "federal holyness" that would be transmitted by descent to his offspring (Gura 1984:114-15; Holifield 1974:153-59; Morgan 1965:134). Like Abraham, visible saints had inward holiness while their descendants, like his, had federal holiness. A recipient of federal holiness had the possibility, but not the certainty, of ultimately receiving inward holiness. Because of this possibility—which the rest of humankind lacked—descendants of visible saints could receive baptism as a seal of the covenant into which they were born and be accepted as part of the visible church.

Those who had not descended from visible saints were in a very different situation. Since baptism was the seal of a covenant relationship, there appeared to be no justification in baptizing individuals who had not received the covenant personally nor been born into it. Nor was there any reason to assume that they had federal holiness. Consequently, it did not seem appropriate to regard these people as part of the visible church. Given these already inauspicious circumstances, many Puritans assumed that there was little hope that God would condescend, as he had with Abraham, to instigate a completely new covenant of grace.

Theologically, Puritans regarded the state of holiness, like the parent-child bond, to be part of the order of nature. Only a natural process could place an individual in either the federal or the inward category of holiness. Federal holiness, transmitted from parent to child, thus followed the only human relationship whose solidarity was still preserved by the primeval law of nature. Acquiring inward holiness was the consequence of sanctification and regeneration, which transformed an individual's nature to correspond more closely with the nature of primeval Adam or Eve.

But while holiness was a condition of nature, the church covenant itself was part of the order of law. It both defined and established the code of conduct that should exist among holy individuals. As there were two levels of holiness, so there were two covenantal orders: the half-way covenant for those who had been granted only federal holiness and the full church covenant for those who had achieved inward holiness.

The policy that servants could become covenant members of their masters' congregations likewise lay within the order of law. Its precedent was that Abraham had circumcised his servants (Genesis 17:23) and thus apparently included them as part of his familial-based church. As a practical matter, though, Puritans generally seemed to regard their servants as "unregenerate"; and after the first few years of colonization, the percentage admitted to covenant membership declined sharply (Morgan 1966:123; Ziff 1973:85-87).

The Ordering of Relationships

Although Ramist logic recognized only one hierarchically paired relationship in a church congregation (pastor and people [Morgan 1966:24]), the concepts of holiness and covenant created a four-tiered hierarchy based on degree of holiness, participation in covenant, or both.

At the most inclusive level were all in attendance at services, both members and nonmembers, all of whom were required by law to attend. This level shared no particular holiness, but all participated in a common national covenant. At the next level were all church members, who were distinguished from nonmembers by possessing federal holiness. The third category included all covenant members, whether half-way or complete. They were not distinguished from the general church membership by holiness but by covenant and code of conduct. The fourth and most exclusive category was the visible saints, distinguished by inward holiness and by complete covenant membership.

This fourth group was the manifestation of the Puritan goal: as the elect of God, they were the embodiment of holiness; as covenant church members, they were the manifestation of ideal conduct.

THE STATE

New England Puritans believed that the Holy Commonwealth had the same covenantal relationship to God as had ancient Israel, in other words, that God had elected them as a nation. The terms of this national or social covenant, simply stated, were these: if the inhabitants of the Holy Commonwealth obeyed God and kept his commandments, he would prosper them; if they turned from him, his wrath would be poured out upon them (Bercovitch 1978:3-61; Gura 1984:180-83; P. Miller 1961:328-431).

Puritans further believed that had Adam and Eve not fallen there would have been no need for a civil government because human beings in that ideal state before the Fall were by nature just and innately capable of maintaining proper relationships (P. Miller 1964: 142-43). In the corruption after the Fall, people lost the natural ability to deal correctly with each other, and God instituted government among human beings as a way to regulate their conduct. In the three-part Puritan system, government was not part of the domain of nature; hence, it could be established only by force or covenant. Most Puritans held strongly that only covenant could produce a just government. As early as the reign of Mary I, Puritans were constructing justifications of tyrannicide on the grounds that valid government must originate in some form of social compact (Morgan 1965:29). After Elizabeth's death, Puritans joined with parliamentarians in opposing the absolutism of the Stuart monarchs. The two groups came to share the belief that "the power of the ruler should be exercised in accordance with established fundamental law, and that the government should owe its existence to a compact of the governed" (P. Miller 1964:146).

The concept of the properly ordered state and the concept of the national covenant resulted in the belief that the inhabitants of New England would remain under God's special protection only to the degree that through mutual consent they established and then complied with laws consistent with God's will. This conception provided the framework for John Winthrop's (1964:201-3) seminal sermon, "A Modell of Christian Charity," delivered in 1630 to Puritans en route with him to Massachusetts Bay:

> For the worke we have in hand, it is by a mutuall consent through a speciall overruleing providence . . . to seeke out a place of Cohabitation and Consorteshipp under a due forme of Government both civill and ecclesiasticall. . . . Thus stands the cause betweene God and us, wee are entered into Covenant with him for this worke, wee have taken out a Commission, the Lord hath given us leave to drawe our owne Articles. . . . Now if the Lord shall please to heare us, and bring us in peace to the place wee desire, then hath hee ratified this Covenant and sealed our Commission [and] will expect a strickt performance of the Articles contained in it, . . . but if wee shall neglect the observacion of these Articles . . . the Lord will surely breake out in wrathe against us be revenged of such a perjured people and make us knowe the price of the breache of such a Covenant.

The same belief justified the strict and exacting laws later established to regulate conduct among the inhabitants of the colony (Bercovitch 1975:91-92).

The Bases of Relationships

Based on these beliefs, the Puritan elite developed a system of civil organization which closely resembled the congregational church structure. First, all inhabitants of the Holy Commonwealth participated in the same national covenant. This covenant was grounded in the order of law and dictated a code of civil regulations that reflected the laws of God. Despite the distinction "between visible saints and all others," the Puritan "federal or social covenant . . . permitted all individuals a role in the construction of the New Jerusalem" (Gura 1984:181).

Non-Puritans who obeyed the civil regulations of the Holy Commonwealth were allowed to settle in Massachusetts, but only the "regenerate" had authority to establish, administer, and enforce the law. Politically, only male visible saints could be freemen, and only freemen could vote on matters affecting public policy and hold significant public office. The theological justification for this exclusionary policy was that only those who had been sanctified and regenerated had the perception and insight into the mind of God necessary to preserve a form of civil government pleasing to heaven (Miller and Johnson 1963:I:200-201; Morgan 1958:84-100; Ziff 1973:52, 88-89).

As a corollary, the citizens of a properly ordered state were bound by covenant to obey the regulations established by their leaders unless these deviated from established law and the commandments of God. As Governor Winthrop explained at a session of the Massachusetts General Court in 1645:

> The great questions that have troubled the country, are about the authority of the magistrates and the liberty of the people. It is yourselves who have called us to this office, and being called by you, we have our authority from God, in way of an ordinance . . . the contempt and violation whereof have been vindicated with examples of divine vengeance. . . . The covenant between you and us is the oath you have taken of us, which is to this purpose, that we shall govern you and judge your causes by the rules of God's laws and our own, according to our best skill. . . . But if a [magistrate] fail in faithfulness, which by his oath he is bound unto, that he must answer for. . . .
>
> There is a twofold liberty, natural (I mean as our nature is now corrupt) and civil or federal. The first is common to man with beasts and other creatures. By this, man . . . simply, hath liberty to do what he lists. This liberty . . . cannot endure the least restraint of the most just authority. The exercise and maintaining of this liberty makes men grow more and more evil. . . . The other kind of liberty, I call civil or federal, it may also be termed moral. . . . This liberty is the proper end and object of authority, and cannot subsist without it; and it is a liberty to that which is just and honest. [It] is maintained and exercised in a way of subjection to authority; it is the same kind of liberty by wherewith Christ hath made us free. The woman's own choice makes such a man her husband; yet being so chosen, he is her lord, and she is subject him, yet in a way of liberty, not of bondage. [If] you will be satisfied to enjoy such civil and lawful liberties, such as Christ allows you, then will you quietly and cheerfully submit unto that authority which is set over you, in all administration of it, for your good. (in Miller and Johnson 1963 I:205-7)

The Ordering of Relationships

Civil administration developed from the original Massachusetts Bay Company into a complex, multiformed, and multilayered system of administration (Morgan 1958). All civil relationships, however, reduce to a simple and consistent pattern: a covenantal relationship of inequality between regenerate magistrates and the rank and file citizens (Breen 1980:24-45; Bushman 1967:3-21; P. Miller 1964:16-47, 141-52; Morgan 1958:84-100; Ziff 1973:57-58).

This pattern follows Ramist logic of affirmative opposition (magistrate-citizen) and resembles the church structure. Although the civil structure itself had no order-of-nature relationships, Puritans understood the qualifying holiness of the elites who occupied both ecclesiastical and civil positions to be an aspect of the order of nature. Consequently, civil organization, like that of the household and the church, consisted of an interrelationship between the order of nature and the order of law.

PURITAN COVENANTAL ORGANIZATION AS A UNIFIED SYSTEM

Subsumption

The covenantal systems that operated for the household, the church, and the state linked on a deeper level to form a unified covenantal organization that served as the basis and the framework for the group identity and solidarity of New England Puritans.

Much of this unity came from, first, the similarity of form in the three subsystems. Second, Puritans believed that all relationships within the three subsystems were established either by nature or by covenant. Third, all three subsystems ordered relationships in similar patterns of inequality. Fourth, most of them also fit within the logical framework of affirmative opposition as husband-wife, parent-child, master-servant, pastor-congregation, and magistrate-citizen. Of course, several group relationships (such as that among covenant church members) did not. These, however, also conformed to the same general structure of inequality when viewed in terms of their relationship to other social groupings—for example, that between covenant church members and individuals who were not part of this covenant group. And fifth, group boundaries within both church and state were based upon the interplay of covenant and holiness.

In addition to these resemblances among the three subsystems, they were also incorporated into a single structure through subsumption, or the incorporation of one covenantal subsystem into a more embracing system. For example, by law, each individual within the Holy Commonwealth belonged to a particular household; thus, everyone in Puritan Massachusetts was related either by nature (parent-child) or by covenant to a small group of individuals in a hierarchically ordered domestic structure.

The household was subsumed by the church congregation. Since by law everyone was required to attend religious services, all the citizens of Massachusetts were under the jurisdiction of a particular church, but the nature of that relationship resulted partially from the domestic structure. Since as a general rule only children of covenant members could themselves qualify for covenant membership status, however, actual membership depended on familial connections.

The church congregation was in turn subsumed by the state, which stood in a covenant relationship with God and was responsible for seeing that citizens performed their covenantal duties. It therefore had the authority to supervise individual congregations, establishing acceptable teachings and practices. Individuals who refused to submit to state religious regulation could face imprisonment, banishment, or death.

But while the state supervised the church, it was also an outgrowth of the church. Freemanship—or the full rights of citizenship—depended on becoming a full covenant member of a church congregation.

Thus, each covenantal subsystem had jurisdiction over covenantal relationships that it subsumed; but simultaneously, critical aspects of each subsystem relied on elements of subsumed order. For example, household solidarity was in large measure based upon the parent-child bond; federal holiness, which qualified one for church membership, was transmitted through this bond; and freemanship within the state was predicated upon the attainment of inward holiness, which was seen as an extension of federal holiness. The natural parent-child bond was thus central to the entire covenantal order. It was consequently with some justification that Cobbert declared the family to be "*the Mother Hive, out of which both . . . State and Church, issued forth*" (Morgan 1966:133-34).

The Distribution of Power

We can further see how the covenantal system was integrated by analyzing how it distributed power, meaning the ability to establish and regulate covenant relationships.

Although the Bay Colony has been characterized by some as a theocracy, very little power was vested in the church itself. First, religious administrators had virtually no ability to enact binding covenants. According to Puritan beliefs, all relationships between God and human beings had to be initiated by God. As a result, rituals like baptism and communion could be administered as seals of a covenant relationship with God, but the ritual could not influence or change the actual establishment of such covenants. If God elected a particular individual to be saved, that individual's salvation was assured regardless of baptism; likewise, the baptism of a nonelected individual availed nothing (Holifield 1974:150-59). While the Puritan church could admonish sinners and seek to separate the holy from the unholy, it had power neither to bind God nor to produce holiness in its membership.

Second, the state, not the church, had ultimate power to ensure religious conformity and participation in the covenantal order. The state established the Puritan congregational system as the only religious organization permitted, required that all citizens attend religious services, and made visible sainthood a requirement for freemen and civil administrators. Such actions ensured the dominance of a particular religious system, but that dominance in large measure remained a function of state power.

Identity and Solidarity

This unified covenant system had important consequences for the group identity and solidarity of the Puritans of the Holy Commonwealth. Most immigrants came in family units and were motivated, at least in part, by a desire to establish a new social order based on religious principles (Breen 1980:46-67). Although they came from diverse backgrounds, in Massachusetts they were incorporated as households into a covenant system that related them strongly to like-minded colleagues and that conferred upon them the identity of Israel reconstituted. They conceived of themselves as a holy nation that existed apart from the rest of the world.

DISINTEGRATION OF THE PURITAN COVENANT ORGANIZATION

Puritan Social Cohesion

Most investigators of New England society agree that one of its most notable characteristics was its high degree of social cohesion. Timothy Breen and Stephen Foster (1977:110, 112) maintain that "the Bay Colony's most startling accomplishment [was] fifty years of relative social peace. . . . Even at its worst moments Massachusetts Bay never lost its extraordinary stability." Darrett Rutman (1970: 87-88) regards Puritan cohesion as a product of "a traditional reality" accepted by the group: "In New England all were children of tradition, born to it by their English origins and the very act of migration, held to it by the augmented traditionalism of the fellowship that lived with them. . . . The wonder is not that New England clung to traditional values to the extent and for so long as the section did, but that there was any tendency at all to depart from tradition." Philip Gura (1984:156-57) defines the same phenomenon as a consequence of the dynamic interaction between the radical minority and the conservative elite:

> New England did not become the veritable New Jerusalem for which its leaders prayed, but the radicals' willingness to read the implications of the New England Way more fully than many of its clerical architects and the New England Puritans' masterful co-option of those readings brought the colonies, if not to the gates of an earthly paradise, then at least to a position enviable in the seventeenth century, for its social and political stability.

By the mid-eighteenth century New England had lost most of its distinctively Puritan characteristics. In "The Deacon's Masterpiece," Oliver Wendell Holmes (Brooks, Lewis, and Warren 1:635-36) apparently attributes Puritanism's decline to its disregard of pragmatic considerations. However, this view is simply not true. New England Puritanism was constantly adjusting to changing circumstances. In fact, its ability to pragmatically adjust contributed both to its stability and to its decline.

Peter Berger and Thomas Luckmann (1966; see also Berger 1967; Berger and Luckmann 1967; Luckmann 1967) have a model for analyzing change in religious belief and practice that can help us better understand this apparent paradox. They define one key term, *pluralism*, as "competition in the institutional ordering of comprehensive meanings for everyday life" that results from an institutional history of "de-monopolization." They continue: "Among the many socially recognized meanings of everyday life there will always be some that are comprehensive in the sense of supplying an overall canopy for all the experiences of individual existence. These are the meanings that allow the individual to make sense of his biography as a whole, particularly to integrate into an intelligible unity his experiences that are marginal to the reality of everyday life."

Secularization, a process often associated with pluralism, is the "progressive autonomization of societal sectors from the domination of religious meanings and institutions" (Berger and Luckmann 1966:73-74).

These rather abstract sociological concepts become vivid when applied to a historical overview of adjustments within New England covenant organization and will be even more important for the analysis of Mormon covenant organization to follow.

Before 1660

Puritan covenant organization provided a framework or "canopy" for such diverse aspects of life as family relationships, church participation, political organization, legal regulations, and civil responsibility. It also existed always in a pluralistic milieu.

However, between 1629 when the Massachusetts Bay Company charter was granted and 1660 when Charles II was restored to the English throne, Puritanism's larger society was in disarray. Religious and political instability led to the outbreak of civil war in 1642, the execution of Charles I in 1649, and the competition among Puritan and parliamentarian groups during the Cromwellian period. Given these internal preoccupations in England, the Massachusetts Bay Colony had thirty years of nearly complete political isolation. Its elites were essentially free to establish the type of government they wished.

Isolation did not mean uniformity, however. Massachusetts had a diverse population, since the only requirement was willingness to accept the civic order, not the religious one. From the beginning, some settlers did not regard themselves as Puritans; others were essentially secular in their outlook. During the founding years, however, most of the diversity stemmed from the religious spectrum represented by the immigrant Puritans themselves. Puritanism encouraged, in effect, such diversity by emphasizing personal religious experience. The result was a pluralistic, religiously oriented milieu.

Given this diversity, it is useful to see how various aspects of New England covenant organization operated to increase stability. Berger and Luckmann (1966:74) point out that pluralism can involve both competition between social institutions and also competition among subjective understandings. Before 1660, we can clearly see such competition among opinions and beliefs.

The Bay Colony's covenantal system allowed for considerable diversity in religious experience while at the same time orienting it toward the values, institutions, and elite of the center. For example, an individual's personal religious experience determined whether he or she had received the covenant of grace. From that point on, however, it became a social experience. The individual was expected to publicly explain that personal experience; and the covenant members passed judgment on its validity. Membership in the church covenant system (a prerequisite for full participation in the political system) depended on interpreting personal religious experience in ways that covenant members would approve. Thus, strong forces for uniformity were at work. Acceptable interpretations were oriented toward the beliefs and values of the colony's elite and of their institutional structures, contributing to rather than detracting from social stability.

A second feature of the covenantal system was its intolerance of nonconformists. The state regulated religious practice, then limited freemanship, and hence political power, to covenant church members who accepted the social order's values and institutions. The exiling of Anne Hutchinson, Roger Williams, and Samuel Gorton, and the persecution of Quakers seem completely out of proportion to the threat they posed to the established order. However, their treatment clearly told the less-peripheral members of the colony where the acceptable boundaries for their own religious expressions lay.

The power to encourage and channel personal charisma on the one hand and punish nonconformity on the other gave the Bay Colony an effective way to promote social stability while allowing for individual expression. It effectively resolved a dilemma Philip Gura (1984:157) pinpointed: "A radically conservative society, New England was faced with the difficult task of maintaining its inhabitants' spiritual fervor even as it sought to channel that enthusiasm into socially acceptable streams."

This equilibrium theoretically could have continued indefinitely if three conditions had been met: (1) if the elite had maintained political control, (2) if the elite had continued to espouse essentially the same values and beliefs, and (3) if the large majority of the population continued to accept or at least acquiesce to those beliefs and values. But none of these conditions lasted.

After 1660

After 1660, two important changes occurred: the colony's secularization and factionalism increased and its political and social isolation decreased. For its first thirty years, the Massachusetts commercial class increased steadily in size and relative wealth. Many were not covenant church members and thus were barred from direct political participation. Even the freemen merchants increasingly felt that it was in their economic interest to see Massachusetts become more legally and socially aligned with England. In 1646 seven prominent Massachusetts merchants petitioned Parliament for English law and civil liberty, including the rights of freemanship. "Although the petitioners lost their legal battle, they did foreshadow a view that the restored Stuarts were to find sensible: English subjects should not form enclaves outside of English law and disregardful of English tradition" (Ziff 1973:98-99).

In the years following the restoration of Charles II to the throne, secularization and pluralism within the Bay Colony increased rapidly. A number of divisions emerged among the inhabitants, based upon both economic and religious differences. The most obvious distinction was between freemen and those who lacked political power. The commercial class oriented itself more toward England and the agricultural class toward its Massachusetts center, with corresponding urban-rural differences. All divisions had religious manifestations, with some ministers and magistrates being more aligned with one faction and others with another (Ziff 1973:128-250).

Meanwhile, English political leaders pressured Massachusetts magistrates to allow more religious tolerance and bring local religious practices more in line with those then developing in England. The imperative for religious tolerance in England was largely forged during the sectarian conflicts of the Interregnum (Gura 1984:185-90). Before the English civil war, the heavy hand of Massachusetts magistrates upon religious practice was not inconsistent with English practices; by the Glorious Revolution of 1689 it appeared anachronistic.

In 1661, one year after his restoration, Charles II announced his intention of promoting "liberty of conscience" in New England and "ordered New England to suspend its recently imposed (and implemented) death penalty for Quakers and to return to England any of this sect whom they still held in prison" (Ziff 1973:158, Gura 1984:324). This action provided a legal basis for gradually establishing religious tolerance in the Holy Commonwealth. The sentiments of some Massachusetts ministers and magistrates is revealed in the contemporary phrase, "that cursed Brat Toleration"; but by the late seventeenth century, this "curse" had "gained the run of all the New England colonies" (Gura 1984:324).

During these years, the Bay Colony's covenantal system underwent important modifications, spurred on by the need to deal with political pressure from England and increased pluralism and secularism in Massachusetts while still maintaining the essential aspects of Puritan society and belief. The 1662 instigation of the half-way covenant is the best known of these changes. Coming as it did when secularization was gaining momentum, it may be seen as a way to preserve church allegiance while accommodating that secularism. Two years later, the colony's leaders broadened the franchise while still retaining the political monopoly of covenant church members. According to Larzer Ziff (1973:153), the majority of magistrates still firmly believed that the state should enforce congregationalism, but "some gesture could be made . . . toward drawing the wealthier into a union with the autocracy." In August 1664, the General Court of Massachusetts extended the vote to men over twenty-four "who could get a ministerial certificate of orthodoxy in religion and unviciousness of life, and who were freeholders of estates ratable at ten shillings."

These stiff requirements sharply limited the number of nonvisible saints who could actually vote; opponents claimed that not three in one hundred could qualify. It is best interpreted, in my opinion, as a pragmatic adjustment designed to increase the central attachments of peripheral colonists while leaving the covenant system essentially unchanged.

Such measures ultimately proved ineffectual. To bring the Bay Colony under more direct English supervision and to counter Massachusetts magistrates' position that their royal charter placed them above current acts of Parliament and royal decrees, in 1684 the Court of Chancery in London annulled the Massachusetts Charter and abolished its elective system. As part of the newly formed "Dominion of New England," Massachusetts was denied all representative government and was ruled from England through Edmund Andros, the dominion's crown-appointed governor, who arrived in Boston in December 1686. As a consequence, the Massachusetts religious elite lost their ability to monopolize political power. Andros allowed an Anglican minister to hold religious services in Boston; and as a matter of course, Congregationalism ceased to be the only recognized religious system in Massachusetts (Breen 1980:92-93; Johnson 1981:3-70; Mead 1956:326).

In 1689, while the English were installing William and Mary on the throne during the Glorious Revolution, Massachusetts citizens deposed Andros and provisionally reestablished the government of the old charter. There was, however, considerable unrest among those denied freemanship on religious grounds. The Act of Toleration in England had granted political rights that very year to all Protestants except Unitarians. Partly because the magistrates' own attitudes toward toleration had changed, the General Court of Massachusetts, on 12 February 1690, opened freemenship to all "adult males who possessed good character, who paid four shillings . . . and who owned a house or lands worth at least six pounds. . . . This seemingly innocuous act opened a floodgate of political participation in Massachusetts Bay" (Breen 1980:95).

In 1691 the Bay Colony's new charter effected a compromise between local colonial leaders and the central government in England. Its provisions allowing freemanship for the unregenerate and tolerance for nonconforming religious groups essentially undermined the basis of unity within the covenant system (Johnson 1981:136-241).

The Puritan elite waged a strong rearguard action, and the 1691 charter certainly in itself did not cause either the collapse of the Puritan covenant order nor the disintegration of New England Puritanism; but it marked a significant point in the transition between the Puritan New England before 1691 and the Yankee New England which followed.

At its most fundamental level, it signaled a basic shift in the orientation of the inhabitants of colonial Massachusetts from a clearly defined and highly regulated local center to the metropolitan center of larger English society. Timothy Breen and Stephen Foster (1977:122) have summarized the consequences of this transformation as follows: "Eighteenth-century Massachusetts looked much like the rest of English society. No longer a peaceful anomaly, the Bay Colony began to experience sporadic internal disorder. The rise of organized violence should be taken not so much as evidence of the Puritan's failure to create the ideal commonwealth, but as testimony that the Bay Colony had rejoined the Western world."

3

The Second Great Awakening
and the Emergence of Mormonism

And now, behold, . . . I bring this portion of my gospel
to the knowledge of my people. Behold, I do not bring it to
destroy that which they have received, but to build it up.

(D&C 10:52)

THE FIRST GREAT AWAKENING

By the eve of the American Revolution, the dominant cultural
orientation throughout New England had shifted from Puritan to Yankee. The mechanisms for this transformation were the disassociation
of state and church and the expansion of pluralism and secularism,
which resulted in a religious landscape characterized by voluntary
affiliation and a choice among many churches. In this landscape arose
the whirlwind of the Second Great Awakening, the religious milieu
of early Mormonism.

The interrelationship of church and state in early Puritan New
England, though jarring to contemporary American values, was fully
consistent with its European roots. Before the Reformation, Europe
saw a symbiotic relationship between religious and civil authority.
A universal church supported civil authority, supplementing it with
sacred sanctions. In turn, the coercion of civil authority was available to maintain religious orthodoxy and solidarity. Universal conformity to a monolithic church was deemed vital for both civil and
religious order.

The Reformation changed the players but not the game. Where
Catholicism still dominated, civil power united with it against Protestantism to ensure religious conformity and orthodoxy. In most Protestant regions, Protestant state churches were established, and civil
power enforced conformity. A good example is the relationship of state
and church in Tudor and Jacobean England.

Sidney Mead (1956) distinguishes between such state churches and the unestablished religious groups like Anabaptists on the Continent and the Brownists in England, who believed that civil power should not enforce religious orthodoxy. Virtually all early colonizing ventures in North America tried to perpetuate the European alliance between an established church and civil power.

By the beginning of the Revolutionary War, however, this pattern had fundamentally changed. Mead (1956:320-26) pinpoints three causes: (1) the vast areas over which settlements spread made consistent enforcement of conformity laws virtually impossible; (2) the self-interest on the part of colonial proprietors and administrators worked against enforcement; and (3) social change in England, culminating in the 1689 Act of Toleration, created pressure to abolish antitoleration laws.

Then in the 1730s and 1740s arose the turmoil of the First Great Awakening which began the fragmentation of New England Puritanism. Its roots begin with Pietism, which had originated in Europe in the late seventeenth century as a movement for religious revitalization through individual emotional transformation (Mead 1954: 328-33). In England, this movement became identified with Methodism, led by such figures as the Wesley brothers. In America it became known as the Great Awakening. Its leading figure in New England was Jonathan Edwards, who in 1734 adopted the fervor of revivalism as a tool for religious conversion. In reaction to Puritanism's increasing intellectualism and complacency, he called for a return to strict Calvinism with its concepts of predestination and an all-powerful deity and repudiated the security and detachment of federal theology.

The ensuing debate generated a schism within Puritanism and contributed ultimately to the separation of the New England populace into a number of religious groupings. Puritan covenant organization ceased to exist as a unified system, and various Congregationalist, Presbyterian, Arminian, Antinomian, Unitarian, Universalist, Baptist, and Methodist groupings gave institutional expression to the religious beliefs and attitudes of New Englanders.

Various Puritan beliefs and practices, however, continued in these religious groupings. This was particularly true of Congregationalism, whose adherents (with considerable justification) regarded it as an extension of seventeenth-century Puritanism. And as Darrett Rutman (1970:125) has suggested, a "covenant fixation" remained "a continuing mark of New England."

THE SECOND GREAT AWAKENING

The First Great Awakening did little to reverse the general deterioration of organized religion in American life. Throughout the eighteenth century, church affiliation steadily declined until, by the Revolutionary War, only some 8 percent of the American people had formal church affiliations (Allen and Leonard 1976:10). Conditions generated by the war created additional difficulties for organized religions. Rationalism, naturalism, and deism gained increasing respectability among large segments of the American population while Anglicanism and Methodism, both English in origin, had to establish American footings. Quakers had become suspect because of their opposition to the war, and Congregationalists were criticized for the state support that they continued to receive in some parts of New England (M. Hill 1968:6-8; Mead 1956:327-34).

Civil authority became increasingly detached from religious matters, culminating in the ratification of the First Amendment in 1791 which prohibited the federal government from establishing a national church or from interfering with the free exercise of religion. Although the Constitution did not forbid established churches in the individual states, no state outside of New England had one by 1800 (Sweet 1952:57); even there, public support was dwindling. Thus, by the beginning of the nineteenth century, each religious organization in America was essentially free to determine its own future, succeeding if it could attract and keep followers, failing if it could not.

The Second Great Awakening began in the early 1790s and continued on into the 1840s. At different times and with varying degrees of intensity, it affected most regions of what was then the United States. In these almost fifty years, hundreds of religiously oriented individuals tried to reverse the decline in religious fervor among the American population through conversion and affiliation. As with the First Great Awakening, their basic tool was the religious revival using emotionalism and psychologically induced enthusiasm. The form of religion they espoused became known as evangelical Protestantism.

The Second Great Awakening and the religious fervor associated with it can best be understood within the context of transformations that were occurring in general American society during this period. The ostensibly chaotic conditions of religion were responses to the democratic transformations occuring during the early years of the republic. As the old order disintegrated "hundreds of thousands of common people were cut loose from all sorts of traditional bonds and found themselves freer, more independent, and more unconstrained than ever before in their history. (Wood 1980:361)

Emerging during the height of the Second Great Awakening, Mormonism has proved difficult to categorize. Sydney Ahlstrom (1972:508) called it "the culminating instance of early nineteenth-century sect formation, and at the same time that period's most powerful example of communitarian aspiration. On the other hand, the transformation brought about by numerical growth, economic adaptation, internal divisions, external hostility, and heroic exploits renders almost useless the usual categories of explanation." Perhaps the best way to begin to comprehend its nature is through an examination of the sociocultural background of its prophet-founder.

Joseph Smith's Family

Richard Bushman (1984:3, 4) has observed: "Mormonism . . . began with one family, the family of Joseph Smith, Sr., and Lucy Mack Smith [and] young Joseph Smith's culture was predominately family culture." That family was unequivocally of Puritan stock. Joseph Smith, Jr.'s, four grandparents were each born in a long-established Puritan village in Massachusetts or Connecticut during or just prior to the First Great Awakening. Three of the four spent most of their lives at least nominally aligned with Congregationalism.

His paternal ancestors had lived for several generations in and around Topsfield, Massachusetts. Great-grandfather Samuel Smith had represented Topsfield in the Massachusetts General Court and was active in public worship (Anderson 1971:89-91, 188-89, note 120). Grandfather Asael Smith was baptized into the Topsfield Congregational Church four days after his birth in 1744 (Anderson 1971:89, 188-89, note 120), and Grandmother Mary Duty Smith had also been baptized into the Congregational church (Anderson 1971:91, 191, note 127). In 1772, they "owned" the covenant when their son Joseph, Sr., was baptized, much as their ancestors would have done a hundred years before (Anderson 1971:91-92, 191-92, note 129).

Although Asael was a pew holder in the Topsfield Congregational church, he had the reputation of being a religious rebel. In 1797, after moving to Tunbridge, Vermont, Asael and sons Jesse and Joseph

joined a Universalist society; but even then, he remained a pew holder in the Tunbridge meetinghouse (Anderson 1971:106, 207-8, note 185). Except for his son Joseph, all his children evidently became active in either Congregational or Presbyterian churches (Anderson, 1971: 105).

Solomon Mack, Joseph Smith, Jr.'s, maternal grandfather, was born in Lyme, Connecticut, in 1732 (Mack 1811:3). From early childhood until about age twenty-one, he was indentured to a master who did not teach him to read and never spoke to him "at all on the subject of religion." Mack describes himself during this period as "totally ignorant of divine revelation or anything appertaining to the Christian religion" (Mack 1811:4).

In 1759 Solomon married Lydia Gates of East Haddam, Connecticut (Anderson 1971:163-64, note 24). The daughter of a deacon in the East Haddam Congregational church, Lydia was baptized shortly after her birth in 1732; and in 1762 she made a formal profession of faith and was "received to communion" (Anderson 1971:26, 177-78, notes 81, 82). They spent much of their married life in wilderness areas of Vermont and New Hampshire, where Lydia gave their children a religious education, evidently imbuing them with deep religious fervor (Anderson 1971:27; L. Smith 1958:9-36). Later, Solomon came under his wife's religious influence and experienced a miraculous conversion to Christianity (Mack 1811:18-23).

The future founder of Mormonism was born 23 December 1805 in Sharon, Windsor County, Vermont. During his early childhood both of his parents were evidently "seekers," one manifestation of the widespread gospel primitivist movement. In its broadest sense, gospel primitivists tried to restore contemporary Christianity to its "primitive" (or earliest) form; thus, even Puritanism might be regarded as a manifestation of gospel primitivism.

Primitivism was never a unified movement; but during the Second Great Awakening, six elements emerged as distinctive features: (1) a strong belief that existing churches were corrupt and apostate; (2) an opposition to the sectarian conflict generated by revivalism; (3) a disapproval of the Calvinist doctrine of election; (4) stress on the authority of the Bible; (5) a belief that restoring the practices and doctrines of the New Testament church would solve Christianity's present difficulties; and (6) a conviction that the millennial reign of Christ was imminent.

Many primitivists organized themselves to replicate what they thought of as original Christianity, but seekers shunned all organized churches. They felt that the true church was different from any form of organized religion of which they were aware (M. Hill 1968, 1969; Latourette 1941:428; Mead 1954:295-99; Murch 1962; Rupp 1844: 166-70, 250-65, 520-21, 730-31; Sweet 1952:190-233).

The term "seeker" dates back to seventeenth-century New England Puritanism and beyond that to English Puritans (Gura 1984: 73-76). Thus, Roger Williams, the best known of the seventeenth-century New England seekers taught that "there is no church, no sacrament, no pastors, no church-officers, or ordinances in the world, nor has been since a few years after the Apostles" (in Gura 1984:74).

Expressing much the same sentiment, Joseph Smith's mother, Lucy Mack Smith, stated that as a young woman she had come to the conclusion: "There was not then upon the earth the religion which I sought. I therefore determined to examine my Bible, and taking Jesus and His disciples for my guide, to endeavor to obtain from God that which man could neither give nor take away" (L. Smith 1958:36). Joseph, Sr., evidently entertained similar views. According to Lucy, he felt that "no one class of religionist . . . knew any more concerning the Kingdom of God than those of the world, or as such as made no profession of religion whatsoever. . . . He [consequently] would not subscribe to any particular system of faith, but contended for the ancient order as established by our Lord and Savior Jesus Christ and His apostles" (L. Smith 1958:48, 46).

While Joseph Smith's parents had thus departed considerably from the Congregational Puritanism of their ancestors, young Joseph had ample opportunity to absorb Congregationalism. As a child he was in close contact with his Grandmother Lydia Gates Mack. In 1814 he spent some time with his Uncle Jesse Smith in Salem, Massachusetts, a strict Calvinist, a "Covenanter," and Asael Smith's only surviving son who did not eventually convert to Mormonism (*JD* 5:103; Anderson 1971:111).

The Burned-over District

In 1816 the Smith family left the New England hill country and migrated to the Finger Lakes region of New York. They settled first in the village of Palmyra and two years later moved two miles south to a farm in the township of Manchester. They were now in the heart of an area nicknamed "the Burned-over District" for its frequent and intense religious revivals. Three factors apparently contributed to this localized fervor.

First was the socioreligious background of the people. Although settlement beyond the Adirondacks and Catskills hadn't begun until the late 1780s, by the time the Smiths arrived the area had some 200,000 people. Over two-thirds of these were from New England (Allen and Leonard 1976:18-19; Cross 1965:3-5), leading Timothy Dwight to call it "a colony from New England" (in M. Hill 1975:5). Most of these Yankee transplants, like the Smiths, had come from the New England hill country, which had a stronger tradition of Pietism than the coastal regions and where religious fervor and revivalism had not experienced the same decline (Cross 1965:7).

Second, the region's economy was different from that of New England, contributing to social disruption. After the revolution, New York experienced rapid economic development. Between 1791 and 1831, its commerce increased tenfold (M. Hill 1975:5). The Erie Canal, begun the year after the Smiths left New England, brought western New York into much closer contact with the industrialized East, accelerating economic development, disrupting traditional trade relationships, opening new markets for agricultural products, undermining home manufacture and local industry and stimulating occupational diversification (Blumin 1976; Cross 1965:55-77; R. Miller 1979; Shipps 1974:7-8). Such a situation created widespread anxiety and frustration, an emotionally charged milieu that fostered both increased religious concern and the appeals of revivalism (M. Hill 1975).

The third, and perhaps most decisive factor, was the presence of revivalistic missionaries. During the Second Great Awakening, individuals in New England and western New York, alarmed at the large number of unchurched settlers, began sponsoring missionary ministers in the area. While it is impossible to establish the precise number of these missionaries in western New York at any given point in time, the following figures provide some indication. In 1814 the Connecticut Missionary Society had 34 preachers in the region; the Massachusetts Missionary Society, 30; the Hampshire Society, 14; and the Berkshire and Columbia Society, perhaps 16. In 1818 the Presbyterian General Assembly was supporting 8 missionaries in the area. In 1827 the American Home Missionary Society reported that it was supporting 120 missionaries in New York State (Cross 1965:21-22). A number of smaller societies were also sending out missionaries. In addition to the ministers sent by the missionary societies, a number of itinerant Methodist and Baptist ministers and assorted revivalist preachers from smaller sects were in the area. Most of the missionary preachers came from New England's western hill country and were trained in its strong revivalistic tradition.

An unexpected consequence of this missionary activity was the emergence of bitter sectarian conflict. The American Home Missionary movement in particular encouraged the proliferation of churches and supported full-time pastors in areas where they could not have survived without external financial assistance. In self-defense, other missionary societies adopted similar tactics. The result was essentially religious warfare, with each denomination attempting to win adherents from competing sects (Cross 1965:47).

Whitney Cross, who has written the standard social history on the region for this period, finds that Palmyra and Manchester "very nearly typified the region" (Cross 1965:140). Settlement in both places had begun about 1790, and the population was primarily from Connecticut and Vermont. The two towns thrived after the construction of the Erie Canal, which passed through Palmyra and was in operation there by 1822. The Smiths thus entered a society "less isolated and provincial, more vigorous and cosmopolitan, than Vermont. It was reaching economic stability but remained on the upgrade, whereas rural Vermont had already started into decline" (Cross 1965:140).

Revivals had begun in the Palmyra-Manchester area as early as the turn of the century (Cross 1965:140). For several decades, waves of intensive revivalist activity succeeded periods of religious calm. These revivals could attract large numbers of people. An estimated 10,000 people attended one Palmyra camp meeting in 1826 (Backman 1969:306).

Mormonism's Regional Roots

Mormonism can be traced, at least in part, to three strong regional religious influences on Joseph Smith: revivalism, primitivism, and Puritanism.

The sectarian conflict generated by the revivalism of the Second Great Awakening stirred deep religious unrest. Many early Mormons could not resolve their religious problems within the revivalistic context; and from its inception, Mormonism was opposed to revivalistic techniques (Ellsworth 1951:339-40).

Joseph Smith himself indicated that one circumstance which motivated him to go to the woods to seek divine guidance was the frustration he felt at a revival where "his Mother, Br. and Sisters got

Religion. He wanted to get Religion too, wanted to feel and shout like the rest but could feel nothing'' (in Backman 1980:[177]). The ensuing theophany resulted in the founding of Mormonism.

Many early converts to Mormonism appear to have struggled with similar issues. As examples, Warren Foote often attended Methodist revivals and even aspired to be a preacher, but

> seeing them ''jump'' and hearing them shout and sing disgusted him, and he became a religious seeker. George A. Smith, after joining the Congregational Church, said he still felt guilty. He went to many revivals, but after he was the only one not converted and was sealed up to damnation, he was in despair. Willard Richards had a similar experience when he was rejected by the local Congregational Church; he wrote later that revivals stir up ''unnecessary fears and torture the mind.'' . . . Lewis Shurtliff drifted from Baptist to Campbellite but still did not feel saved, having had no conversion experience. . . . [And] Parley P. Pratt . . . ''felt anxious to be saved.'' . . . [With this object in mind he] attended Baptist meetings but was unable to ''tell them of any particular experience of religion.'' (M. Hill 1980:425)

Such experiences were probably typical for early Mormon converts, for most were apparently recruited from evangelical Protestantism. In a study of Mormon missionary activity before 1860, George Ellsworth (1951:339) found that a large proportion of early Mormon converts had belonged to evangelical churches. In a demographic analysis of 100 early Mormon converts, Laurence M. Yorgason (1974:42) singled out those affiliated with another church at conversion; 89 percent belonged to churches that employed revivalistic techniques.

Second, early Mormonism shares many characteristics with the broader gospel primitivist movement (Hill 1968; 1969). Many early converts had a gospel primitivist orientation similar to that of Joseph Smith's parents. Wilford Woodruff, for example, later president of the church, had not joined a church earlier because ''I could not find any denomination whose doctrines, faith and practices agreed with the Gospel of Jesus Christ.'' Newel Knight, one of the earliest converts, felt that there had been a falling away from pure Christianity but had faith that the gospel would be restored (in M. Hill 1968:57-58). Fifty-seven percent of Yorgason's sample had a primitivistic orientation (1974:45-47).

Third, certain aspects of Mormon doctrine and practice have a close affinity with Puritanism. Of the twenty-six men who were formally ordained to positions of high leadership in the church during Joseph Smith's life, twenty-two had been born either in New England or New York (Ellsworth 1951:392). Seventy-five percent of Yorgason's sample (1974:32) were likewise born either in New England or New York. Ellsworth (1951:341) corroboratively concludes that pre-1860 missionaries "made the greatest number of . . . converts and organized the greatest number of congregations in the middle-sized, settled communities of New York and New England."

For well over a hundred years, observers have assumed a link between Puritanism and Mormonism. As early as 1867, English editor William Hepworth Dixon quoted an unidentified American journalist as saying that "everybody in this country has got into the habit of calling . . . [the Mormons] the spawn of our New England coventicles"; while in 1871 Ralph Waldo Emerson characterized Mormonism as "an after-clap of Puritanism" (Mulder and Mortensen 1958:366, 384).

More recent investigators share similar opinions: Fawn Brodie (1977:1) writes that Joseph Smith "was as much a product of New England as Jonathan Edwards." Mark Leone (1979:11) holds that "New England Calvinism . . . formed one mainstream from which Mormonism flowed." Robert Bellah (1978:3) recommends studying Mormonism "with the example of Puritan New England in mind."

Yet there has been little systematic attempt to investigate the precise nature of this association beyond listings of shared traits. Granted, the list is extensive, but few include detailed analyses. Some of the suggested parallels are: (1) an emphasis on reason and an orderly relationship among ideas (Cross 1965:145; DePillis 1966:84); (2) an interest in theorizing and speculation (DePillis 1966:84); (3) a belief in human perfectibility (David Davis 1972:21); (4) an ethic of thrift and industry (Allen and Leonard 1976:21); (5) an emphasis on the importance of a Christian calling (David Davis 1972:21); (6) a sense of social obligation (Cross 1965:145); (7) an institutional cast of mind (DePillis 1966:84); (8) the desire to establish a well-ordered close-knit community, an ideal theocracy, and a church of saints (Allen and Leonard 1976:21; David Davis 1972:21; K. Hansen 1981:92; Jamison 1961:213, Wood 1980:384); (9) belief in providential history, in predestination, in a restoration of the "ancient order of things," and in America as a chosen land (Allen and Leonard 1976:21; David Davis 1972:21; Jamison 1961:213); (10) a belief in continuing revelation coupled with an element of mysticism and superstition (David Davis 1972:21); and (11) a positive attitude toward marital sex (K. Hansen 1981:147, 153).

However, perhaps the most significant parallel, similar covenant structure, has received only scant attention.

MORMON COVENANT ORGANIZATION AND GROUP COHESIVENESS

Mormon historian Marvin Hill (1975:4-5) characterizes early Mormonism as a "quest for refuge." He explains:

> It seems likely that the Mormons reacted against the disintegration of the rural, socially harmonious village community with its dominant religious orientation which its leaders had known in New England, and the triumph of a commercially oriented, acquisitive, openly pluralistic and competitive, and implicitly secular social and religious order in western New York. The early Mormons, I would argue, were fugitives from social change and political and social conflict, their Kingdom of God a refuge.

Klaus Hansen (1981:51, 52, 20, 69) comes to similar conclusions. He essentially accepts Perry Miller's (1965:3-95) and William G. McLoughlin's (1974; 1978) position that the Second Great Awakening helped create the political, economic, and religious pluralism of contemporary America and sees Mormonism as a "counterideology" to this development. It was a "revitalization movement" of sorts that "appeared on the American religious scene at precisely that moment when external religious authority, both intellectually and institutionally, was in headlong retreat before the forces of individual responsibility." Thus, argues Hansen, Mormonism was a reactionary response to the divisive nature of American pluralism and "a quest for order."

The Hill-Hansen hypothesis is a useful one. From its inception, believers have regarded Mormonism as an authentic restoration of primitive Christianity; but one of its distinctive attributes is a system of order reminiscent of Puritan covenant structure. "Mormons reversed America's separation of church and state," wrote Gordon Wood, "and tried to reestablish the kind of well-knit commonwealth that John Winthrop had envisioned two hundred years earlier" (1980:384). John Dillenberger (1978:185-86) goes further:

> Mormonism belonged to an English type of Christianity as compared with a Continental type. . . . From the medieval Lollards to the Puritans . . . the identification with Israel, the creation of a new Israel, the identification of the land and people with Israel has been constant [in English Christianity]. . . . The impossibility of creating such a society in England led, of course, to New England, the real new Israel. The Puritan experiment in New England was more successful in its ethos

than its theology, which increasingly divided and fragmented the very society it was intending, in analogy to Israel, to create. It was the Mormons who found and made the place a society in genuine analogy to Israel. The religious-social experiment which was frustrated in London, and abortive in Boston, succeeded in Salt Lake City.

He hypothesized that Joseph Smith and other early Mormons drew on persisting aspects of the Puritan tradition in establishing a religious system that they hoped would unite them despite the centrifugal forces of the Second Great Awakening.

An alternative explanation is that the Mormon covenant system developed independent of Puritanism. The structural similarities stemmed from a common goal (establishing ideal human relationships) using a common source (biblical patterns).

Believing Mormons usually see continuing revelation as the cause of the similarities: God inspired the Puritans to establish their social order as preparation for the restoration of the gospel and the establishment of the kingdom of God upon the earth through the Prophet Joseph Smith.

The strong similarities between the two covenant systems can be meaningfully compared regardless of their source. In the following chapters, I will examine Mormon covenant organization, compare it to the Puritan system, describe how it established social order amid the religious flux of the Second Great Awakening, and trace its historic function in providing unity and a distinctive identity for the Mormons while pragmatically adjusting to changing conditions.

4

Israel's Promised Lands: Mormon Covenant Organization, 1830-38

We believe that God has set his hand the second time to recover the remnant of his people, Israel; and that the time is near when he will bring them from the four winds . . . and reinstate them upon their own lands which he gave their fathers by covenant.

Oliver Cowdery (*MA* 1:2)

One of the most comprehensive and characteristic aspects of Mormon group life is its pervasive covenant organization, flexibly undergoing modifications and transformation in response to historical demands. This chapter discusses that system between the organization of the church in 1830 and the expulsion of the Mormons from Missouri in the winter of 1838-39. I also compare it with its Puritan counterpart.

It is easier to grasp the underlying premises of Mormon covenant organization when that system is viewed from the Mormon historical perspective. This perspective reflects basic Mormon understandings that were similar to those of the Christian Primitivist movement: (1) existing Christianity was in apostasy; (2) Christ's millennial reign was imminent; and (3) the restoration of the primitive church was both possible and crucial.

Early Mormons found evidence of apostasy in the sectarian conflict and social upheaval of antebellum America. Thus, in 1832 Joseph Smith (1984:5) related that between the ages of twelve and fifteen he had come to the conclusion that "mankind . . . had apostatised from the true and liveing faith and there was no society or denomination that built upon the gospel of Jesus Christ as recorded in the new testament."

Believers felt that this apostasy would bring the judgments of God upon the world, then usher in Christ's millennial reign. In a revelation that Joseph Smith dictated in November 1831, the Lord exclaims:

> Prepare ye, prepare ye for that which is to come, for the Lord is nigh;
>
> And the anger of the Lord is kindled, and his sword is bathed in heaven, and it shall fall upon the inhabitants of the earth. . . .
>
> For they have strayed from mine ordinances, and have broken mine everlasting covenant. (D&C 1:12-13, 15)

In such a context, the restoration of the primitive church was vital. Those who embraced the true and uncorrupted religion would escape divine wrath and be prepared for Christ's millennial reign (*HC* 1:11-14; L. Smith 1910). Faithful Mormons saw the Church of Jesus Christ of Latter-day Saints, established by Joseph Smith, as this promised restoration. Thus, in the same revelation, the Lord declares:

> I the Lord, knowing the calamity which should come upon the inhabitants of the earth, called upon my servant Joseph Smith, Jun., and spake unto him from heaven, . . .
>
> That mine everlasting covenant might be established. (D&C 1:17, 22)

According to the Mormon view, history can be divided into various "gospel dispensations." At the head of each dispensation stands a pivotal prophet to whom the Lord reveals His will and with whom He establishes His covenant. Under divine authorization, the prophet organizes his followers according to the provisions of this covenant. As long as they adhere to the covenant and comply with the gospel, the Lord blesses them and regards them as his people. In time, however, they cease to live the gospel and depart from the covenant. The resulting apostasy requires the Lord to call a new prophet, instigating yet another gospel dispensation, and again restoring the covenant. The Saints believed that the final dispensation, referred to as "the dispensation of the fulness of times," commenced with the divine calling of Joseph Smith (D&C 27:13; 76:106; 110:12, 16; 112:30; *EJ* 1:39-42).

THE DISTRIBUTION OF POWER

The Mormon Concept of Priesthood

The claim of ultimate religious authority distinguished Mormonism from its inception. Mario DePillis (1966) speculates that the voluntaristic pluralism of the Second Great Awakening required any new religious movement to present credentials establishing its divine validity, and many primitive gospel groups did so by showing how their doctrine and organization paralleled those of the New Testament church. Joseph Smith claimed more. He announced Mormonism as not only a reinstatement of biblical teachings and organizational patterns but as a unique restoration of the actual power of God. Accepting his position, his followers believed that Mormonism monopolized divine authority.

Such a position provided the basis for the belief that Mormonism was unique—the only church endowed with divine authority. Its elaborate organizational system embodied that authority, thus producing, in the Mormon view, an institutional structure independent of all other organizational forms and solely approved by God. It thus became for them the "only true and living church upon the face of the whole earth" (D&C 1:30).

Mormons employed the term *priesthood* for their conception of God's power and authority. Endowed with the priesthood, mortal men became God's authorized agents, empowered to fulfill his purposes on earth. While priesthood was seen as the power of God, "the keys of the priesthood" authorized the exercise of that power in certain prescribed offices or functions.

According to Mormon belief, only males were eligible for priesthood, and it could be conferred only by formal ordination performed by someone who already possessed the priesthood and had "the keys" to ordain others. Mormons held that in every gospel dispensation, at least some mortal men have had the priesthood. In the primitive Christian church, Christ's apostles had the priesthood and the keys to confer it on others. Following the death of the apostles, no one had the keys of conferral. Living priesthood bearers died.

There then ensued the Great Apostasy, a period of some sixteen hundred years during which the priesthood was absent from the earth. However, at the opening of the "dispensation of the fulness of times," Joseph Smith and his associate Oliver Cowdery were ordained to the priesthood by John the Baptist and by the ancient apostles, Peter, James, and John, now resurrected beings (D&C 13; 107:8, 20; *HC* 1:39-42).

These ordinations restored general priesthood power and also the keys of conferral to earth. A series of visitations from a number of divine personages over the next several years delegated the priesthood keys of specific functions to Joseph Smith "all declaring their dispensations, their rights, their keys, their honors, . . . and the power of their priesthood" (D&C 128:21).

Priesthood Ordinances

Administratively, the existence of priesthood in the Mormon system permitted the bearers to perform such "saving ordinances" as baptism and also regulate church organization and administration. Integral to most priesthood ordinances was a covenant, a binding relationship among individuals and between individuals and God. If the participants kept the covenant, the relationship thus established was ratified by the authority of God delegated to the priesthood holder officiating in the ordinance.

Like the Puritans before them, Mormons believed covenant making to be among the most serious acts that mortals could perform. However, they went beyond their Puritan ancestors in maintaining that God, by delegating priesthood power to mortal men, also permitted himself to be bound by covenants initiated under that authority (i.e., *MA* 1:10:146).

Mormons also used the Puritan term *seal*. To Puritans it meant the visible symbol of a covenant; to Mormons it meant the authoritative ratification of convenantal promises, in a sense similar to that of Matthew 16:19, in which Christ gives Peter the keys of the kingdom and promises, "Whatsoever thou shalt bind on earth shall be bound in heaven." The term *seal* appears in the Book of Mormon to describe the binding power of God, Satan, and prophets (Mosiah 5:15; Alma 34:35; Hel. 10:7). After the church was organized in 1830, the term appears to have first been employed about assurances of eternal salvation. Thus, in October 1831, Joseph Smith declared that Mormon elders holding the "high priesthood . . . have power given them to seal up the Saints unto eternal life" (Cannon and Cook 1983:20-21).

The concept of sealing was later generalized to include bestowing various promises. For example, Joseph Smith relates that on 21 January 1836 he anointed his father's "head with . . . consecrated oil, and sealed many blessings upon him . . . [after which] my father anointed my head and sealed upon me the blessings of Moses, to lead Israel in the latter days" (*HC* 2:379-80).

Consistent with their belief that the priesthood had been lost at the beginning of the Great Apostasy, Mormons did not recognize religious rituals performed by individuals outside the LDS church as valid. Thus, when converts who had been baptized by non-Mormon ministers sought to join the church without undergoing rebaptism by Mormon priesthood holders, Joseph Smith received a revelation announcing that to participate in the "new and . . . everlasting covenant," they would have to be baptized by the priesthood authority that had been conferred on Joseph Smith (D&C 22).

Church Administration

Eleven months after Joseph Smith received priesthood authority, he organized the church. While he affirmed that the procedures he followed in organizing the church had been received by revelation (*HC* 1:60-61), they closely resembled Congregationalist practices of church government. On 6 April 1830, Smith met with five other men in a farmhouse at Fayette, New York. He asked these men if they would accept him and Oliver Cowdery "as their teachers" and "whether they were satisfied that we should proceed and be organized as a Church according to [the] commandment which we had received." When they formally agreed, Smith ordained Cowdery an elder of the church and was himself ordained by Cowdery to the same office. Smith and Cowdery then "proceeded to call out and ordain some others of the brethren to different offices of the Priesthood, according as the Spirit manifested unto us" (*HC* 1:77-79).

Joseph Smith thus established a dual claim to authority: (1) by ordination from divine beings; and (2) by the common consent of the membership of the church to his ordination. It seems to be a practical solution to a practical problem: in a society characterized by voluntaristic pluralism, even a man claiming authority through divine ordination could exercise religious influence only over those willing to accept his leadership.

These early years saw considerable conflict over the issue of whether a man's authority resulted from the collective will of the people or from his possession of priesthood power and keys. By the Nauvoo period (1839-44), a consensus had generally emerged that priesthood existed logically prior to the church, which existed operationally to fulfill the objectives of inspired priesthood leaders. Thus the Congregational-like procedure of sustaining ecclesiastical officers became essentially a formality; position and authority within the church were understood as products of divine authority.

Although Mormonism traced its origins to the early revelations of Joseph Smith and to his divine priesthood, his position as head of the church emerged in stages. Among the steps were establishing his revelations as alone authoritative for the church, formal sustainings by the church membership, and his monopoly on all priesthood keys. He could delegate priesthood keys to others, allowing them to fill particular positions, perform specific ordinances, and receive revelation for their jurisdictions; but priesthood authority and keys ultimately resided in him as president of the high priesthood, a position to which he was formally ordained at Amherst, Ohio, on 25 January 1832 (Cahoon 25 Jan. 1832; JH, 25 Jan. 1832).

Furthermore, in addition to his monopoly on priesthood, he also had a monopoly on revelation for the church as God's solely authorized mouthpiece. Thus, all doctrines and policies came from God through Smith's pronouncements. The Saints were then expected to sustain such pronouncements by formal vote and obey them.

Beginning in the earliest years of the church's existence and clearly by the settlement of Nauvoo in 1939, the joint office of president of the church and of the high priesthood, together with the complex organization over which it had jurisdiction, showed many of the characteristics Weber (1968:1139-41) identified as aspects of office charisma. As a mechanism for regulating religious conformity, Mormon priesthood organization is analogous to the Puritan state. Mormon hierocrats in this highly centralized system were empowered to regulate the affairs of the church, determine correct doctrine, and expel unrepentant nonconformists through excommunication.

Simultaneously Mormon priesthood organization also fostered personal religious experience while channelling it toward the localized Mormon center. All members were entitled to personal revelation and encouraged to seek spiritual gifts. Many converts, frustrated in their quest for religious experience in evangelical Protestantism, found personal religious fulfillment in Mormonism.

The hierarchy, however, retained the right to interpret the meaning and significance of religious experiences. As early as September 1830, six months after the organization of the church, a member named Hiram Page began claiming that he was receiving revelations from a seer stone. A revelation to Oliver Cowdery through Joseph Smith instructed him to tell Page that ''those things which he hath written from that stone are not of me, and that Satan deceiveth him'' (D&C 28:11, see also *HC* 1:109-15). Given this procedure, believing Mormons would likely interpret their personal religious experiences in ways that were consistent with those of the hierocracy.

Like New England Puritanism, the Mormon method of containing charisma did not prevent charismatic radicalism; but the system was essentially stable. The personal religious experience of most Mormons was contained in a way that reinforced the Mormon social order, while those who continued to interpret their religious experiences in potentially disruptive ways were excommunicated.

MYTHOLOGICAL UNDERPINNINGS

Mormons, like the Puritans before them, linked their current covenants with a mythical past. They believed that all the covenantal promises made in previous dispensations would at last be fulfilled in the "dispensation of the fulness of times." The foundation myth for Mormons appears in the Book of Mormon, from which the common name is taken.

The Book of Mormon sets forth in broad contours the Mormon pattern of redemptive history and the basic structures and processes within Mormon covenant organization. A significant number of Book of Mormon themes broadly resemble those of Puritan redemptive history: (1) the Abrahamic covenant dominates God's dealings with both individuals and groups; (2) this covenant can be transmitted to Abraham's offspring; (3) believing Gentiles can participate in this covenant; (4) the Jews will be converted as a nation; (5) American Indians are the biological descendants of biblical Hebrews; (6) America is a chosen land with a divine mission; (7) God has made a national covenant with the inhabitants of America collectively; and (8) the New Jerusalem will be established in America in the last days.

Furthermore, the Book of Mormon is replete with covenantal imagery. *Covenant* occurs 145 times, while *swear*, *oath*, and *promise* appear 173 times (Shapiro 1977:216-17, 678, 768, 938, 940). Sometimes the context describes covenantal relationships among individuals in the narrative, but often these terms appear in passages that might be regarded as prophetic commentary on the Abrahamic covenant. From these passages, we can identify a prophetic history of fulfilling the Abrahamic covenant, the social groups involved, and the rights and obligations associated with that covenant.

The Book of Mormon describes the Abrahamic covenant thus: God established a covenantal relationship with Abraham that was transmitted by hereditary right to his son Isaac and grandson Jacob. The same covenant was then extended to all the descendants of Jacob, who collectively became known as the house of Israel. In time, the entire house of Israel fell into apostasy and was temporarily disqualified to receive the divine promises that its members might otherwise

have claimed by right of descent. They were consequently "scattered
upon all the face of the earth, and . . . among all nations." Many
eventually forgot that they were members of the house of Israel and
ceased to have any knowledge of the provisions of the Abrahamic covenant. To remedy this situation, in the last days "the Lord will proceed to do a marvelous work" by again making known "the covenants
of the Father of heaven unto Abraham." Many of Abraham's descendants will again become qualified to receive the covenantal blessings
that are theirs by hereditary right, and "all the kindreds of the earth
[shall] be blessed" (BM 1 Ne. 22:3-12; see also 1 Ne. 10:2-14; 3 Ne.
20:12-21; 29; Morm. 5:20; Eth. 13:5-11).

The Book of Mormon describes two basic social groups affected
by the covenant: biological descendants of the patriarch Jacob are
the house of Israel while all else are the Gentiles, who (because they
are not descended from Jacob) have no hereditary rights to the Abrahamic covenant. The house of Israel is subdivided into the descendants of Judah and Joseph, both of them sons of Jacob. The
descendants of Judah are essentially identical with the Jews (BM 2
Ne. 3:12; 29:5), while part of the descendants of Joseph (through his
son Manasseh) are the families whose history it records, a branch who
immigrated to the New World (BM 1 Ne. 5:14; Alma 10:3). The
American Indians (called Lamanites) are at least partially descended
from these colonizers (1 Ne. 13:12-14; see also *HC* 1:12; *TS* 3:707).

The Book of Mormon further implies that Joseph Smith is a
descendant of the biblical Joseph (2 Ne. 3:7-9, 14-15), suggesting that
part of the patriarch Joseph's descendants were "scattered" among
the Puritans and other Europeans who colonized America in the seventeenth century.

Among the various promises associated with the Abrahamic covenant in the Book of Mormon, probably the most frequently repeated
and most important is land. God promises to gather the righteous
together (BM 1 Ne. 19:16, 3 Ne. 20:13) on "choice" and "promised
lands" (BM 1 Ne. 5:5; 7:13; 13:30; 2 Ne. 1:5; 9:2; 10:7; 3 Ne. 20:29),
and to "prosper" them in the land (BM 1 Ne. 4:14; 2 Ne. 1:9; Mosiah
1:7; 2:22).

Other promises involve a quality of religious life. Those who obey
the covenant will come to a correct understanding of God (BM 2 Ne.
10:2; 3 Ne. 20:13), will receive the gospel (BM 3 Ne. 16:12), and
will bless "all the kindreds of the earth" (BM 1 Ne. 15-18; 3 Ne.
20:25).

Although these promises depend on obedience and can be extended to others who comply with the commandments, they are presented as hereditary rights for the descendants of Jacob. The Book of Mormon compares the house of Israel to an olive tree from which all recalcitrant Israelites will eventually be cut off and upon which repentant and worthy Gentiles will be grafted so that they may become eligible for the Abrahamic promises (BM Jac. 5-6; see also 1 Ne. 14:1-2; 2 Ne. 10:7-10; 3 Ne. 21:20-24). Thus, while the Book of Mormon clearly indicates that convenantal promises can be biologically transmitted, it emphatically maintains that their fulfillment is predicated upon personal worthiness. "For behold, I say unto you that as many of the Gentiles as will repent are the covenant people of the Lord; and as many of the Jews as will not repent shall be cast off; for the Lord covenanteth with none save it be with them that repent and believe in his Son, who is the Holy One of Israel" (BM 2 Ne. 30:2).

BASES OF THE RELATIONSHIPS

The Book of Mormon was published less than a month before the church was organized (Bushman 1984:110). For many Saints, the book and the church became inextricably linked: the church with its priesthood power was the vehicle by which the book's covenantal promises would be fulfilled, while the Saints themselves were the groups who could claim the book's covenant promises. Such a view became the basis for solidarity within the church.

The Book of Mormon's covenantal ideology quickly became a foundational principle in the Latter-day Saint world view. For example, the church's earliest periodical, the *Evening and Morning Star*, was published only a little more than two years (June 1832 to September 1834), but it contains the complete text of the Book of Mormon allegory of the tame and wild olive tree, with a commentary on its significance (*EMS* 1:4:[26-28]; see also *EMS* 1:5:[33]). It devotes considerable space to the relationship between Gentiles and Israelites and how both may qualify for Abrahamic promises (e.g., *EMS* 1:5:[34]; 2:16:126-27; 2:19:148; 2:23:178; 2:24:188). One article discusses the whereabouts of the lost ten tribes (*EMS* 1:5:[33-34]), while another traces the history of the tribe of Joseph (*EMS* 1:6:[41-43]). One of the most persistent themes is the "gathering of Israel" in the last days (e.g., *EMS* 1:2:[13]; 1:3:[21]; 1:7:[51-53]; 1:9:[67, 72]; 2:13:100; 2:14:106-7). In this context, articles discuss the migration of Jews to Palestine (*EMS* 1:7:[51]; 1:9:[67-68]; 2:14:106-7; 2:16:127) and the effects of the Indian Removal Act of 1830 on the gathering of the Lamanites (*EMS* 1:7:[54]; 1:8:[62]; 1:9:[71]; 2:13:101).

Varying passages in the Book of Mormon identify "God's covenant people" as (1) all who obey God's commandments and (2) all the literal descendants of Jacob. Both concepts became basic to Mormon group identity, producing a pattern that lends itself to analysis in terms of David Schneider's (1968) American kinship model. The first, which coincides with Schneider's category of law-established relationships based on a "code of conduct," consists of accepting church discipline as symbolized by baptism. The second, which corresponds to Schneider's concept of shared genetic substance, is manifest in the understanding that Mormons should ideally possess the blood of Israel.

The Baptismal Covenant and the Relationship in Law

Baptism for Mormons officially had a dual purpose (BM Mosiah 18:8-13; Moro. 6; D&C 20:37). First, it established a covenant with God. Baptized men, women, and children over eight covenanted to forsake their sins, take upon themselves the name of Christ, and henceforth keep the Lord's commandments; the Lord in turn covenanted that, if the recipients proved faithful to their promises, God would forgive their sins, bestow the Holy Ghost, and accept them into the kingdom of heaven. Second, baptism was the means of achieving membership in the Mormon church, the earthly manifestation of God's kingdom.

Because of these two purposes, Mormon baptism became a boundary mechanism separating the faithful covenanters from those who had either rejected the covenant or those who lacked ability to comply with its provisions (e.g., infants).

Covenanters were bonded through the Mormon order of law. In contrast, Puritan baptism had expressed the order of nature in its aspect as a "seal" of the covenant of grace. The covenant of grace had set in motion an essentially biological process to transform the recipient's nature to correspond with that of pre-Fall Adam and Eve. Administered to the infant children of church members, baptism transmitted federal holiness to them. As a result, the Puritan church community was essentially bound together in hereditary charisma.

Mormons saw the effects of their baptismal covenant differently. They did not believe that the guilt of the Fall was transmitted biologically (e.g., BM Moro. 8:19-26; D&C 93:38) and, hence, did not believe in natural depravity. Children were born "in a state of innocence" and did not need baptism until they were morally responsible agents, capable of personally committing themselves to the baptismal covenant (D&C 20:71). Eight was defined as this point of moral responsibility (D&C 68:25). While one might question whether eight-year-old children actually comprehended the significance of the baptismal covenant to which they were formally committing themselves, this practice contributed to the Mormon self-definition that the church consisted exclusively of individuals who by covenant had committed themselves to comply with the commandments of God. Mormon baptism thus created solidarity based on a common code of conduct rather than heredity or biology.

The "Blood" of Israel and Relationships in Nature

The solidarity of voluntary participation in a code of conduct was not particularly different from that found in various religious organizations that emerged during the Second Great Awakening. However, Mormon solidarity was enhanced from a second element of self-definition: membership in the house of Israel.

According to the Book of Mormon, a complex relationship exists between Gentiles and Israelites. In the last days the Lord will "proceed to do a marvelous work among the Gentiles," who will restore to the house of Israel a correct understanding of their covenant relationship with God (BM 1 Ne. 22:8-12). Repentant Gentiles will be "numbered among the house of Israel" and be gathered with them (BM 2 Ne. 10:18; 3 Ne. 16:13; 21:22-25).

Believing Mormons tried to understand this sacred history within the context of their own history. What was the marvelous work? Who were the Israelites and who were the Gentiles? How was the work to go from the Gentiles to the Israelites? How were the Gentiles to be numbered with the Israelites? What was meant by the gathering? The resolution of these questions produced a complex descent ideology that became central to the Mormon conception of religious identity. In the process of formulating and articulating this ideology, the Mormons developed a "genetics of salvation" which was even more intricate than that of seventeenth-century New England.

As might be expected, the "marvelous work" was the Mormon restoration, particularly the Book of Mormon (D&C 19:26) and the distinctive Mormon gospel (D&C 14:10). Mormonism thus became the vehicle to restore the house of Israel to its proper covenantal relationship with God. This conception was made explicit in another visitation from divine messengers on 3 April 1836 in Kirtland, Ohio. During that visitation, Joseph Smith received, with Oliver Cowdery, "the keys of the gathering of Israel" from Moses, "the dispensation of the gospel of Abraham" from Elias, and keys to "turn the hearts of the fathers to the children, and the children to the fathers" from Elijah (D&C 110:11-16).

Before the Missouri expulsion in 1838-39, there seem to have been two different understandings about the identity of Gentiles and Israelites. The first definition was that Gentiles were all individuals of non-Jewish European descent, while the Israelites were composed essentially of three different groups: the Jews; the "Lamanites," or American Indians; and the "ten lost tribes," who some Mormons believed were located in an undiscovered region close to the North Pole (D&C 109:60-67; 133:26-35); *EMS* 1:5:[33-34]; 2:13:101; 2:16:126; 2:19:148; *MA* 2:1:193-95). In terms of this definition, Mormons saw themselves as repentant Gentiles entrusted with the responsibility of taking the "marvelous work" to the house of Israel, then receiving with them the covenant blessings of the Lord. They anticipated that large numbers of Jews and American Indians would accept the message of the Mormon restoration and participate in the Mormon conception of the Abrahamic covenant. Thus, in December 1833, Oliver Cowdery rhetorically asked, "Who . . . can doubt for a moment the near approach of that day when Israel shall be gathered to his own land, and the captivity of Jacob's tents return?" (*EMS* 2:15:113). In October 1835, William W. Phelps wrote that "the Indians are the people of the Lord; they are of the tribes of Israel; the blood of Joseph . . . and the hour is nigh when they will come flocking into the kingdom of God" (*MA* 2:1:193).

Consistent with the Book of Mormon teaching that the "marvelous work" would go from the Gentiles to the house of Israel, Joseph Smith sent a group of missionaries in October 1830 to the Lamanites (*HC* 1:118-20). These missionaries met with little success. For many years thereafter, the church made little attempt to convert either American Indians or Jews, the two categories with which the Book of Mormon most closely associated the fulfillment of the Lord's covenant promises in the last days. Had Mormons continued to define themselves only as Gentiles, this situation could have presented the church with conceptual and theological difficulties. This, however, never became an issue. Part of the reason was that throughout the 1830s Mormons came more and more to regard themselves as actual biological descendants of Abraham. Thus, the events of their own lives became manifestations of the fulfillment of the Lord's covenant with the house of Israel.

The establishment of this second definition regarding Mormon identity occurred early in the history of the church, and it is difficult to trace its development. The Book of Mormon itself suggests the possibility that Mormons might be descendants of biblical Israel by identifying Joseph Smith as the literal descendent of the biblical patriarch Joseph (BM 3 Ne. 3:11-16). Thus, it would be logical to assume that he and his immediate family were not the only church members with this characteristic.

The evidence at hand gives no indication that Mormons were making this connection during the earliest months of the church's existence; by late 1832, however, this situation was changing. In November of that year, W. W. Phelps, editor of the *Evening and Morning Star*, published an article entitled "The Tribe of Joseph." In it he suggests that "Joseph or Ephraim, may be mixed among the nations, so that feet have scarce trod where he hath not been" and that Joseph's descendants will be "brought from the east and gathered from the west, ready to meet the Redeemer when he brings again Zion" (*EMS* 1:6:[41-43]. Although he never explicitly states that current members of the church are literally of the tribe of Joseph, he seems to be coming very close to this position.

In a revelation Joseph Smith received the following month, the biological connection between ancient Israel and at least some rank-and-file members seems to be made explicit. In it the Lord addresses certain unnamed members of the church: "Thus saith the Lord unto you, with whom the priesthood hath continued through the lineage of your fathers—For ye are lawful heirs, according to the flesh. . . . Therefore . . . the priesthood . . . must needs remain through you and your lineage until the restoration of all things" (D&C 86:8-10). A revelation received the following June of 1833 explicitly names early church member John Johnson as "a descendant of . . . Joseph and a partaker of the blessings of the promise made unto his fathers" (D&C 96:7). In February 1834, a revelation addressed to the general membership of the church declares, "Ye are the children of Israel, and of the seed of Abraham" (D&C 103:17).

Such general statements became more specific through the practices of giving "patriarchal blessings" to individual Saints after January 1833, when Joseph Smith, Jr., ordained his father to the office of "patriarch." This office has persisted in the church, and nearly all active members receive a patriarchal blessing.

While over time there has been some evolution in the nature of patriarchal blessings, they have always primarily considered in a number of promises that the patriarch feels inspired to make to the recipient. One of the most interesting features of these promises is that they are often stated as hereditary prerogatives that are transferable from generation to generation. Here, for example, are typical excerpts from blessings pronounced by Joseph Smith, Sr., in 1834-37:

> The blessings of the fathers shall rest upon thee. . . . Thy seed shall be blessed and thy seed's seed, after thee, till the last generation (R. Smith 1954:42).

> I lay my hands upon thy head . . . and confirm the blessings of a father upon thee and for thy posterity also, for thou shalt raise up children and the Lord will bless them and they shall be kept in the covenant of Abraham. . . . Thou art of the seed of Israel, even an Ephraimite. (Crosby, blessing dated 2 Feb. 1836)

> I now ask my heavenly Father . . . to bless thee with the same blessing with which Jacob blessed his son Joseph, for thou art his true descendant, and thy posterity shall be numbered with the house of Ephraim. (H. Smith and Sjodahl 1965:23)

The general context in which these hereditary promises often appear is that of "a declaration of lineage": the recipient is informed that he or she is a descendant of a biblical patriarch and as such is entitled to the covenant promises bestowed upon that individual. At present, the declaration of lineage is regarded as essential in a patriarchal blessing. However, in a sample of fifty-four patriarchal blessings given between 1834 and 1838, only 46 percent contained a declaration of lineage. A break-down by years reveals this pattern: in 1834 and 1835, only 31 and 32 percent, respectively, declared lineage; in 1836, 66 percent; in 1837, 74 percent; and in 1838, 100 percent. This pattern suggests that during this period it became increasingly common for rank and file members to be regarded as the literal descendants of biblical Israel.[1] There was little variation

---

[1] The LDS archives contain transcripts of virtually all patriarchal blessings pronounced by ordained patriarchs. These are not open for public examination, but the patriarchal blessing index is available. Among other

in categories of descent among those receiving declarations of lineage. The range was from the broader designation of descent from Jacob to the more restricted descent from Ephraim, the son of Joseph. Thus, 20 percent were declared to be descendants from Jacob, 20 percent descendants from Joseph, and 60 percent as descendants from Ephraim. The importance of Ephraim seems to be associated with the belief that because he had received the "birthright blessing" his descendants were entitled to the most important covenantal promises of all the tribes of Israel (1 Chron. 5:1; D&C 133:26-32; *EMS* 1:6:[42]; Gen. 48:15-22).

The Mormon belief that an individual had special rights to blessings divinely bestowed on an ancestor had some affinity to the Puritan concept of federal holiness and was basically an aspect of the domain of nature. Mormons thus understood such rights to be a consequence of the genetic transmission of blood. For instance, Joseph Smith, Sr., declared to Wilford Woodruff, later president of the church: "I confer on thee all the blessings of Abram. . . . God has looked on thee from all eternity and has known thy blood. Thou art a descendant of Joseph. . . . Thou art of the blood of Ephraim" (Woodruff, Journal, 15 Apr. 1837). And to Erastus Snow, he stated: "Thou art an Ephraimite, a son of Joseph that was sold into Egypt; and thou hast claim by blood to the priesthood and also to an inheritance in Zion among thy brethren" (Erastus Snow, entries for 1837).

---

information, this index contains the name of each person whose blessing is on file in the church archives, the date the blessing was given, and the recipient's lineage declaration. By identifying individuals known to have been members of the church during the 1830s and then searching in the index to see if and when they had received a patriarchal blessing, I was able to compile information on fifty-five individuals who had received patriarchal blessings from Joseph Smith, Sr., between 1834 and the Mormon expulsion from Missouri in the winter of 1838-39. (The sample contained only five examples of patriarchal blessings given in 1833, four of them members of Joseph Smith, Sr.'s family). In cases where the index left the space for the declaration of lineage blank, I inferred that no such declaration was made. I was able to verify that this was the case both by discussing the issue with a member of the archive staff and by locating copies of a number of these blessings from sources other than the patriarchal blessing file in the church archive; they indeed contained no declaration of lineage. Because the process of using the patriarchal blessing index for collecting information on 1830s blessings was very time-consuming, I did not attempt to increase the sample size. A more complete sample could substantiate or falsify these conclusions.

In a manner reminiscent of their Puritan ancestors, Mormons also believed that an individual's biological makeup could be modified as a consequence of supernatural intervention. During the 1830s, this concept was discussed in terms of changes in skin pigmentation as the result of divine cursings and blessings. Thus, the Book of Mormon teaches that because of the wickedness of the early Lamanites, the Lord cursed them and "did cause a skin of blackness to come upon them" (2 Ne. 5:21). This same condition was then to be genetically passed on to their descendants until they returned to their proper relationship with the Lord and again became "a white and delightsome people" (2 Ne. 30:5; 1948 ed.).

The Lamanites were not unique in having the color of their skin changed. The Joseph Smith Inspired Version of the Bible (written between December 1830 and June 1833) indicates that the descendants of both Cain, the son of Adam, and Canaan, the son of Ham, experienced similar pigmentation transformations (J. Smith 1970: Gen. 7:10, 29; 9:30). By 1835 William W. Phelps was suggesting that a dark skin was prima facie evidence of spiritual deterioration (*MA* 1:82).

Thus, Mormon theology included a connection between an individual's relationship to God and aspects of his or her biological condition. Consequently, having blood in common with Abraham or some other biblical patriarch could logically imply also having a favored relationship with God. The implications of this genetics of salvation would be developed more fully later.

But while Mormons and Puritans shared these understandings of hereditary charisma, there were also marked differences. First, the Puritans narrowly equated the endowment of federal holiness with an increased likelihood of receiving the covenant of grace, but a Mormon with the blood of Abraham might be eligible for a wide range of blessings. Joseph Smith, Sr., continuing his blessing to Wilford Woodruff promised him "all the blessings of Abram, Isaac and Jacob which includes all blessings both temporal and spiritual, the blessings of heaven and the blessings of earth. Thou shalt have all the power and authority of the Melchizedek Priesthood."

Second, because Mormons rejected the Puritan concept that the fall of Adam resulted in genetically transmitted depravity, Mormons likewise did not accept that through a covenant relationship, God could transform an individual into the state of pre-Fall Adam or Eve.

Third, most Puritans could not look further than one or two generations for the source of hereditary sanctity, while Mormons believed themselves entitled to blessings enunciated thousands of years before. By making such a genealogical leap, Mormons could regard themselves, not as "surrogate" Israel, but as legitimate biological heirs to the Abrahamic covenant. The end result of this process resulted in a new self-conception for Mormons—not Gentiles "numbered with the house of Israel," but rather literal descendants of Jacob, gathering again after their long dispersion.

Solidarity: Covenant and Blood

By the 1838-39 expulsion from Missouri, a code of conduct evident in the behavioral qualifications associated with the baptismal covenant, and substance or blood (as manifest in the concept of Abrahamic descent) had clearly emerged as conceptual bases for two forms of solidarity within the Mormon group. The first might be referred to as normative solidarity and the second as biological solidarity. They defined two distinct but overlapping social categories established by different covenants between God and humanity.

The first of these categories—the baptized and still-affiliated—was a well-defined group with precise boundaries. The church was composed exclusively of individuals who had committed themselves to its code by publicly receiving baptism. The social category based on blood was more nebulous. It had its basis in God's covenants with the founding patriarchs of the house of Israel and thus theoretically included all their descendants, including not only Mormons whose patriarchal blessings assured them that they belonged to this category, but also Lamanites and Jews.

These two covenantal categories created four logical cultural categories of persons: baptized Israelites, nonbaptized Israelites, baptized Gentiles, and nonbaptized Gentiles. Only baptized Israelites combined both code and substance and were thus linked to the Mormon group through two patterns of solidarity. Such persons were regarded as possessing all the essential aspects of Mormonness. At the other extreme were nonbaptized Gentiles who possessed neither code nor substance and, consequently, no covenant relationship with God. Nonbaptized Israelites were viewed as kin to Mormon Israelites with a hereditary claim to the blessings restored during the final dispensation. The most ambiguous type was baptized Gentiles, individuals linked to the Mormon group by code but not by substance. During the 1830s, however, this type of person seems to have presented

few difficulties for Mormon group solidarity. Most Mormon Israelites were just beginning to perceive their own Abrahamic heritage,
and there were as yet no well-developed concepts regarding either
the identity of Mormons devoid of the blood of Israel or of consequences that such a condition might have for their position within
the Church. This situation was later to change.

Normative solidarity was more fundamental to Mormon group
unity than biological solidarity. This might be demonstrated in two
ways. First, a baptized Gentile was regarded as part of the Mormon
group, but not an unbaptized Israelite. And second, excommunication placed an individual outside the Mormon group regardless of
what claims he or she might make regarding Israelite ancestry or biological relationship to fellow Mormons; thus, blood ties were not
regarded as fundamental so far as Mormon group solidarity was
concerned.

Baptism as Adoption

Mormon solidarity was further reinforced as the Saints came increasingly to view themselves as a sort of kinship group by understanding baptism as a ritual of adoption, a rebirth by which they
became heirs to the kingdom of God. Parley P. Pratt (1837) developed this theme extensively in his *Voice of Warning*, a publication that
was to play a decisive role in the subsequent development of Mormon ideology. Pratt describes God's "organized government on
earth" as a "kingdom" in which there are "no natural born subjects" (1837:96, 103). Candidates become citizens only by "the law
of adoption" as executed through baptism (1837:103-10).

Thus, although normative solidarity was more fundamental than
biological solidarity to Mormon group identity, Mormons employed
a kinship idiom to discuss some of its most salient aspects. This had
a tendency to fortify the interrelationships between the two forms of
solidarity.

THE ORDERING OF RELATIONSHIPS AND THE
STRUCTURE OF SUBSUMPTION

While the baptismal covenant expressed Mormon normative
solidarity, Joseph Smith felt a need for an even stronger mechanism
to create the moral unity which he believed should characterize the
covenant people of God. Baptism related each separate believer to

God and to the group as a whole but produced only a collectivity of Mormons. The Mormon concept of a covenantal community entailed a way to unify the individual members of the group through a network of explicit covenantal ties.

The basic elements of this covenantal network emerged during the first sixteen months of the church's existence and employed two basic forms of social interaction: locality (building the City of Zion) and economic cooperation (the law of consecration and stewardship). The result was a pattern of social organization designed to unite Mormons in an exclusive and interdependent body.

The City of Zion

Prominent among the prophetic promises of the Book of Mormon is the assurance that in the last days the righteous will be "gathered together" in a "choice land" and there establish a holy city called "the New Jerusalem," where they will dwell in peace awaiting the second coming of the Lord (BM 3 Ne. 21:22-24; Eth. 13:4-8). Early Mormons felt that one of the principal reasons for which the church had been restored was to fulfill this promise.

Thus, in a letter dated 6 January 1831, Lucy Mack Smith (1910:545) wrote that God "has now established His Church upon the earth [and] has made a new and everlasting covenant, and all that will hear His voice and enter, He says they shall be gathered together into a land of promise." And in April of 1832, a citizen of Lyman, New Hampshire, observed that "there has been in this town and vicinity, for about a week, two young . . . Mormonites. . . . They say they are commanded by God to preach . . . that all who do not embrace their faith . . . and go with them to a place of safety, which is in the state of Missouri, where they are about building a city, will be destroyed . . . and that reformation . . . unless it be accompanied with a speedy removal to their city of refuge, will be of no avail" (in Mulder and Mortensen 1958:72).

In July 1831 Joseph Smith received a revelation designating Missouri as "the land which I have appointed and consecrated for the gathering of the saints. Wherefore, this is the land of promise, and the place for the city of Zion. And . . . the place which is now called Independence is the center place" (D&C 57:1-3). On 2 August, Sidney Rigdon dedicated the site, and the Mormons immediately began constructing their sacred city.

Mormons understood two purposes for the City of Zion. First, echoing John Winthrop's understanding of Massachusetts Bay Colony as a holy commonwealth, it would be a refuge from the wicked and from the judgments of God that were to precede Christ's millennial reign (D&C 45:66-68).

Second, it would be the locale for the reconstitution of the house of Israel which, in the last days, would involve the physical migration of the tribe of Judah to the old Jerusalem in Palestine and of the other tribes to the New Jerusalem in Missouri (*EMS* 1:9:[67]. Believing Gentiles in the New Jerusalem would be numbered among the house of Israel and thus become eligible for the promises associated with the Abrahamic covenant (BM 3 Ne. 21:21-24).

The Law of Consecration and Stewardship

As part of the dedication ceremonies in Independence, the assembled Saints pledged to "keep the law of God" (*HC* 1:196). This "law" was a specific revelation given February 1831 as "the law for the government of the church" (*Book of Commandments* 1833:89). Mormons believed that the principles underlying this law were fully consistent with those which governed the highest kingdom of heaven (the celestial kingdom) and that by following this law strictly they could create a perfect society (D&C 105:5).

The economic aspect of the law, known as "the law of consecration and stewardship," required believers to consecrate all their properties to the Lord with "a covenant and deed that cannot be broken." These properties were to be laid before the bishop of the church and subsequently could "not be taken from the church." Each consecrator, however, would then be appointed steward over sufficient property to maintain his family, while the church used surplus property to help the poor and buy land to establish additional stewardships. Members who sinned and did not repent were "to be cast out" and "not receive again" the properties that they had consecrated (*EMS* 1:2:9; *Book of Commandments* 1833:92-93).

One week after the land of Zion had been dedicated, Joseph Smith and ten other elders who had been in Independence for the dedication left to return to church headquarters at Kirtland (*HC* 1:202). The Mormons remaining in Independence (primarily the Colesville Branch consisting of about sixty members) were expected to implement the "law for the government of the church" immediately and to prepare for the Saints who would soon arrive to receive their inheritance in Zion and build up the New Jerusalem (*HC* 1:196). Implementing the new system of economic redistribution and regulation was the responsibility of Edward Partridge, the newly appointed bishop of the church.

Partridge devised a printed form to facilitate this objective (Arrington, Fox, and May 1976:28-29), which essentially followed the procedures outlined in the revelation. Upon arriving in Jackson County, each Mormon household head was expected to transfer rights in fee simple over all his property to Bishop Partridge. The consecrator would then receive his stewardship—rights in usufruct over sufficient income-producing property to provide for the needs of his family.

While he could manage his stewardship as he saw fit, he was not permitted to accumulate or reinvest any profits. Instead, they went to the bishop who would then either create additional stewardships or provide for the various financial needs of the inhabitants of Zion.

An individual could maintain rights in usufruct over his stewardship only so long as he followed this economic system and remained a member in good standing. An excommunicate would lose his stewardship property and not be able to repossess the property that he had originally consecrated.

The faithful widow and minor children of a deceased steward could retain rights in usufruct over his property. The orphans, however, would lose these as they reached adulthood and became eligible to receive their own stewardships.

According to Mormon belief, a chief purpose of this law was to create righteousness and spiritual unity among the inhabitants of the New Jerusalem. Such a condition was essential before the city would be acceptable to the Lord. Thus, an 1830 revelation indicates that the Lord would designate his people "Zion" only when they were "of one heart and one mind and dwelt in righteousness" (PGP Moses 7:18), while a January 1831 revelation commands Mormons who are anticipating the establishment of the New Jerusalem to "be one" and then adds, "if ye are not one ye are not mine" (D&C 38:27).

The law of consecration and stewardship was based on the understanding that economic equality contributes to spiritual unity, while economic inequality produces social divisions. The Book of Mormon contains numerous examples of the spiritual plight of societies that permitted sharp divisions between the rich and the poor. Various early revelations reiterate the same philosophy. Thus, a March 1831 revelation states, "It is not given that one man should possess that which is above another, wherefore the whole world lieth in sin" (D&C 49:20), while a revelation the following year declares that "if ye are not equal in earthly things ye cannot be equal in obtaining heavenly things" (D&C 78:6; see also D&C 38:24-27; 51:9; 70:14-16; 82:17).

By providing each household head with a stewardship "sufficient for himself and family" and then by not permitting him to accumulate and use investment capital derived from that stewardship, the law of consecration and stewardship was seen as an instrument of economic parity among the inhabitants of Zion. As William W. Phelps explained in December of 1832, in Zion "one cannot be above another in wealth, nor below another for want of means, for the earth is the Lord's and the fulness thereof" (*EMS* 1:7:[54]).

DOMESTIC ORDER

The law of consecration and stewardship also established each household as a discrete economic entity in which the wife and children were dependent upon the male head for economic maintenance.

This basic pattern resembled the Puritan concept of the ideal household. Many Americans also accepted this general model as normative during the early days of the republic, but the social and economic changes associated with the development of antebellum America caused disruption on the household level; and during the 1830s, many regarded American domestic organization to be in general disarray (Berthoff 1971:204-17; Gordon 1973; Kett 1977; Rosenberg 1971; 1972; Sklar 1973).

Various statements by Mormon leaders on proper domestic relationships attest to the persistence of the Puritan ideal. For example, an 1835 directive by Joseph Smith instructed missionaries to proselyte wives only with the consent of their husbands, children only with the consent of their parents, and servants/slaves only with the consent of their masters. When such permission was granted, they were to teach the members of the household "to be kindly affected one towards another; that the fathers should be kind to their children, husbands to their wives; masters to their slaves or servants; children obedient to their parents, wives to their husbands and slaves or servants to their masters" (*MA* 2:2:211; see also D&C 101:4, 1835 ed.).

Later in Nauvoo, the Puritan pattern of domestic inequality would be linked explicitly to the Abrahamic covenant; but patriarchal blessings of the 1830s indicate that the connection was already being made. In addition to declarations that children participated in the covenant God had established with their ancestors, various blessings also indicated that wives often participated in the blessings bestowed upon their husbands. Husbands and wives often came together to receive patriarchal blessings. On such occasions it was not uncommon to first give the husband his patriarchal blessing and then to state in the wife's blessing that she participated in the promises already made to her husband. For example, Joseph Smith, Sr., after giving Jonathan Crosby his patriarchal blessing, next pronounced a patriarchal blessing for Jonathan's wife, Caroline Barnes Crosby, in which he said: "I seal blessings for thee in common with thy husband. Thy life shall be as his life and thy years as his years" (Crosby, blessing dated 2 Feb. 1836). Such blessings implied a divine origin for the hierarchical pattern in which women were covenantally subordinate to their husbands and children to their parents.[2]

Priesthood Marriages

Perhaps the most important difference between Puritan and Mormon patterns of domestic organization stemmed from the role of priesthood authority in establishing and maintaining covenant relationships, a role which contributed to a distinctively Mormon conception of the order of law.

Beginning in the mid-1830s, leaders of the church simultaneously promulgated two definitions of marriage. The first of these was similar to that of Puritans and most mainline American Protestants: marriage is essentially a legal contract established under the auspices of the state. Marriages performed by non-Mormons are as valid as those performed by Mormon elders, and thus "all legal contracts of marriage made before a person is baptized into the church, should be held sacred and fulfilled." Furthermore, even when a Mormon elder performed a marriage, he was to do so "by virtue of the laws of the country and the authority vested in him" (D&C 101, 1835, ed.).

The second definition, however, maintained that Mormon priesthood holders, by virtue of their authority, could establish a special

---

[2] For other examples of this practice, see the blessings of Orson Hyde and Marinda Nancy Johnson Hyde (Barron 1977:314-16), Samuel Smith and Mary Baily Smith (R. Smith 1954:41-43), and Newel Knight and Lydia Goldthwaite Knight (K. Knight, ms a, blessings dated 8 Apr. 1836).

form of marriage independent of the state and regardless of existing civil marriage contracts. This concept of marriage would have considerable impact on the subsequent development of Mormon covenant organization.

During the years that Kirtland, Ohio, was the ecclesiastical headquarters of the church (1831-38), practical problems about state-regulated marriages developed. First, the local county would not authorize Mormons to perform marriages; and second, some Saints who had separated from their spouses without obtaining legal divorces desired to remarry (Brodie 1977:183-84; *HC* 2:408).

For example, in late 1835, Newel Knight, a New York convert, and Lydia Goldthwaite Baily wished to marry. Before her conversion to Mormonism, Lydia had separated from her husband, Calvin Baily, but had never obtained a legal divorce. Although she wanted to marry Newel, she felt that such an arrangement would be improper and immoral. When they laid the problem before Joseph Smith, he stated that it was right that they should marry and performed the ceremony himself on 24 November 1835. In the course of the ceremony, Joseph Smith remarked that "marriage was an institution of heaven, instituted in the garden of Eden; [and] that it was necessary it should be solemnized by the authority of the everlasting Priesthood" (*HC* 2:320). Newel recorded: "Joseph Smith a few days later stated that "he had married Brother Newel Knight to Lydia Baily . . . although the laws of Ohio had not yet granted him the right to marry. But said he 'I have done it by the authority of the holy priesthood, and the Gentile law has no power to call me to an account for it' " (Knight, fall 1835).

Mormon marriage "by the authority of the priesthood" produced ideological problems. What was the precise nature of marriage by priesthood authority? How did such a marriage differ from that performed by the state? What was the relationship between priesthood marriage and civil marriage? Since it was "necessary" that marriage "be solemnized by the authority of the everlasting Priesthood," what was the status of civil marriage in the eyes of God?

Mormonism would have to confront such issues more directly after 1838-39; but during the Kirtland and Missouri periods, the chief importance of marriage as a priesthood ordinance was to identify the ideal Mormon conjugal relationship as established through a power independent of and superior to legal authority.

While such power was still within the Mormon order of law, it was clearly based on a concept that priesthood law transcended human convention. It is analytically useful to see the Mormon order of law as containing two categories: the suborder of human law and the suborder of priesthood or divine law. I hypothesize that ambiguities centering on the relationship between civil and priesthood authority resulted from the fact that Mormons recognized two suborders of law but had yet to determine fully those aspects of human organization to which each applied.

Consecration Community

The consecration community that emerged from the economic law of consecration and stewardship shared at least three structural similarities with Puritan church covenant groups: restrictive admittance procedures, a unique covenant, and a shared charisma within this group that the general church population did not share. Each factor contributed to the structural isolation of the consecration covenant community.

An individual technically was required to receive written authorization from local priesthood leaders who had a confirming revelation that he or she should be permitted to "go up unto Zion" and there commence living the law of consecration and stewardship (D&C 72:24-26; *EMS* 1:1:[2]). While one rationale for this procedure was to regulate the speed of gathering (*EMS* 1:2:[13]), there is some indication that those not regarded as capable of abiding by the laws of Zion had difficulty receiving certificates of authorization (*EMS* 1:8:[6]).

Entrance into the community was signaled by "a covenant and a deed which cannot be broken." While the printed consecration agreement constituted the "deed," the covenant of consecration became the basis for a distinctive relationship between the consecrator and both the Lord and his earthly representatives—the Mormon hierocracy. The exact terms of such a covenant were not articulated in much detail at the time but would remain an active part of Mormon theology.

The process of subsumption is clearly visible in these arrangements. The consecrator, who had surrendered all of his property, thus placed himself in perpetual economic dependency on the hierocracy. Since rights in usufruct over stewardship property were granted by the bishop dependent upon obedience to the hierocracy, hierocratic and economic domination were conjoined.[3] Thus, households participating in the law of consecration and stewardship were subsumed by the hierocratic organization of the church. The law of consecration and stewardship thus provided an economic basis for the development of the Mormon structure of religious authority which saw such subsumption as the divine order.

Upon making the consecration covenant, an individual thereby covenanted with the Lord to abide by the various provisions of the law for the government of the church. What the Lord covenanted in return is perhaps best summarized in the 2 January 1831 revelation:

> And this shall be my covenant with you, ye shall have [the land of Zion] for the land of your inheritance, and for the inheritance of your children forever, while the earth shall stand, and ye shall possess it again in eternity, no more to pass away.
>
> But, verily I say unto you that in time ye shall have no king nor ruler, for I will be your king and watch over you.
>
> Wherefore, hear my voice and follow me, and you shall be a free people, and ye shall have no laws but my laws when I come, for I am your lawgiver, and what can stay my hand? (D&C 38:20-22)

Correspondingly, a disobedient Saint could expect not only to lose his stewardship and be excommunicated from the church, but also to be "delivered over to the buffeting of Satan until the day of redemption" (D&C 78:12; see also D&C 85:9). Furthermore, if the Saints in Zion did not collectively live up to their covenants, they would jointly experience the wrath of God (see D&C 84:55-59). Such a conception was similar to the Puritans' national covenant. In both cases, the judgments of God would be poured out collectively upon the group who violated the covenant.

Surely an added incentive of the covenant was the distinctive religious specialness it conferred upon the consecrator. In Mormon terms, such individuals could be "sealed up unto eternal life." The minutes of an October 1831 church conference in which various elders covenanted to live the law of consecration and stewardship recorded:

> Br. Sylvester Smith said that he had a testimony to the effect that it was the will of the Lord to seal his Saints and also covenanted to give all to the Lord. . . . Br. Daniel Stanton said that he had a long time

---

[3] Weber (1968:53) defines domination as "the probability that a command with a given specific content will be obeyed by a given group of persons."

since covenanted to do the will of God in all things and also said that it was his desire to be sealed with the Holy Spirit of promise. . . .

Brother Joseph Smith, Jr., said . . . until we have perfect love we are liable to fall and when we have a testimony that our names are sealed in the Lamb's book of life we have perfect love. (Cannon and Cook 1983:21, 23)

The operating mechanism seemed to be this sequence: consecration would produce economic equality; economic equality and continuing harmony in the community would produce "perfect love" toward God and one's fellows; once possessed of such love, an individual was worthy of the gift of eternal life; that gift, offered to a mortal, did not eliminate death but assured salvation on the other side of death. They believed, as Joseph Smith had taught, "When a man has offered in sacrifice all that he has . . . he does know most assuredly, that God does and will accept his sacrifice and offering and that he has not nor will not seek his face in vain" (D&C pp. 60-61, 1835 ed.).

Given such assumptions, it became easy to conclude that those who failed to make the consecration covenant were not religiously qualified to obtain eternal life. Joseph Smith wrote in November 1832:

It is contrary to the will and commandment of God, that those who receive not their inheritance by consecration . . . should have their names enrolled with the people of God. . . .

And they . . . whose names are not found written in the book of the law . . . shall not find an inheritance among the saints of the most high. (*EMS* 1:8:[61]; also D&C 85:1, 3-4, 11; *HC* 1:298-99)

PURITAN/MORMON COVENANT ORGANIZATION

Mythological Underpinnings

Associated with both Puritan and Mormon covenant organization was a mythological narrative summarizing a covenant relationship between Abraham and the Lord. Both groups explained and justified many covenantal practices in terms of this myth, and it thus became the ideological model for many aspects of the two covenant systems.

There were, however, important differences in how the two groups interpreted the Abrahamic myth. For Puritans, it was part of their understandings of the Fall and Redemption, part of the process by which an individual might achieve sanctification and by which groups of sanctified individuals might be organized into church congregations and national entities. While early New England society looked forward to the second coming of Christ and such associated events as the national conversion of the Jews, these beliefs were not integral to their understanding of the Abrahamic myth. In contrast, Mormons explicitly linked the Abrahamic myth with the redemptive history of the Book of Mormon. The gathering of Israel was an integral aspect of their concept of salvation.

Bases of Relationships

Both Puritan and Mormon systems of covenant organization manifest Schneider's basic division between the order of nature and law. As in Puritan New England, solidarity within the Mormon family and within the Mormon larger community were both based on the interface between these two orders. The parent-child relationships within the Mormon family and the concept of Abrahamic descent within the larger Mormon community both involved the concept of shared genetic substance and were thus aspects of the order of nature. The husband-wife bond (established through civil or religious covenant) and boundary mechanisms defining church membership (established through the baptismal covenant and its associated code of conduct), on the other hand, were aspects of the Mormon order of law.

The most fundamental difference between the Puritan and Mormon orders of nature and law was that while Puritan covenant organization presupposed two suborders within nature, Mormon covenant organization presupposed two suborders within law. The dichotomization of nature was essential to the Puritan concept of sanctification while the dichotomization of law was essential to the Mormon concept of priesthood authority. These basic distinctions were manifested in many of the different ways the two groups were organized and in the goals they pursued.

Ordering of Relationships

Covenant making in both Puritanism and Mormonism established a complex network of asymmetric and symmetric relationships. The formal structure of inequality within the Mormon household resembles the Puritan pattern of domestic order while inequality within the hierocracy derived from the church president's supreme position and was maintained through the need to formally delegate priesthood keys. Household and hierocratic inequality were formally conjoined by the consecration covenant between the household head and the bishop.

In Mormonism there were two instances in which the enactment of formal covenants resulted in establishing symmetrical relations. The baptismal covenant united all Mormons and separated them from the world. The consecration covenant created a separate group of the more dedicated, who sought to achieve spiritual unity and ultimate salvation. Like the church covenant group within Puritanism, the consecration group appears to have been central to the Mormon covenant system and its establishment a chief reason for which the entire apparatus existed.

Subsumption

Both Puritan and Mormon convenantal organization maintained order by subsumption. In Puritanism, households were subsumed by church congregations and church congregations by the state. In early Mormonism, subsumption of household by the hierocracy occurred primarily for the consecration group.

Distribution of Power

Puritans did not believe that God delegated power to human beings; rather human power and ability to establish and regulate covenant relationships were ultimately derived from their collective will. In Puritan New England, this power had two loci: the congregation of visible saints bound together by church covenants; and the state, which received its authority from the visible saints as freemen.

In sharp contrast, Mormons saw religious power and authority, including the ability to establish and regulate covenant relationships, as derived from a divinely restored priesthood. Through ordination to various offices in the priesthood, adult male members could possess aspects of that power. But the president of the church maintained a monopoly over priesthood power by possessing ultimate control over priesthood keys.

The Puritan system became fragmented when the visible saints lost control of state power. Lacking any centralized authority structure except the state, each congregation was essentially set free to determine its own course. In contrast, Mormonism possessed a highly developed centralized system of religious authority. It expanded independent of state sponsorship. Although both individuals and organized groups removed themselves from the control of the Mormon priesthood, its hierarchical structure not only remained intact but became increasingly centralized over time. Thus, while Puritan unity was ultimately based upon political domination, Mormon unity was predicated upon hierocratic domination; in Mormonism, then, priesthood replaced the Puritan state as the fundamental basis of religious order.

Group Charisma

In both Puritanism and early Mormonism, group charisma was an important element; and in both groups, it was unequally distributed. In Puritanism, group charisma was grounded in inward and federal holiness with the distinctions that resulted from each. For Mormons, group charisma stemmed from personal righteousness as manifest in baptismal and consecration covenants and descent as revealed in patriarchal blessings.

The unequal distribution in both groups resulted in more complex internal differentiations than Weber's model of the ideal sect. Both groups had subgroups based on the common possession of charismatic endowments which were not shared by the larger religious communities. In Puritanism, covenant church groups were such a subgroup; in early Mormonism the consecration community of Independence, Missouri, was such a subgroup.

Center and Periphery

Both Puritanism and Mormonism were ideally structured within their larger societies to produce a cohesive peripheral group with members attached to localized values, institutions, and elite personnel. New England Puritanism became peripheral to larger English society, although that relationship changed depending on its relative political, social, and economic isolation from metropolitan England. During its early developmental period, it experienced its greatest isolation; serious and permanent reversals came after Charles II had been restored to the throne.

Early Mormonism, on the other hand, was surrounded by a much larger Gentile population which had no attachment to Mormonism's localized values, institutions, and elite. In many ways, the premises of Mormonism were at odds with this larger American society. One important consequence was that Mormonism developed within a milieu of external conflict that the early New England Puritans, despite their dissidents and Quakers, never faced.

The Second Great Awakening was but one aspect of the social changes which were occurring in antebellum America. The post-Revolutionary period saw economic change, large-scale migration, and the alteration of political processes on a scale that transformed the new republic and disrupted long-established patterns of social interaction (Berthoff 1971; Littell 1962; Nye 1960; Somkin 1967; Tyler 1962; Wood 1980). Although it is certainly possible to exaggerate the social fragmentation during this period, late seventeenth-century Massachusetts would have appeared almost homogeneous in comparison.

While various aspects of Mormon covenant structure have correlates in seventeenth-century Puritan social organization, the elements of Mormon covenant organization were ordered to counter aspects of the disruptive social milieu in which it emerged. At its foundation, believers saw a system of exclusive religious authority that existed independent of human convention with power to establish divinely sanctioned convenants. On the basis of such authority, Mormons perceived their religious organization as the one true and living church, distinct from the contending sects that characterized American voluntaristic pluralism.

While American social institutions and mobility produced a milieu in which, to quote de Tocqueville (1969:507), "the woof of time is ever being broken and the track of past generations lost," Mormons fixed their position in history and linked themselves to biblical patriarchs through lineage pronouncements in patriarchal blessings. And while economic development, migration, settlement, and family organization at large were experiencing "freedom's ferment" (Tyler 1962), the Saints created order by bringing all four under the aegis of priesthood authority and by weaving them into their covenant system. In Peter Berger and Thomas Luckmann's terms (1966:73), this system provided a paradigm for "the institutional ordering of comprehensive meanings for everyday life."

Mormonism was one of several religious organizations of the period with the same goal—order amid the chaos of American democracy. Mormonism, however, more than most, was fundamentally at odds with the dominant trend of American society.

One year before the Mormon church was organized, Andrew Jackson was inaugurated president of the United States. His administration has often been regarded as a response to the social changes that had occurred during the republic's early years. It has been viewed as a triumph of individualism, as the beginning of stability for various political, economic, and religious institutions and the coalescence of those institutions around the individual as an autonomous unit in society (Fish 1927; Pessen 1969; 1971; Remini 1976; Schlessinger 1945). Without exaggerating these tendencies in the Age of Jackson, *individualism* is perhaps as good a term as any to denote both the institutional and subjective manifestations of this era's pluralism and secularization. It is in this milieu that Mormonism and its conflicts developed.

The Mormon blueprint for group solidarity was the point of immediate disagreement. It required the Saints to gather to the New Jerusalem, where they would enter the law of consecration and stewardship, a plan that logically entailed several provisions the Missourians found unacceptable: (1) the Saints would exclusively occupy the area designated as the site of the New Jerusalem, (2) they would have the means to enforce the law for the government of the church, (3) they would expel all who failed to comply with its requirements, (4) they would gain control over large tracts of agricultural land, and (5) they would possess the power and authority to perpetuate an economic system that recognized no rights in fee simple.

Although the Mormons expended a great deal of effort on this Missouri endeavor from mid-1831 through the fall of 1838, the attempt was racked by internal dissension and threatened by external persecution (Bushman 1955; 1960; Gentry 1965; Jennings 1962; 1973; McKiernan 1973; Parkin 1966). As difficulties persisted and intensified, they either modified or abolished various aspects of the scheme until, by their expulsion in the winter of 1838-39, little of the initial Mormon covenant system remained. The message from the American center was clear: Mormonism's most distinctive social values belonged on the periphery.

THE MISSOURI EXPERIENCE

Jackson County, 1831-33

Because of the intensifying resistance, it was only from August 1831 to November 1833 that the Mormons were able to focus their primary energies on establishing their New Jerusalem in Jackson County.

A practical problem that the church failed to solve was regulating the rate of migration to Jackson County. As might be expected, those most anxious to go were the economically less fortunate. Thus, John Corrill (1839:19) recalled that "the church got crazy to go up to Zion . . . and the poor crowded up in numbers, without having any places provided, contrary to the advice of the bishop."

Unregulated migration of the poor taxed the bishop's ability to provide adequate stewardships for all who had entered the consecration covenant. When the church asked unconsecrated members still in the East to contribute to the Jackson County stewardship fund, there was apparently little response. Corrill (1839:19) indicated that "the rich were afraid to send up their money to purchase lands." As a result, the stewardships seemed to average around thirty acres of land, "and thirty acres in that county, is little enough for wood and timber land" (Ezra Booth in Howe 1834:196).

Even more disruptive to the covenantal system was the issue of granting only nontransferable rights in usufruct over individual stewardships while the church as a corporation retained rights in fee simple. The practice generated internal conflict and raised serious legal issues. As Arrington, Fox, and May (1976:25) have indicated, "Judges on the frontier viewed properties held in trust with noticeable disfavor." The issue was finally resolved by the directive Joseph Smith sent Bishop Partridge on 3 May 1833 instructing him to grant individuals rights in fee simple over their stewardship properties (O. Whitney 1884:7).

The retreat to private property had a serious impact on the Mormon covenant system. Solidarity within the covenant community was primarily structured in terms of economic relationships. If each household held its stewardship as private property, the household would no longer be subsumed by the hierocracy, nor could the bishop enforce the requirement that households turn over their surplus. From that point, there was no way to maintain economic equality among households or ensure that the bishop could continue to provide additional stewardships. Furthermore, with stewardships as private property, the covenant community no longer had a way to remove the unrepentant from the City of Zion.

A decisive blow came in 1833 when a member named Bates successfully sued to regain possession of consecrated money (*EMS* 2:110), making the whole covenantal system legally vulnerable and challenging the rights of the church to control consecration property before dispensing it as stewardships.

Whatever its objectives, the Mormon law of consecration and stewardship thus appears to have been incompatible with Jacksonian America.

There is no way to determine the ultimate form that the law of consecration and stewardship might have assumed had the Saints in Jackson County been granted enough time and freedom to continue the experiment. Armed Jackson County residents forced them from the county in November 1833.

Independence had been settled four years before the Saints' arrival and by 1831 was something of a boom town (Brodie 1977:109). Although the Saints were commanded by revelation "to purchase this whole region of county" (D&C 58:52), such a task was manifestly impossible, given their financial strictures; and they probably never composed more than about one-third of the total population of Jackson County (Allen and Leonard 1976:82). The non-Mormon "settlers were primarily from the mountainous portions of the border states" (Jennings 1973:100) and, by virtually any measure, appeared to qualify as individualists, a trait that frontier Missouri would only intensify. From their perspective, Mormon solidarity was not only different but wrong.

Many Gentiles were particularly concerned about Mormon political and economic domination of the area. In August 1833, anti-Mormons in Jackson County wrote that "when we reflect on the extensive field in which the sect is operating, . . . it requires no gift of prophecy to tell that the day is not far distant when the civil government of the county will be in their hands" (*HC* 1:397).

Mistrust of Mormons and their ways turned into vigilante action until, to gain a respite from mob action, Mormon leaders in Missouri signed an agreement that the Saints would leave Jackson County before the following April. Joseph Smith and other leaders in Kirtland countered with instructions for the Saints in Jackson County to neither sell nor move (*HC* 1:417). Mob activity intensified and, early in November 1833, approximately twelve hundred Mormons were forced from Jackson County.

Clay County, 1834-36

The exiled Mormons found temporary refuge in neighboring Clay County and there awaited direction from Kirtland. On 16 December, Joseph Smith received a revelation that was both bitter and hopeful: "I, the Lord, have suffered the affliction to come upon them . . . in consequence of their transgression" (D&C 101:2). Their transgression in part was failure to properly implement the law of consecration and stewardship.

However, the designation of Jackson County as the site of the New Jerusalem remained unchanged. "Zion shall not be moved out of her place, notwithstanding her children are scattered" (D&C 101:17). If the Saints repented "and are pure in heart, [they] shall return, and come to their inheritances . . . to build up the waste places of Zion" (D&C 101:18).

In practical terms, the revelation continued, they were to "importune at the feet of the governor; and if the governor heed them not, let them importune at the feet of the president; and if the president heed them not, then will the Lord arise and come forth out of his hiding place, and in his fury vex the nation" (D&C 101:87-89).

Church leaders in Missouri wrote Governor Daniel Dunklin of Missouri and President Andrew Jackson, formally requesting that they take measures that would enable the Mormons to regain their lands in Jackson County and to maintain them without fear of mob action.

Jackson responded by way of Lewis Cass, the Secretary of War, pointing out a jurisdictional problem: "The offences of which you complain are violations of the laws of the State of Missouri, and not of the laws of the United States. . . . The President cannot call out a military force to aid in the execution of State Laws, until the proper requisition is made upon him by the constituted authorities" (*TS* 6:1073). This position, though discouraging, was consistent with Jackson's advocacy of states' rights, which applied individualism to federal-state relationships.

Dunklin's response appeared more hopeful. On 4 February 1834 he wrote: "I am very sensible indeed of the injuries you people complain of, and should consider myself very remiss in the discharge of my duties were I not to do everything in my power consistent with the legal exercise of them, to afford your society the redress to which they seem entitled" (*HC* 1:476:78). He promised a "military guard" to escort the Mormons to their holdings in Jackson County, warned that the state could not maintain a permanent peace-keeping force in Jackson County, but suggested that "should your men organize according to law . . . and apply for public arms, the Executive could not distinguish between their right to have them, and the right of every other description of people similarly situated" (*HC* 1:476).

Based on this assurance, Joseph Smith mustered Mormons in the Kirtland area into a militia called "Zion's Camp" and marched with them to western Missouri. Upon their arrival, however, in June 1834, Dunklin refused to call up the state militia to assist the Mormons. He stated that while the citizens of Jackson County had the right to arm themselves independent of his authority as commander-in-chief, the Mormons had no right to march into Jackson County under arms without his authorization, which he never granted (*HC* 2:86).

About two weeks later, Joseph Smith received a revelation prohibiting armed conflict, postponing "the redemption of Zion . . . for a little season," and suspending the commandments pertaining to the governing of the New Jerusalem, presumably including the laws of consecration and stewardship (D&C 105:13-14, 34).

Thus, the endeavor to establish the New Jerusalem and the law of consecration and stewardship, two of the fundamental elements of Mormon covenant organization, were deferred.

There is little indication that Joseph Smith or others foresaw negative results for the development of the church, probably because they expected to repossess their Zion within a short time. However, unity steadily deteriorated between the disbanding of Zion's Camp in June 1834 and the final expulsion from Missouri. From a sociological perspective, at least, abandoning two of the principal bases for solidarity within the covenant structure seriously undermined Mormon group cohesiveness.

Caldwell County, 1837-38

The residents of Clay County first welcomed the refugee Mormons from Jackson County; but as the Mormon population steadily increased, the Gentiles of Clay County became alarmed and formally requested the Mormons to leave (*HC* 2:448:55). The Mormons petitioned the state legislature to establish a new county in an unsettled region of the state where they might settle as a body; and during the winter of 1836-37, Caldwell County was organized in a virtually unpopulated area. There was apparently a tacit understanding that the Mormons would be left alone if they restricted their colonizing efforts exclusively to that county (Allen and Leonard 1976:106-7).

Some ten thousand Mormons moved to Caldwell County during 1837 and there attempted to establish a semicommunal economic order that embodied some of the principles of the law of consecration and stewardship (Arrington, Fox and May 1976:34-38, Rockwood 1988:20). Throughout 1837 the Mormons in Missouri lived in relative peace, and the plan to establish a separate county for their occupancy appeared to be working.

The year 1838, however, was disastrous. A basic reason for this was the Mormon hierocracy's continuing attempt to maintain economic and territorial control despite the exile from Jackson County and the abandonment of the law of consecration and stewardship.

In 1837 Joseph Smith became involved in an ill-advised scheme to establish an "anti-banking society" among the Mormons in the Kirtland area (*HC* 2:470-73). The project was not presented as a revelation or linked to a covenant order designed to produce a perfect society. Many investor-Saints, however, felt that the society had divine sanction (Partridge 1972; Sampson and Wimmer 1972). When the bank failed in the general economic collapse of 1837, a number of Saints suffered considerable financial loss. Many regarded Joseph as a "fallen prophet" and attempted to depose him (Allen and Leonard 1976:112-15; *HC* 2:528-29). Fearing for his life, he fled from Kirtland on 12 January 1838 and came to Far West, the principal Mormon settlement in Caldwell County (*HC* 3:1).

There he and loyal followers took strong measures to intensify internal unity. Excommunication trials ousted prominent Saints then in Missouri who opposed various church policies (Cannon and Cook 1983:146-49, 162-78). Part of the evidence presented was their unwillingness to follow church directions on economic matters. Both the Kirtland Anti-Banking Society and the Far West trials thus increased dissension over an economic pattern that the hierocracy tried to establish.

There is still considerable controversy surrounding the events that resulted in the expulsion of the Mormons from Missouri. Much of what happened, however, can be interpreted as consequences of attempts by Mormons to achieve unity and control within a territorial context. These attempts become understandable only when it is realized that a significant number of Mormons during this period felt that the church as a corporate body as well as its individual members were in grave danger from Mormon dissenters and hostile Gentiles.

During the spring of 1838, a number of Mormon dissenters residing in Far West were taking various actions to discredit Joseph Smith and other church leaders (Gentry 1974:422-23). Their activities engendered counter-responses by more orthodox members. According to John Corrill (1839:30), "The church, it was said, would never become pure unless these dissenters were routed from among them. Moreover, if they were suffered to remain, they would destroy the church. Secret meetings were held, and plans contrived, how to get rid of them. . . . Some time in June [1838] a few individuals began to form a society that . . . entered into solemn covenants, and bound themselves under oath to keep the secrets of the society."

It was apparently this society which circulated a petition signed by eighty-four citizens of Caldwell County. The petition demanded that five of the most prominent dissenters (Oliver Cowdery, David Whitmer, John Whitmer, William W. Phelps, and Lyman E. Johnson) leave the county: "For out of the county you shall go, and no power can save you" (Gentry 1974:424-25).

While these events were transpiring in Caldwell County, Gentile attitudes toward the Mormons were becoming more hostile. There were two basic reasons for this: (1) following Joseph Smith's directions, Mormons were beginning to extend settlements beyond the county boundaries and (2) statements made by the dissenters and the actions that the Mormons had taken against them had increased the negative feelings that many Gentiles in the area had toward the Mormons.

When verbal threats from unfriendly Gentiles began to circulate, Mormons vowed to fight back. In a Fourth of July oration, 1838, Sidney Rigdon (1838:12) declared:

> We take God and all the holy angels to witness this day, that we warn all men in the name of Jesus Christ to come on us no more forever. . . . Our rights shall no more be trampled on with impunity. The man or the set of men who attempts it, does it at the expense of their lives. And the mob that comes on us to disturb us; it shall be between us and them a war of extermination, for we will follow them, till the last drop of their blood is spilled, or else they will have to exterminate us.

Actual fighting broke out on 6 August when some Saints attempted to vote in an election being held at Gallatin, Daviess County (*HC* 3:56-58). The next few weeks saw several pitched and running battles (Rockwood 1988:21-26). Since both the Gentile and the Mormon combatants were involved in both defensive and offensive operations, the state should probably have regarded issues of guilt and innocence as moot. On 27 October, however, Governor Lilburn Boggs issued a proclamation that has become known as the "extermination order": "The Mormons must be treated as enemies and must be exterminated or driven from the state, if necessary, for the public good'' (*HC* 3:175). By the first week of November, Joseph Smith and other leaders were under arrest, Far West was occupied by the state militia, the Mormons had delivered up their arms, those Mormons who had taken up arms had signed over to the state all rights to their property to pay their debt and for ''damages done by them,'' and the Mormons as a body had agreed to leave Missouri (*HC* 3:149-95; 203; Rockwood 1988:26, 34-35). All that winter, groups struggled across the state, ferried across the Mississippi, and sought refuge in Illinois.

While the difficulties in Missouri had many causes, this episode provides ample evidence of American resistance to economic and territorial domination by a religion. While the hierocracy, the baptismal covenant, and the concept of Abrahamic descent endured, the internal dynamics of Mormon covenant structure collapsed. Indeed, to an outside observer, the church's survival seemed highly unlikely.

5

The Basic Structure
of the Patriarchal Order

The order of God's government, both in time and in eternity is patriarchal: that is, it is a fatherly government. Each father who is raised from the dead and made a partaker of the celestial glory in its fulness, will hold lawful jurisdiction over his own children, and over all the families which spring of them to all generations, forever and ever.

Parley P. Pratt (*MS* 5:189)

From December 1838 to April 1839 between twelve and fifteen thousand Mormons left Missouri (Allen and Leonard 1976:128-29, 134). Many sought refuge in Adams County, Illinois; and Quincy, its largest city, became the temporary headquarters of the church. During the winter and early spring, all of the Mormons imprisoned by the Missouri militia either escaped or were released, including Joseph Smith, evidently with the connivance of his guard (*HC* 3:320-21, 327).

He arrived at Quincy on 22 April, and the church began to purchase large tracts of land along the Mississippi waterfront in Hancock County, Illinois (Allen and Leonard 1976:141-42; Flanders 1965:25-42; *HC* 3:342). There they laid out a city which Joseph Smith named Nauvoo and designated as the new gathering place. Drawing Mormon converts from the United States, Canada, and Britain, Nauvoo would become one of the largest cities in Illinois, then dwindle to a sleepy river town when the Mormons left in 1846.

By the time Nauvoo was established, Joseph Smith had been painfully educated in the limitations of locality and economic ties when used as devices of unification. The Missouri expulsion served strong notice that a New Jerusalem in Jackson County was not probable within the foreseeable future. The practical problems of the law of consecration and stewardship, together with the economic chaos of geographic dislocation, underscored the instability of covenantal relationship based primarily upon economic factors.

Thus, in Nauvoo, Joseph Smith decreased the doctrinal importance of both the New Jerusalem and the law of consecration and stewardship. First, a revelation in January 1841 indefinitely suspended the commandment to build the New Jerusalem (D&C 124:49-51), but the promise of a return to Jackson County at some unknown future time remained. Second, the concept of Zion was generalized. While still a prisoner in Missouri, Smith wrote to apostles Heber C. Kimball and Brigham Young in January 1839 that though "the gathering of necessity [has] stopped, . . . America will be a Zion to all that choose to come to it" (J. Smith 1839). Perhaps as early as July 1840, Joseph Smith publicly preached that "the Land of Zion . . . consists of all N. & S. America [and] that any place the Saints gather is Zion" (J. Smith 1980:415). Such geographical vastness coupled with a shift from geography to metaphor meant that locality ceased to be a divinely mandated component of Mormon identity, though throughout the nineteenth century the Mormon concept of gathering included a locale.

The de-emphasis of the law of consecration and stewardship, begun when the Saints failed to recolonize Jackson County in the spring of 1834, continued during the Nauvoo period. In March 1840 when certain Saints expressed the desire to reinstitute some form of this law, Joseph Smith actively opposed them, declaring that "the law of consecration could not be kept here, and that it was the will of the Lord that we should desist from trying to keep it; and if persisted in, it would produce a perfect defeat of its object, and that he assumed the whole responsibility of not keeping it until proposed by himself" (*HC* 4:93).

Abandoning the New Jerusalem and the law of economic unity could have eroded the foundations of Mormon group identity and solidarity. Prior to the settlement of Nauvoo, Mormons had seen themselves as the covenant people of God gathering to the New Jerusalem, where they would achieve unity and perfection through the law of consecration and stewardship while awaiting the imminent return of the Savior. This vision, checked in 1833 and postponed through the mid- and late-1830s, had now been declared inoperative by the prophet who had initially articulated it.

Mormonism's continued vigor rests largely in Joseph Smith's ability to construct and articulate a new covenantal system—"the patriarchal order." From the mid-1840s to the present, this kinship-based

covenant system has remained fundamental to Mormon group identity and solidarity.[1]

This chapter and the next two will examine the patriarchal order
in detail. This chapter analyzes the structural aspects of the system
according to its mythological underpinnings, bases of relationship,
and ordering of relationships. Although various aspects of the patriarchal system have developed through time, my analysis will be essentially ahistorical for the sake of clarity. The following two chapters
deal with the changing consequences of the patriarchal order for Mormon group identity and solidarity in two categories: the distribution
of power and changes in the pattern of subsumption.

MYTHOLOGICAL EXPANSIONS

During the Nauvoo period, Mormon covenantal myth underwent
considerable refinement and expansion. During the 1830s, it had focused primarily on a covenantal pattern drawn from the relationship
established between God and Abraham. During the 1840s, the basis
of the myth shifted to an eternal covenantal order that predated mortal existence, had been instituted with Adam and Eve, and that would
continue into the celestial kingdom, final destination for the most
righteous.

The Preexistence

The Mormon doctrine of the preexistence, or existence before mortality, bears some relation to the Puritan concept of the preexistent
platform. A revelation covering the same basic area as the Genesis
creation account that Joseph Smith recorded in the summer and fall
of 1830 states that God had created all individuals, animals, and plants

---

[1] Although Joseph Smith turned the church's energies from the realiza-
tion of the New Jerusalem and the law of consecration and stewardship,
Mormonism did not abandon territorial and economic concerns. Indeed,
much of Mormon history to 1890 can be interpreted as a struggle for such
control. A divine imperative to do so, however, was no longer basic to Mormon ideology; and when the church eventually discontinued much of its
attempt to maintain economic and territorial control, it did so without a
fundamental loss in its sense of mission (Arrington and Bitton 1979:243-335;
Leone 1979; Shipps 1985:131-49). At least part of the reason that it was
able to make this transition was that territoriality and economic ties had
long since ceased to be integral to the essential covenantal system of the
church.

"spiritually, before they were naturally upon the face of the earth" (PGP Moses 3:5). These teachings had their greatest impact on Mormon covenant organization during the 1840s and after.

The amplification of the doctrine of premortal existence established (1) that the preexistent spirits of mortals were hierarchically ordered and (2) that prior to the creation of the physical earth, they had been organized into social patterns which should, ideally, be reflected in mortality. Thus, two fundamental Puritan concepts—divinely ordained hierarchy and correspondence between preexistent archetype and existent entype —were rearticulated in 1840s Mormon ideology.

The concept of hierarchical ordering first appears in the Book of Abraham, which Joseph Smith translated in a revelatory manner from scrolls that arrived in Kirtland with some Egyptian mummies. Published in March 1842 (*TS* 3:704-6, 719-22), the Book of Abraham contains this declaration from God to Abraham: "If two things exist, and there be one above the other, there shall be greater things above them. . . . These two facts do exist, that there are two spirits, one being more intelligent than the other; there shall be another being more intelligent than they (PGP Abr. 3:16, 19).

Joseph Smith interpreted this statement in part to mean that individuals within a species are hierarchically ordered by biological or spiritual connections; human beings and gods are thus linked in a continuous hierarchy:

> I want to reason a little on this subject. I learned it by translating the papyrus. [In them Abraham] reasoned concerning the God of heaven. "In order to that," said he, "suppose we have two . . . men on earth, one wiser than the other. [That would] logically show that another who is wiser than the wisest may exist. Intelligences exist one above the other, so that there is no end to them."
>
> If Abraham reasoned thus [then it follows that] if Jesus Christ was the Son of God . . . you may suppose that He had a Father also. Where was there ever a son without a father? And where was there ever a father without first being a son? Whenever did a tree or anything spring into existence without a progenitor? And everything comes in this way. (*HC* 6:476)

Joseph Smith further taught that individuals were capable of attaining godhood and that God, the father of human spirits, had once been mortal: "God himself was once as we are now, and is an exalted man. . . . And you have got to learn how to be gods yourselves, and to be kings and priests to God, the same as all the gods have done before you" (*HC* 6:305-6).

Joseph Smith's stress on the literal parenthood of God led many of his followers to believe that there was a Heavenly Mother as well as a Heavenly Father and that the spirits of human beings were their joint offspring (Wilcox 1980). Thus on 31 December 1844, Joseph Smith's successor, Brigham Young, addressed a gathering of Saints on "the relationship we held to our father in Heaven and our mother the Queen" (Hovey, Journal).

According to Joseph Smith, mortal existence was a probationary state in which men and women could prepare for godhood and prove their worthiness. Before the creation in a grand council (*HC* 3:387; 6:307-8, 314; D&C 76:25-28; PGP Moses 4:1-4; Abr. 3:22-28), all preexistent spirits who would later experience mortality were present, accepted this plan, and also accepted Jesus as their Savior while rejecting the alternative claims of Lucifer, or Satan, who also wished to become the savior. Lucifer was thereafter cast out with his followers, who were committed to thwarting this grand plan by enticing human beings into rejecting Christ and following evil.

According to their spiritual intelligence, various preexistent spirits were foreordained to the positions they would occupy in mortality (*HC* 6:364). In at least a few cases, Joseph Smith taught that this fore-ordination included familial and kinship ties. Mary Elizabeth Rollins Lightner (1902), one of Joseph Smith's plural wives, later attested that he had told her, "I was his before I came here."

Brigham Young's (1971:530) journal records that on 23 February 1847 he was visited in a dream by the then-deceased Joseph Smith who instructed him: "Be sure to tell the people to keep the Spirit of the Lord; and if they will they will find themselves just as they were organized by our Father in Heaven before they came into the world. Our Father in Heaven organized the human family, but they are all disorganized and in great confusion."

John Taylor, Brigham Young's successor as president of the church, held that premortal familial organization included specific husband-wife and parent-child selections. In an 1857 article addressed to a woman who wrote asking, "Where did I come from?" he replied:

> Knowest thou not that eternities ago thy spirit . . . dwelt in thy Heavenly Father's bosom and in His presence, and with thy mother, one of the Queens of heaven. [While there thou] made a covenant . . . with two others, male and female spirits, that thou wouldest come and take a tabernacle through their lineage, and become one of their offspring. You also chose a kindred spirit whom you loved in the spirit world . . . to be your head, stay, husband and protector on earth and to exalt you in eternal worlds. (*Mormon* 3:28:[2])

The Adamic Order

In ordaining Joseph Smith, Sr., to the office of patriarch in January 1833, Joseph Smith, Jr., referred to a "patriarchal order" established in the days of Adam. During his years at Nauvoo, he would develop this order into a basic pattern for the Mormon concept of dispensational history.

According to Joseph Smith's teaching (*HC* 3:385-90; 4:207-9; J. Smith 1980:13), Adam had been Michael the Archangel in the preexistence, foreordained to preside over the human race under direction and guidance from Jesus Christ. As the first mortal man, he entered a covenant relationship with God, underwent the saving ordinances, and received all the keys of the priesthood. As a compassionate and loving parent, he desired to use his priesthood power to save his descendants and bring them into a proper relationship with their Heavenly Father. He ordained various of his righteous descendants to the priesthood and, as presiding high priest, directed their affairs.

Then three years before his death, he called a family council of all his righteous posterity at the Valley of Adam-ondi-Ahman, which Joseph Smith located in Missouri. He there bestowed patriarchal blessings on his descendants and expressed his desire to bring them into the presence of God. His desire was fulfilled, because the Lord appeared to them in the valley. Adam's gathered descendants than "rose up and blessed Adam and called him Michael, the prince, the archangel. And the Lord administered comfort unto Adam, and said unto him: I have set thee to be at the head; a multitude of nations shall come of thee, and thou art a prince over them forever" (D&C 107:54-55).

Since then, in the Mormon view, Adam has continued to preside over his descendants. He remains concerned for their welfare, and his "bowels yearn over" them (*HC* 3:389). After each apostasy, the priesthood keys to inaugurate a new dispensation have always been restored under Adam's supervision. Thus, the divine messengers who gave Joseph Smith their priesthood keys did so at the direction of Adam, the grand patriarch and presiding high priest of the human race. Although Joseph Smith heads the dispensation of the fulness of times, Adam continues to maintain control of the keys of that dispensation.

Patriarchal Organization in the Celestial Kingdom

At some future day, according to Joseph Smith's teachings, Adam will again call a meeting of his righteous posterity at the Valley of

Adam-ondi-Ahman to prepare for the second coming of Christ. All who have received keys in the various gospel dispensations will there return them to Adam, Christ will appear, Adam will report his stewardship, Christ will confirm his eternal role as head of the human family, and those present will be organized in a patriarchal hierarchy that will exist eternally in the celestial kingdom (*HC* 3:386-87).

Shortly after the death of Joseph Smith, Apostle Parley P. Pratt (*MS* 5:191) described this event:

> First: His most gracious and venerable majesty king Adam, with his royal consort queen Eve, will appear at the head of the whole great family of the redeemed, and will be crowned in their midst as a king and priest for ever after the order of the Son of God. . . .
>
> This venerable patriarch and sovereign will hold lawful jurisdiction over [the] saints of all ages and dispensations. . . .
>
> They will then be organized, each over his own department of the government according to their birthright and office, in their families, generations and nations. Each one will obey and be obeyed according to the connexion which he sustains as a member of the great celestial family.
>
> Thus the gradation will descend in regular degree from the throne of the Ancient of days . . . down to the least and last saint of the last days, who may be counted worthy of a throne and scepter, although his kingdom may, perhaps, only consist of a wife and single child.

This organizational pattern will have the same form as that established in the preexistent council in heaven and introduced among mortals in the days of Adam. In Puritan parlance, archetype and entype will then match perfectly. Thus the "restoration" will at last be complete.

To summarize: First, the spirits of human beings are descended from the gods and thus are "biologically" part of a divine hierarchy. Second, prior to mortal existence, humanity was organized into a pattern which included a form of lineage and perhaps familial association. Third, in the days of Adam's mortality, a patriarchal order was established which gave Adam everlasting supervision over all his posterity. And fourth, this form of patriarchal organization would exist eternally in the celestial kingdom.

These concepts provide mythological justification for the kinship-based Mormon covenant order that emerged during the 1840s. The church's *raison d'etre* thus became establishing this same organizational pattern among the righteous. While describing his 23 February 1847 vision of Joseph Smith, Brigham Young (1971:530) continued: "Joseph . . . showed me the pattern, how [the human family was] in the beginning. This I cannot describe, but I saw it, and saw where the Priesthood had been taken from the earth, and how it must be joined together, so that there would be a perfect chain from Father Adam to his latest posterity.''

The New Covenantal Ordinances

As these mythological elaborations were developed to provide the theological basis of the new system, Joseph Smith also introduced new covenantal ordinances: baptism for the dead, eternal marriage, the endowment, and the second anointing. For my purpose, it will be most useful to consider such ordinances as the ritual enactment of the new mythology and also as the means of establishing the relationships and roles identified in that mythology. As the Saints understood these ordinances, they provided the way to organize the human family according to the preexistent pattern established in heaven.

In each ordinance, priesthood power operated to seal the ordinance. As discussed in chapter 4, sealing ratified the covenantal promise. It had both a general and a specific sense: generally, it was the process by which a priesthood officiator extended various promises to a recipient. In its more restricted sense, it was the act which ultimately secured salvation. During the Nauvoo period, four additional terms were current which also meant sealing in this second sense: (1) being sealed up to eternal life; (2) having one's calling and election made sure, (3) receiving the Second Comforter; and (4) obtaining the more sure word of prophecy.

Patriarchal blessings apparently began the process which linked sealing in both its general and specific senses merged with kinship. For example, the patriarch often "sealed" various blessings upon the recipient such as, "You are sealed up to eternal life" (i.e., Barron 1977:315, 316; Crosby 2 Feb. 1836; Knight 6 Apr. 1836; Mills 1917:92; R. Smith 1954:43; Erastus Snow 1837; Woodruff 15 Apr. 1837). Second, as we have seen, some patriarchal blessings indicated that such promises could be transferred to children and from a husband to his wife.

The concept of sealing was more firmly linked with kinship during the 1836 appearance of the biblical prophet Elijah in the Kirtland Temple. Believers accepted his transmission of priesthood keys to Joseph Smith as the fulfillment of Malachi 4:5-6. Joseph Smith, recording a version of this scripture quoted by a heavenly messenger in 1823, rendered this passage somewhat differently, which made the prophecy more applicable to Mormon ideology:

> Behold, I will reveal unto you the Priesthood, by the hand of Elijah the prophet, before the coming of the great and dreadful day of the Lord.
> And he shall plant in the hearts of the children the promises made to the fathers, and the hearts of the children shall turn to their fathers.
> If it were not so, the whole earth would be utterly wasted at his coming. (D&C 2)

The full explication of this passage required nearly twenty years, but then became an integral part of the kinship-based covenant system. The keys restored by Elijah were, broadly, the power to have sealed in heaven that which is sealed on earth. In the context of Malachi's prophecy, these keys were the power to establish familial ties on earth that would endure in heaven. Individuals thus united were said to be "sealed" to one another.

The keys restored by Elijah empowered Mormons to establish the patriarchal order of Adam. Joseph Smith explained the sealing powers of Elijah in these terms:

> The earth will be smitten with a curse unless there is a welding link . . . between the fathers and the children. . . . For we without them cannot be made perfect; neither can they without us be made perfect. Neither can they nor we be made perfect without those who have died in the gospel also; for it is necessary in the ushering in of the dispensation of the fulness of times . . . that a whole and complete and perfect union, and welding together of dispensations, and keys, and powers, and glories should take place, and be revealed from the days of Adam even to the present time. (D&C 138:18)

The sealing rituals were, by divine commandment, to be performed in sacred temples that had been constructed for that purpose. The Saints had completed such a building at Kirtland, Ohio, even though the ordinances performed there differed from those that would be developed in Nauvoo. Joseph Smith had planned other temples for Independence, Far West, and Adam-ondi-Ahman in Missouri.

During the settlement of Nauvoo, however, the rationale for temple building expanded greatly. In a revelation dated 19 January 1841, the Lord urgently commanded the Saints, at the risk of their own salvation and that of their ancestors, to build a temple at Nauvoo to perform these new rituals (D&C 124:31-32).

Simultaneously, Joseph Smith redefined the purpose for the gathering of Israel as receiving these sacred ordinances within a temple. In an 11 June 1843 discourse, he rhetorically asked the congregation:

What was the object of gathering the Jews, or the people of God in any age of the world? . . .

The main object was to build unto the Lord a house whereby He could reveal unto His people the ordinances of His house and the glories of His kingdom, and teach the people the way of salvation; for there are certain ordinances and principles that, when they are taught and practiced, must be done in a place or house built for that purpose. (*HC* 5:432)

Baptism for the dead was the first ritual Joseph Smith introduced at Nauvoo which was explicitly linked with the sealing power of Elijah. As early as August 1840, he taught that Mormons might be baptized by proxy for their deceased relatives. At first, the Saints performed such baptisms in the Mississippi River; but within five months, the January 1841 revelation designated the baptismal font in the new temple as the proper location for this ritual (D&C 124:30-32).

Eternal marriage, the endowment, and the second anointing together comprise the ritual process by which one becomes sealed up to eternal life. Like baptism for the dead, these rites were introduced prior to the completion of the temple but were to be ideally performed in the temple. Unlike baptism for the dead, however, these rituals were always practiced in secret, and participants took a solemn vow to maintain that secrecy. This procedure, like the ordinances, has persisted to the present time. My analysis of these rituals, even though it is based on published or publicly available sources, avoids details that might be regarded as violations of these ordinances' private nature.

On 12 July 1843 Joseph Smith dictated a revelation to William Clayton which links the act of being sealed up to eternal life with the concept of godhood as a state that righteous mortals can achieve, most notably by participation in a form of eternal marriage established by the sealing power of the priesthood (D&C 132; Clayton 1982:20). This revelation is consistent with Joseph Smith's 1835 statement that marriage "should be solemnized by the authority of the everlasting Priesthood" (*HC* 2:320).

The revelation first establishes that all relationships and obligations not conducted by priesthood authority and "sealed by the Holy Spirit of promise" will not exist after death, including marriage (vs. 7, 15). However, through proper priesthood authority, a marital relationship can be established between a man and woman that will persist after death, allowing them to become gods, and continue to procreate (vs. 19-20). Furthermore, such a marriage sealing can also lead to a situation in which the husband and wife are jointly sealed up to eternal life (v. 26). A final, and controversial provision, is that through priesthood power a man may be simultaneously married to more than one woman (vs. 61-62).

On 4 May 1842, approximately one year after beginning the practice of eternal marriage, Joseph Smith met with nine of his closest male followers in a room above his store in Nauvoo and organized them into a secret society that contemporary sources refer to as the Holy Order, the Ancient Order, Patriarchal Priesthood, Council Pertaining to the High Priesthood, the Quorum of the Anointed, the First Quorum of the Priesthood, or simply as The Quorum (Allen 1979:47; Fielding 1979:156 note 65; Quinn 1978:85).

The induction ceremony consisted of a complex rite that Mormons now call the endowment. Although the details of the endowment ritual were to be kept secret, some participants in this organizational meeting left partial records of some aspects (Ehat 1982:28-29, 254 note 61; *JD* 2:31; H. Kimball in Buerger 1983:18, note 24; Mills 1917:120). The endowment initiated participants into the "order pertaining to the Ancient of Days," or Adamic order, conferred upon them special priesthood keys including "Patriarchal Priesthood" which empower them to "come up and abide in the presence of . . . Eloheim in the eternal worlds" and thus gain their "eternal exaltation in spite of earth and hell."

For some eighteen months, the Holy Order consisted only of Joseph Smith and the original nine participants. Beginning in the fall of 1843, however, new members of both sexes were brought into the order through participating in the endowment. At this point, a new ritual was introduced, "the second anointing." It was and remains the most sacred of all Mormon ordinances. Only those couples who are both endowed and united in eternal marriage are candidates, but relatively few of such endowed and sealed couples do, in fact, participate in this ordinance.

According to Brigham Young, when Joseph Smith gave members of the Holy Order the second anointing, he "said he had given us all that could be given on the earth" (H. Kimball 1982:26 Dec. 1845). According to historian Andrew F. Ehat (1982:94-96), recipients of the second anointing received what they termed "the fulness of the priesthood." The husband was ordained "a priest and king," his wife "a queen and priestess unto her husband," and they were jointly "sealed up to eternal life."

The Relationship between Myth and Ritual

The ordinances of the endowment, eternal marriage, and second anointing fit neatly with the mythic developments of the 1840s. The endowment inducted the participants into the patriarchal Adamic order and united them with the posterity of Adam and Eve in the Valley of Adam-ondi-Ahman. As Adam there gave his offspring the power and instructions necessary to reenter the Lord's presence, the endowment similarly supplied its participants with the same keys and similar instructions.

Eternal marriage established the participants' position within the patriarchal order. A man and woman united by this ordinance not only shared an eternal relationship with one another but also with their offspring. Eternal marriage thus became the means for weaving the network of eternal relationships upon which the patriarchal order within the celestial kingdom would be established. Finally, the second anointing sealed upon the participants the most awesome of all power—eternal life, which in Mormon theology was the equivalent of godhood.[2]

---

[2] There does not appear to have been complete agreement among nineteenth-century Mormons whether the promises associated with "being sealed up to eternal life" and receiving one's second anointing were unconditional (Buerger 1983:37-39). Doctrine and Covenants 132:26, officially dated at 12 July 1843, seems to take this position as long as one did not commit the "unpardonable sin" of murder or denying the Holy Ghost.

However, the rank and file members of the church at the time of Joseph Smith seemed to understand that these blessings depended on their personal worthiness. Nine months after Joseph Smith told William Clayton (1982:53) that "nothing but the unpardonable sin" could prevent him "from inheriting eternal glory," Clayton recorded in his journal: "May the God of Joseph preserve me and mine house to walk in the paths of righteousness all the days of my life. . . . For thou oh God knowest my desire to do right that I may have eternal life." Joseph Hovey (ms a) and his wife received their second anointings in the Nauvoo Temple on 16 January 1846; but when she died a few months later, he recorded in his journal on 16 September 1846: "If I am faithful I anticipate meeting her and embracing her when she comes forth in the morning of the resurrection. . . . My daily prayer is that I may hold out until the end and enjoy the glories of the Celestial kingdom with her and reign with my brethern throughout all eternity." Such statements clearly imply that the speakers felt that the promised blessings were conditional.

After the death of Joseph Smith, General Authorities in Utah made other statements supporting this understanding. For example, on 6 October 1855, Heber C. Kimball, speaking at a public gathering in the Bowery on Temple Square, warned:

As Joseph Smith (1980:247) succinctly asked and answered in a single sentence: "What was the design of the Almighty in making man, it was to exalt him to be as God." Joseph Smith's enunciation of this three-ritual complex assured exaltation for the individual within an eternally binding kinship network.

The Abraham-Elijah Synthesis

A potentially confusing aspect of 1840s sources on Mormon rituals is that the term *seal* can refer to three distinct ordinances: the sealing together of husbands and wives in eternal marriage, the process of being sealed up to eternal life associated with receiving one's second anointing, and the sealing of children to parents. As already indicated, Joseph Smith introduced the first two ordinances. Brigham Young introduced the third in the Nauvoo Temple after the death of Joseph Smith and just before the Mormon exodus from Illinois.

> Some will come with great zeal and anxiety, saying, "I want my endowments; I want my washings and anointings; I want my blessings; I wish to be sealed up to eternal lives. . . ." What good will all this do you, if you do not live up to your profession and practise your religion? Not as much good as for me to take a bag of sand and baptize it, lay hands upon it for the gift of the Holy Ghost, wash it and anoint, and then seal it up to eternal lives, for the sand will be saved, having filled the measure of its creation; but you will not, except through faith and obedience. (*JD* 3:124)

Brigham Young seemed to have a similar understanding. In 1866, he observed that some women had been sealed to their husbands and received their second anointing with them but that the men were "not worthy of a wife." In such cases, the women were to be sealed to righteous men and receive their second anointing again in conjunction with their new husbands (Woodruff 26 Dec. 1866).

The closest nineteenth-century position to affirming the unconditional nature of such promises may have been that of Orson Pratt, an apostle, who evidently took the position that once an individual was sealed up to eternal life he might have to suffer in hell for his sins but would eventually receive all that had been promised. On 7 April 1855, he declared:

> The Saint who has been sealed unto eternal life and falls into transgression and does not repent, but dies in his sin, will be afflicted and tormented after he leaves this vale of tears until the day of redemption; but having been sealed with the spirit of promise through the ordinances of the house of God, those things which have been sealed upon his head will be realized by him in the morning of the resurrection. (*JD* 2:260)

The juxtaposition of the term *seal* in reference to the first two ordinances occurs in a number of sources written before the death of Joseph Smith. For example, William Clayton (1982:27) records in his journal on 20 October 1843: "J[oseph] gave us much instruction, showing the advantages of the E[verlasting] C[ovenant]. He said there was two seals in the Priesthood. The first was that which was placed upon a man and woman when they made the [marriage] covenant & the other was the seal which alloted to them their particular mansion [i.e., the second anointing]. Wilford Woodruff wrote in his journal on 11 November 1843: "Br. Hirum Smith . . . sealed the marriage covenant between me and my wife Phoebe W. Carter for time and eternity." He later records that on 26 January 1844, he and his wife "received our 2d anointing and sealing."

During his lifetime Joseph Smith taught that when a man and woman were sealed, it established an eternal relationship, not only between them, but also between them and the children who were subsequently born to them. Existing sources, however, give no indication that he discussed the relationship between that couple and the children born prior to their being sealed as husband and wife. After ordinance work commenced in the Nauvoo Temple in December 1845, the Twelve Apostles introduced an ordinance by which offspring born to them prior to their matrimonial sealing, as well as individuals who were not their biological children, could be eternally linked to them as children. This ordinance was referred to as sealing or adoption. I will refer to this ordinance as "adoptive sealing" to distinguish it from matrimonial sealing and being sealed up to eternal life. The eternal tie between parents and children (whether from being born to matrimonially sealed parents or from being adoptively sealed to such individuals) will be termed "lineal sealing."

The relationship between these forms of sealing becomes clearer when examined as aspects of the fusion between the Abrahamic covenant concept and the concept of the sealing power of Elijah during the Nauvoo period.

After the expulsion from Missouri, the Abrahamic covenant was modified to become one link of the chain of promises God had made with his forefathers back to Adam. It implied patriarchal jurisdiction over territorial rights. Both developments are articulated in the Book of Abraham, published in 1842. In the opening verses, Abraham declares:

> I became a rightful heir, a High Priest, holding the right belonging to the fathers. It was conferred upon me from the fathers; it came down from the fathers, from the beginning of time, . . . even the right of the firstborn, or the first man, who is Adam, our first father, unto me. I sought for mine appointment unto the Priesthood according to the appointment of God unto the fathers concerning the seed. (PGP Abr. 1:2-4)

When God later established his covenant with Abraham, he made only passing reference to the possession of a promised land (PGP Abr. 2:6). Rather, fundamental to the covenant was the promise that Abraham's rights to the priesthood and to the blessings of eternal life would be transferred to his posterity: "In their hands they shall bear this ministry and Priesthood unto all nations. . . . As many as receive this Gospel shall be called after thy name, and shall be accounted thy seed, and shall rise up and bless thee, as their father" (PGP Abr. 2:9-10).

In a crucially important sermon delivered 18 August 1843, Joseph Smith (1980:240-41) extended the Abrahamic covenant concept even further by linking it to the sealing power of Elijah and associating it with being sealed up to eternal life. This sermon synthesizes the developing doctrines and reaches to the very core of the meaning behind the Nauvoo rituals:

> Malachi 4th ch [v. 1] Behold the day cometh that shall burn as an oven and all . . . that do wickedly shall be as stubble . . . but before that God shall send unto them Elijah the prophet and he shall reveal unto them the covenants of the fathers in relation with the children and the covenants of the children in relation to the Fathers that they may have the privilege of entering into the same in order to effect their mutual salvation And I saw another angel ascending from the east having the Seal of the living God and he cried &c saying Hurt not the Earth . . . till we have sealed the servants of our Go[d] [Rev. 7:2].
>
> Now I would ask who know[s] the seal of the living God. . . .
>
> A measure of this sealing is to confirm upon their head in common with Elijah the doctrine of election or the covenant with Abraham— which when a Father & mother of a family have entered into their children who have not transgressed are secured by the seal wherewith the Parents have been sealed. And this is the Oath of God unto our Father Abraham and this doctrine shall stand forever.

This sermon clarifies a number of aspects of sealing: First, the promise or covenant "made to the fathers" is equated with being sealed up to eternal life. Second, this covenant secures one against the forces that will destroy the wicked at the end of the world. Third, when a husband and wife enter a covenant by which they are sealed up to eternal life, their children are included in that covenant. Fourth, the relationship thus established between parents and children will effect their mutual salvation. Fifth, this process is equated with the Abrahamic covenant. And sixth, because of the coming of Elijah, children can once again participate in the covenant of their fathers.

The relationship between eternal marriage and the second anointing provided the system behind these statements. First, matrimonial sealing included the promise that children subsequently born would be eternally bound to the parents as husband and wife were to one another. Second, the sealing of the second anointing jointly assured them that they would be preserved during the destruction of the wicked at the Second Coming, that they would inherit eternal life, and that they would achieve godhood. Third, the blessings of their second anointing could be transmitted to their offspring.

Furthermore, proxy adoptive sealings, when performed on behalf of deceased families, would extend the ritual linkages of sealing back through time, uniting all the descendants of Adam into one vast patriarchal order.

This formulation is closer to the Puritan concept of the Abrahamic covenant than any previous concept in Mormonism. Both promised salvation—for the Puritan elect through the covenant of grace, and for Mormons through being sealed up to eternal life. Both included children with parents in the covenant—for Puritans through the federal holiness conferred upon their children, and for Mormons through "the seal wherewith the Parents have been sealed" (J. Smith 1980:241). Not surprisingly, Mormons soon began referring to children born to matrimonially sealed parents as having been "born in the covenant."

Despite these similarities, the Mormon understanding of salvation remained essentially Arminian, not Calvinist. Only after an individual had demonstrated that he or she was "determined to serve [God] at all hazards" (*HC* 3:380) could he or she expect to be sealed up to eternal life, and only children who had "not transgressed" would be "secured by the seal wherewith the Parents have been sealed." Puritans did not include eternal familial relationships as part of their theology, nor did they have an eschatological emphasis, with the covenant of grace preserving them from the physical destruction that would consume the wicked.

It was the concept of eternal family relations that would have the most far-reaching consequence for Mormon covenant organization. The Puritan process of salvation ultimately required severance from one's family. John Bunyan's (1628-88) Christian could not begin his quest for salvation without leaving behind his wife and children: "So I saw in my Dream that the Man began to run. Now he had not run far from his own door, but his Wife and Children, perceiving it, began to cry after him to return; but the Man put his fingers in his ears, and ran on crying, *Life! Life! Eternal Life!*" (1909:15) In contrast, a Mormon man would, according to Joseph Smith, take his wife and children with him in his search for eternal life, achieving salvation interdependently.

The basis for this interdependency was the Mormon concept of patriarchal authority. As Adam had received the priesthood keys to effect the salvation of his righteous posterity, so might the worthy Mormon priesthood bearer. Marital sealing included the understanding that a righteous man's wife and children would participate with him in his exaltation in an eternal family unit over which the patriarch would have eternal jurisdiction. Thus, each man could establish a "family kingdom"; and the more individuals over whom he had eternal jurisdiction, the "higher" would be his exaltation.

GROUP IDENTITY AND THE COVENANT SYSTEM

Doctrines of Descent

While the 1830s concepts of Abrahamic descent and the baptismal covenant were incorporated into the patriarchal order, beliefs regarding descent developed and expanded—resulting in a more complex understanding of Mormon identity than had existed in the 1830s.

The system of descent that Mormon thought produced during the 1840s and shortly thereafter, divided the world's population into Israelites, Gentiles, and Blacks, based on the blessings and cursings Noah pronounced on Shem, Ham, and Japheth, his three sons (Gen. 9:24-27). Israelites were the descendants of Shem, Gentiles were the descendants of Japheth, and Blacks were the descendants of Ham (*HC* 4:445-46); Woodruff 7 Nov. 1841; *TS* 6:857).

The Israelites were subdivided into tribes, based roughly on the twelve sons of Jacob. Three of them had particular significance for Mormon covenant organization: Ephraim and Manasseh (the two sons of Joseph), and Judah. All Israelites, as descendants of Jacob, were heirs to the Abrahamic covenant, while the descendants of Ephraim, who held the birthright blessing, were singled out for special distinction. Blacks, believed to be the descendants of Cain through

Ham's wife, were subject to the curse that God pronounced on Cain after he had murdered his brother Abel.

Nineteenth-century Mormon statements on descent currently appear racist to many Mormons and non-Mormons alike. They were not, however, inconsistent with understandings within the general population or within the scholarly community regarding the relationship between genetics and behavior during the time in which they were made (see Boas 1974:219-54; Durant and Durant 1968:25-31; Lowie 1937:10-29; Myrdal 1944:83-112; Pagden 1982; Stocking 1968; 1988). They perhaps might best be seen as attempts to identify Mormon distinctiveness within the context of Mormon genetics of salvation rather than as manifestations of deep-seated racial antipathy.

Hierarchically, Israelites occupied the superior position; Gentiles held an intermediate position; and Blacks were assigned the most inferior position. Israelites were also organized hierarchically, with Ephraim first, Manasseh second, and Judah third.

Mormons ascribed distinctive characteristics to each descent group. Brigham Young, for instance, characterized Blacks as basically servile (*JD* 2:184; 10:190), "uncouth, uncomely, disagreeable and low in their habits, wild, and seemingly deprived of nearly all the blessings of the intelligence that is generally bestowed upon mankind" (*JD* 7:290). Gentiles he regarded as "disobedient and rebellious" (*JD* 2:268), while Israelites would have a special attraction to the Mormon gospel (*JD* 25:172). Ephraimites, he maintained, had great leadership ability and were "upon the face of the whole earth, bearing the spirit of rule and dictation" (*JD* 10:188).

As adjuncts to the understanding that God had pronounced hereditary blessings and cursings upon the founding ancestors of the various descent categories, two explanations were put forth to account for the distinctive behavior propensities that were understood as characteristic of the different groupings. Both explanations had been articulated before the Mormons left Nauvoo.

The first assumed an interconnection between biology and spiritual qualities and might be regarded as a form of Lamarckism. It seems to have been based upon the following premises: (1) there is a relationship between behavior and "blood" or genetic descent; (2) through personal achievement or divine intervention, an individual's blood can be changed; and (3) this altered blood can be genetically transferred. Joseph Smith articulated this position as early as June 1839: "The Holy Ghost . . . is more powerful in expanding the mind . . .

of a man who is of the literal seed of Abraham, than one that is a Gentile, though it may not have half as much visible effect upon the body. . . . The effect of the Holy Ghost upon a Gentile, is to purge out the old blood, and make him actually of the seed of Abraham. That man that has none of the blood of Abraham (naturally) must have a new creation of the Holy Ghost." And in 1854 Brigham Young declared: "If a Jew comes into this Church and honestly professes to be a Saint, . . . and if the blood of Judah is in his veins, he will apostatize. . . . There is not a particle of the blood of Judaism in him, if he has become a true Christian . . . ; for if there is, he will most assuredly leave the Church of Christ or that blood will be purged out of his veins" (*JD* 2:142).

The second was based upon Joseph Smith's teachings regarding the preexistence and foreordination. While there appears to be no good evidence that Joseph Smith taught that behavior distinctions between different races and categories of individuals were consequences of their pre-earth life, it was easy for his followers to make this inference. Thus, in September 1844 Apostle Orson Hyde stated: "At the time the devil was cast out of heaven there were some spirits that . . . were not considered bad enough to be cast down to hell, and neither were they considered worthy enough of an honorable body on this earth. [They were consequently] required to come into the world and take bodies in the accused lineage of Canaan; and hence the Negro or African race" (in J. S. Hyde 1933:56). And in 1853, Apostle Orson Pratt wrote: "Some spirits take bodies in the lineage of the chosen seed . . . ; others receive bodies among the African negroes or in the lineage of Canaan whose descendants were cursed. [The reason is that there were] certain callings . . . which were conferred upon spirits [and which] were promised to them because of their good works in the spirit world" (*Seer* 1:56, 55).

Foreordination on the basis of preexistent merit and the genetic transmission of behavioral propensities are essentially complementary concepts; and by at least the early twentieth century, the two had become fused. For example, in 1919 Apostle Orson F. Whitney (1927:143) stated: "Through . . . acts of deportation, enforced exile, and voluntary wandering, the blood of Israel, the blood that believes, with choice spirits answering to that blood, and no doubt selected for the purpose, were sent into those nations where the Gospel has since been preached." And more recently, Apostle Bruce R. McConkie (1966:81) has written: "In general, the Lord sends to earth in the lineage of Jacob those spirits who in the pre-existence developed an especial talent for spirituality and for recognizing the truth. Since much of Israel has been scattered among the Gentile nations, it follows that millions of people have mixed blood, blood that is part Israel and part Gentile. The more of the blood of Israel that an individual has, the easier it is for him to believe the message of salvation.''

Priesthood Prerogatives

In addition to establishing the importance of lineal descent for covenantal qualification, the Nauvoo period also saw the essence of the covenantal promise as residing in priesthood prerogatives. In an 1841 discourse, Joseph Smith (1980:74) first read verses from Romans 9 dealing with the Abrahamic covenant and the position of descendants of Jacob in redemptive history, then stated: ''All election that can be found in the scripture is according to the flesh and pertaining to the priesthood.''

The publication of the Book of Abraham the following year further established the concept that Abraham's priesthood, received from ''the fathers'' back to Adam, could continue in his seed after him (PGP Abr. 1:2-4; 2:8-11). As Abraham's ''literal seed'' through his favored son Isaac and grandson Jacob, Israelites were lawful heirs to the priesthood. This, of course, included Mormons who were regarded as Israelites. Apostle Parley P. Pratt explained in 1853: ''From the days of Abraham until now, if the people of any country, age, or nation, have been blessed with the blessings, peculiar to the everlasting covenant of the Gospel, its sealing powers, Priesthood, and ordinances, it has been through the ministry of that lineage, and the keys of Priesthood held by the lawful heirs according to the flesh'' (*JD* 1:261).

Among the various tribes of Israel, Ephraim had the right to preside and to hold the keys belonging to the Melchizedek Priesthood. Thus, Apostle Erastus Snow stated, ''Ephraim, the peculiar and chosen son of Joseph, was the one whom the Lord had named . . . to inherit the keys of presidency of this High Priesthood'' (*JD* 23:84).

Patriarchal blessings from the early Nauvoo period to the present have expressed this concept. For example, an 1840 blessing given by Joseph Smith, Sr., declared: ''Thou art of the blood of Joseph, and confirmed in his covenant, even in Ephraim, and if thou art faithful thou mayst become mighty, and be one of the horns to push the people together" (Mills 1917:91). Patriarchal blessings being received over 100 years later were still saying much the same thing. A blessing given in the mid-1950s announces: "You are of the house of Israel through the loins of Ephraim and you are entitled to the blessings promised to Ephraim, the blessings of leadership in Israel" (Andrus 1959).

Gentiles had no lineage rights to the priesthood or to other aspects of the Abrahamic covenant but could be adopted into the family of Abraham by Mormon baptism and thus acquire rights to the Abrahamic covenant. Parley P. Pratt made a distinction between the literal descendants of Jacob who "are of the royal blood . . . of Jacob and have a right to claim the ordination and endowments of the Priesthood, inasmuch as they repent, and obey the Lord God of their fathers" and "those who are not of this lineage" but can accept the gospel as preached by Jacob's literal descendants: "Through this Gospel they are adopted into the same family, and are counted of the seed of Abraham; they can then receive a portion of this ministry under those (literal descendants) who hold the presiding keys of the same" (*JD* 1:262).

Blacks, the third major descent category, did not acquire rights to the priesthood blessings by baptism. The Book of Abraham provided much of the mythological justification for this exclusion (PGP Abr. 1:21-27), although there is no conclusive evidence that such an exclusionary policy existed before the abandonment of Nauvoo in 1846 and at least one Black (Elijah Abel) had been ordained to the priesthood in the 1830s. By the late 1840s, however, church officials were saying that, as descendants of Cain, Blacks were not to be ordained to the priesthood. Apparently the earliest recorded statement to this effect was made by Apostle Parley P. Pratt on 25 April 1847 at Winter Quarters. In a public address, he contrasted the faithful who will want to go west with the less valiant "who may want to follow this Black man who has got the blood of Ham in him which lineage was cursed as regards to the priesthood" (in Esplin 1979:395). The second is a statement which William Appley records in his journal on 19 May 1847 while on a mission in New York: "In this branch there is a coloured Brother, An Elder ordained by Elder Wm. Smith while he was a member of the Church, contrary, though[,] to the order of the Church on the Law of the Priesthood, as Descendants of Ham are not entitled to that privilege" (in Bush 1973:56, note 85). The fact that Pratt and Appley made essentially the same statement at approximately the same time although they were separated by several hundred miles, both seeming to take priesthood denial to Blacks for granted would strongly indicate that the policy had been established at some earlier point. The policy appears to have become clearly authoritative by 13 February 1849 when Brigham Young declared that "the Lord had cursed Cain's seed with blackness and prohibited them the priesthood" (in Bush 1973:25).

Natural Inequality

Unlike earlier Mormon descent ideology, Nauvoo theology provided the structure for a well-developed pattern of inequality. Like the Puritans, Mormons believed that an encounter with the Divine could affect a person's state of being in a way that could also be transmitted to his or her offspring. For Puritans, this transmitted characteristic could be either natural depravity or federal holiness. Mormons believed that religious inclinations could be transmitted by blood inheritance, ranging from righteous susceptibility for Abraham's descendants on the one hand to something very close to natural depravity on the other for Cain's descendants.

This system of natural inequality for Mormons resulted in hierarchical orderings as a result of their distinctive states of being. The potential conflict between the kinship conceptual model and the church's ecclesiastical structure did not arise; believers held that Israelites would be especially attracted to the church but that Gentiles would not. Thus in 1855 Brigham Young declared at a general conference: "The Elders who have arisen in this church and Kingdom are actually of Israel. Take the Elders who are now in this house, and you can scarcely find one out of a hundred but what is of the house of Israel. It has been remarked that the Gentiles have been cut off, and I doubt whether another Gentile ever comes into this church" (*JD* 2:268).

Ephraimites, Mormons believed, were the most likely Israelites to join the church because, as leaders, it was their particular mission to prepare for the eventual gathering of the rest of the house of Israel (*JD* 2:268). Blacks, at the other end of the spectrum, were not actively proselyted. While a few might join the church, they were barred from ordination to the Mormon priesthood. Sociologically, they played the important role of validating the claim of other Mormons that they were full members by inheritance. As such they exemplified the category of individuals whose covenantal ties to the church and to fellow Mormons were grounded purely in the order of law.

Out of a sample of seventy-four patriarchal blessings listed in the patriarchal blessing index for the Nauvoo period, 85 percent gave Abrahamic lineage declarations while the remaining 15 percent had no lineage declarations. Interestingly, there was more variation in house of Israel lineages during this period than either before or after. Out of sixty-three blessings with lineage declarations, twenty-seven were declared to be descendants of Ephraim, twenty-three of Joseph, three of Abraham, three of Jacob, two of Manasseh, and one each of Benjamin, Judah, Zebulun, Naphtali, and Caleb. In the sample drawn from blessings given after 1847, virtually everyone receiving a patriarchal blessing was declared a member of an Israelite lineage.

There could have been ideological justification for recipients of patriarchal blessings to assume that they were adoptive members of these lineages rather than biological members. There was, however, little incentive for a Mormon convert to assume that he or she was anything other than a literal descendant of Jacob. The identity of the Mormon group was thus essentially that of Israel who had been gathered out from among the Gentiles and united through participation in the baptismal covenant.

The genetics of salvation embodied in Nauvoo ideology thus provided Mormons with strong group identity. Except for the few Black members at the periphery, Mormons believed themselves to be bound together both by common blood and by the distinctive qualities that they had brought with them from the preexistence. As such, they were not only distinct from but superior to the non-Mormons who surrounded them. Brigham Young declared to a congregation of Mormons in 1855: "You understand who we are; we are of the House of Israel, of the royal seed, of the royal blood" (*JD* 2:269).

SEALING RELATIONSHIPS IN THE PATRIARCHAL ORDER

The system of specific covenants associated with the patriarchal order created three basic relationships: husband-wife, parent-child, and master-servant. Although the theology governing their significance has evolved over the years, the relationships themselves and the understandings that created them began in Nauvoo and have persisted to the present.

The Husband-Wife Relationship

Matrimonial sealing in the patriarchal order creates the husband-wife relationship through a specific priesthood ritual. Its ultimate purpose is to effect the mutual exaltation of the man and woman so joined (D&C 131:1-2), establish an everlasting union between them and their offspring, and create an eternal "family kingdom" ruled over by the husband.

Unlike Puritan marriage or contemporary American marriage, Mormon matrimonial sealing is created by priesthood authority, not civil authority; it forms a relationship that may endure eternally; and it does not have to be consummated by sexual intercourse.

The third aspect requires additional comment. Nonconsummation constituted legal grounds for annulment among the Puritans and still does in contemporary American society. In Mormon thought, however, a living person can be matrimonially sealed to a dead one, even though no conjugal relationship had existed between them while living. For example, several hundred women who had not been married to Joseph Smith in his lifetime were sealed to him as wives after his death (Tinney 1973), while living women were sometimes sealed as wives to living men without the expectation of a sexual relationship. Rhoda Richards, for example, remained a "maiden" throughout her life, although she had been sealed as a living wife to Joseph Smith in 1843 when he was thirty-seven and she was fifty-nine. She later explained, "In my young days I buried my first and only love, and true to that affiance, I have passed companionless through life; but am sure of having my proper place and standing in the resurrection, having been sealed to the prophet Joseph, according to the celestial law" (in Tullidge 1877:422).

In view of such situations, it might be argued that within the context of the patriarchal order, the union between husband and wife is conceptualized in terms of patriarchal priesthood power rather than in terms of lawful sexual intercourse—which David Schneider (1968:37) sees as the root symbol of American kinship. Despite such ideological conceptions, at least some nineteenth-century Mormons regarded matrimonial sealings that did not involve sexual intercourse to be incomplete marriages. Susa Young Gates (1977:273-75) thus writes that her mother, Lucy Bigelow, was "sealed to Brigham Young for time and all eternity" in March 1846 but became "a wife indeed" in 1850 when she evidently first began to have sexual relations with him.

The domestic order established by matrimonial sealing places the wife perpetually under her husband's jurisdiction, even though they participate jointly in exaltation. Such a conceptualization is reminiscent of both the Puritan concept of domestic order and structurally consistent with the law of consecration and stewardship of the 1830s. However, female subordination had been based, during the 1830s, on economics. In the 1840s, it was based on the fact that the husband was ordained to the Melchizedek or higher priesthood, which served as the basis for his patriarchal authority. Women were never ordained to the priesthood. As an aspect of the marriage ceremony, the husband received priesthood keys that gave him ''patriarchal'' authority over his wife.

From the mid-1840s to the present, the official ideological position of the Mormon church includes female subordination. The model is usually explained in this way: (1) men hold the priesthood while women participate in the blessings of the priesthood by following their husband's directions; (2) a marriage will be close and harmonious as men attempt to be righteous leaders and wives righteous followers; and (3) God developed this pattern in heaven and established it on earth in the days of Adam.

Although such beliefs are certainly at odds with current feminist thought and generate conceptual and emotional difficulty for a number of liberal Mormons, they are not inconsistent with general nineteenth-century American understandings regarding domestic relationships. In recent years, various church leaders have sought to soften some of the more difficult aspects of such teachings by stressing that while the husband formally presides in the family, marital harmony must be based on mutual agreement and respect.

The Parent-Child Relationship

When a child is ''born in the covenant'' (born to parents who were previously matrimonially sealed), the parent-child relationship contains aspects from both the order of nature and the order of law. In a general sense, a child thus born might be understood to be related to his or her father primarily through the order of law and to his or her mother through the order of nature. The reason for this distinction can be simply stated. When a couple is matrimonially sealed, the man acquires patriarchal jurisdiction over the children subsequently born to the women, whether or not he is their biological father.

A woman, on the other hand, does not acquire priesthood jurisdiction over the children. Her relationship to them consequently is grounded in the order of nature.

Except in cases when there were no offspring from this union and the sealing is posthumously canceled by special permission, if the husband of a sealed couple dies and the wife remarries, she cannot be sealed to the second husband but is rather considered inalienably joined to the first. All children born to the second union are born in the covenant to her and the first husband who will thus be their father in the celestial kingdom. As Orson Pratt explained, the second husband "is obliged to enter into a covenant to deliver her up with all her children to her deceased husband in the morning of the first resurrection. In this case, the second husband would have no wife only for time, neither could he retain his children in the eternal worlds, for they, according to the law of Heaven, would be given up to the wife and her first husband" (*Seer* 1:142).

Furthermore, such a father-child relationship can be established by sealing even if the sealed husband and the child's mother were never married in life and never had sexual intercourse. The most notable example is that of Heber J. Grant, seventh president of the church (1918-45). After his mother, Rachel Ridgeway Ivins, migrated to Utah in 1853, she was sealed for eternity as a wife to Joseph Smith, who had died in 1844, and was married "for time" to Jedediah M. Grant, a counselor to Brigham Young. Heber, their only child, born the next year, was clearly known and acknowledged as the genetic offspring of Jedediah but as the covenant or legal son of Joseph.

As a final variation, it is technically possible for an individual born in the covenant to be the biological son of a man to whom his mother has been married neither for time nor for eternity as when a woman sealed to her husband conceives a child through rape by another man or adultery. In 1851 Salt Lake resident Howard Egan (*Deseret News* 15 Nov. 1851; *JD* 1:95-103) returned from an extended trip to California to discover that his sealed wife had given birth to the son of her seducer. Egan killed the man and, in the ensuing trial, was acquitted on the grounds of justifiable homicide. For some years, however, the status of the child remained moot. Had he been born in the covenant? In 1894, the First Presidency declared that he had because the mother had been matrimonially sealed to Egan.

Another case is created by the modern medical technology of artificial insemination. In a 1977 statement the First Presidency discouraged but did not forbid artificial insemination with other than the husband's semen, then stated: "A child born by means of artificial insemination after parents are sealed in the temple is born in the covenant. A child born by artificial insemination before parents are sealed may be sealed subsequent to the sealing of parents" (Bush 1979:101).

As these examples illustrate, a child born in the covenant is the child of the father, whether biologically so or not, as a function of the order of law. Until recently all children born in the covenant shared genetic substance with their mothers. With the development of in vitro fertilization, however, the possibility now exists for women to give birth to children with whom they share no genetic material. In an 1989 directive, church leaders stated that such children were born in the covenant. It thus appears that the act of birth itself, rather than the sharing of genetic material, has become identified as the critical natural link between a woman and a child born to her in the covenant. It is unclear how church leadership would resolve the issue in a conflict between a surrogate mother and a woman who had contracted with her to give birth to a baby in her behalf. Despite such anomalies the parent-child relationship in the Mormon covenant system conceptually includes elements from both the order of law and the order of nature.

This union of law and nature helps explain why Mormon leaders often present priesthood and motherhood as complementary terms. For example, Gordon B. Hinckley, a member of the First Presidency, stated in September 1983:

> Priesthood is the power by which God works through us as men. . . . Motherhood is the means by which God carries forward his grand design of continuity of the race. Both priesthood and motherhood are essentials of the plan of the Lord.
>
> Each complements the other. Each is needed by the other. God has created us male and female, each unique in his or her individual capacities and potential. (*Ensign* 13:11:83-84)

As an aspect of the order of law, the duty of the father toward his children is logically extended from his role as husband. He is to exercise authoritative leadership over them and on their behalf by virtue of his patriarchal priesthood. The 1978-79 study manual for Melchizedek Priesthood holders instructs:

> Fatherhood is leadership, the most important kind of leadership. It has always been so; it always will be so. Father, with the assistance

and counsel and encouragement of your eternal companion, you preside in the home. It is not a matter of whether you are most worthy or best qualified, but it is a matter of law and appointment. . . .

A righteous husband and father exercises spiritual leadership in the same way that he performs all his priesthood responsibilities. (*Prepare Ye the Way of the Lord* 1978:9)

In contrast to and consistent with the characteristics of the order of nature, the duties of motherhood are associated with the giving of substance. Mothers are defined as procreators, sometimes to the extent of giving the impression that the father has virtually no role. N. Eldon Tanner (1979:4), a member of the First Presidency, wrote: "From the beginning God has made it clear that woman is very special. . . . One of her greatest privileges, blessings, and opportunities is to be a co-partner with God in bringing his spirit children into the world."

Correspondingly, she is to give these children spiritual substance. Brigham Young declared in 1852: "If your children do not receive impressions of true piety, virtue, tenderness, and every principle of the holy Gospel, you may be assured that their sins will not be required at the hands of the father, but of the mother. Lay it to heart, ye mothers, for it will unavoidably be so" (*JD* 1:67).

In a special category of parent-child relationships comes that of adoptive sealings. A child born to a man and woman who have not been maritally sealed is not born in the covenant and will not automatically have the relationship of a child to those parents after they are all dead. To ensure his or her proper place in the patriarchal order, he or she must be sealed as a child to a man and woman who have been matrimonially sealed. A child cannot be lineally sealed to only a mother or a father, even though one or both parents may be dead. As in the case with matrimonial sealing, proxies can take the part of deceased individuals.

To believers, adoptive sealing gives an individual the same rights and duties within the patriarchal order as an individual born in the covenant, with one exception. Under certain circumstances, an adoptive sealing can be "cancelled" by proper priesthood authority. Being born in the covenant cannot.

The Master-Servant Relationship

The 1843 revelation on eternal marriage underscores the importance of matrimonial sealing by specifying that individuals who are not so sealed but who are otherwise worthy of admittance to the celestial kingdom will remain unmarried and be appointed "ministering servants, to minister for those who are worthy of a far more, and an exceeding, and an eternal weight of glory"—saved but single (D&C 132:15-17).

The revelation does not specify their actual relationship to those with eternal marriages; but by the mid-1850s, Apostle Parley P. Pratt (1855:173) was describing their situation as something like that of domestic servants in a wealthy nineteenth-century American family:

> All persons who attain to the resurrection, and to salvation, without these eternal ordinances, or sealing covenants, will remain in a *single state*, in their saved condition, to all eternity, without the joys of eternal union with the other sex, and consequently without a crown, without a kingdom, without the power to increase.
>
> Hence, they are angels, and are not gods; and are ministering spirits, or servants, in the employ and under the direction of THE ROYAL FAMILY OF HEAVEN—THE PRINCES; KINGS, AND PRIESTS OF ETERNITY.

Some Mormons believed that such persons would be attached as servants to particular individuals within this "royal family." Thus in October 1857, Erastus Snow declared that "no woman will get into the celestial kingdom, except her husband receive her, if she is worthy to have a husband; and if not, somebody will receive her as a servant" (*JD* 5:291).

Peter Hansen (autobiography) records a statement made by Brigham Young in 1868 or 1869 that "the mechanic or merchant who instead of working for the kingdom of God sought to aggrandize himself could never enter into the celestial kingdom, unless some other faithful man would take him by the hand and ask permission to take him in with him as a servant."

While some nineteenth-century Mormons thus believed that those exalted in the celestial kingdom would have personal servants, there is only one known instance of an attempt to establish such a relationship by sealing. Jane Elizabeth Manning James (1893), a devoted Black woman, joined the church in the late 1830s and, while living in Nauvoo, worked as a maid in Joseph and Emma Smith's home. A close relationship developed between her and the Smith family; she declined Emma's offer to become their adopted child. After she came to Utah with the Saints, she repeatedly petitioned leaders of the church that she be permitted to receive her endowments, be sealed to her husband, and have their children sealed to them (Bush 1973:32). Her requests were denied; but in 1894, the First Presidency decided that "under the circumstances it would be proper to permit her to go to the temple to be adopted to the Prophet Joseph Smith as his servant and this was done" (Excerpts, 26 Aug. 1908; also 2 Jan. 1902). In the process, she was declared to be eternally a servant to Joseph Smith and his household.

Given this single example of a master-servant sealing, it may be regarded as irrelevant in the patriarchal order, except to illustrate that, ideologically and actually, sealing was capable of including all basic nineteenth-century domestic relations: husband, wife, parent, children, masters, and servants. Mormons continue to believe that righteous individuals who are not matrimonially sealed will not receive the same glory in the celestial kingdom as those who are. The term "ministering angels," rather than the Doctrine and Covenants expression, "ministering servants," however, is generally employed to designate their situation. Furthermore, there seems to be no understanding that as such they will have a sealinglike relationship with the individuals who have undergone a complete ordinance sequence. Furthermore, it is believed that women who, through no fault of their own were not married and matrimonially sealed in mortality, will have that opportunity in the next life.

Kinship and Group Identity

The patriarchal order has a much simpler system of relationships than the Puritan covenant system, which included many levels of relationships within the household, church, and state. In contrast, all patriarchal order relationships are at least ostensibly domestic in nature.

Not surprisingly, relationships within the patriarchal order resemble those found in the Puritan household, in the Mormon domestic organization of the 1830s, and in American society at large. What is distinctive about the patriarchal order is how such relationships have contributed to the development and preservation of Mormon group identity and solidarity. Two basic aspects of these relationships are primarily responsible for this phenomenon.

First, within the context of the patriarchal order, aspects of nature and law are fused with aspects of nature and law within kinship per se. As demonstrated by the example of Puritan federal holiness, such a development is not unique to Mormonism. The Mormon relationship between religious identity and kinship, however, is more com-

plex than that found in Puritanism. The relationship of an individual
Saint to the Mormon group and of a child born in the covenant to
his or her parents is conceptualized in almost identical terms. Both
involve a similar interrelationship between the orders of law and
nature.

The group relationship established through the baptismal covenant and the father-child relationship both involve solidarity based
upon priesthood authority, and both may be seen as aspects of the
Mormon order of law. Once an individual is baptized into the church,
he or she is expected to obey the rules articulated by the priesthood
leadership of the church. His or her adequacy as a member of the
group is understood in part to be a function of how well those rules
are complied with.

A child born in the covenant is likewise bound to his or her father by priesthood authority. The father is expected to direct the conduct of the child as leaders of the church direct individual church
members. If the child fails to follow the father's rules and regulations,
that parent-child relationship will be terminated in the next life; and
the disobedient child will find himself or herself outside the patriarchal order and the celestial kingdom.

The group relationship based upon the concept of Abrahamic descent and the traditional mother-child bond are likewise intimately
connected. As aspects of the Mormon order of nature, both establish
unity and identity by sharing biological substance. Indeed, the child's
genetic or "blood" inheritance from his or her mother is the identical genetic or "blood" connection shared with other descendants of
Abraham in the Mormon house of Israel.

For a Mormon born in the covenant, there is no identifiable point
at which kinship identity stops and Mormon group identity begins.
Both are part of the same totality.

Second, like Puritan relationships, Mormon covenant relationships also can be described as Ramist relates or affirmative opposites.
The category of husband, for example, cannot exist unless there is
also a complementary category of wife. In the Puritan system, this
concept produced clear social positions and equally clear hierarchical orderings.

Mormonism follows this system in its patriarchal order and goes
further by creating a covenant relationship between categories of affirmative opposites. Thus, a fully qualified member of the order must
simultaneously be sealed as a child to a mother and a father, as a

spouse to a husband or wife, and as a parent to at least one child. If any of these conditions is not met, the individual is an anomaly in the order.

All of these relationships are hierarchically ordered. The wife and children are formally subordinate to the husband/father. Any attempt to change this situation is regarded as contrary to the order of heaven. For example, Apostle Orson Pratt stated in 1857: ''The order of heaven places man in the front rank. . . . Woman follows under the protection of his counsels, and the superior strength of his arm. . . . No man can be exalted to the celestial glory . . . whose wife rules over him [and] it follows as a matter of course that the woman who rules over her husband, thereby deprives herself of a celestial glory.'' And over a hundred years later, Apostle David B. Haight (1979:13-14) stated that ''the stewardships assigned to man and woman are part of God's eternal plan to prepare for godhood, and we cannot disregard them without risking our positions in that plan.'' No husband/father, however, has independent authority. Each must be sealed to a father who in turn has authority over him, and so on back to Adam, who is under the jurisdiction of God, his father. Mormon theology continues this system: God also has a father, though not one with whom mortals have any direct dealings, who in turn has a father. This model of hierarchy extends back infinitely (*HC* 6:476).

Such elements have contributed to a complex social network that has had far-reaching consequences for Mormon group identity and solidarity. Because the leaders of the hierocracy hold the ''keys'' relating to the development and organization of the order, developments in the patriarchal order can illuminatingly be analyzed by changes in the pattern of subsumption. These developments are the focus of the next two chapters.

6

The Patriarchal Order
and Mormon Group Cohesion:
The Nauvoo Period

I would advise all the Saints to go to with their might and
gather together all their living relatives to this place, that they
may be sealed and saved, that they may be prepared against
the day that the destroying angel goes forth; . . . and my only
trouble at the present time is . . . that the Saints will be *divided,
broken up, and scattered,* before we get our salvation secure.

Joseph Smith (*HC* 6:184)

The patriarchal order can accurately be regarded as a mechanism
for maintaining Mormon group identity and solidarity. It defines the
boundaries of the religiously qualified Mormon community. A believing Mormon accepts an identity that includes Abrahamic descent
and association with Adam's righteous posterity. This identity makes
a Mormon distinct from the rest of humankind; and through the network of relationships that form the basis of the order, the same Mormon is linked both to member Mormons and to the regulating
hierocracy who supervises both individual conduct and the order's
development.

Subsumption, or the system of interlocked hierarchies, was an
important factor in maintaining the Puritan covenant order; the household was subsumed by the church congregation, and the congregation was subsumed by the state. Under the law of consecration and
stewardship, the 1830s Mormon household was subsumed by the hierocracy as a function of the economic and ecclesiastical relationship
established by covenant between the household head and the bishop.
The system was integrated and unified because the locus of power
within the church at large (the president's monopoly of priesthood
keys) was also the locus of power for the more exclusive consecration
community.

During the 1840s, Mormon thought produced double centers of
power: one theoretical and the other pragmatic. In this system, theo-

retical power centers in Adam and the priesthood keys that he monopolizes as the presiding patriarch of the human family. In the celestial kingdom where order will be perfect, this power will pass by patriarchal succession from Adam to his righteous male descendants.

Pragmatic power, on the other hand, centers in the living president of the church and the priesthood keys he monopolizes as the temporary presiding high priest of the visible Mormon kingdom. By this power alone, sealing relationships can be established and dissolved. The portion of this power delegated to Mormon males theologically qualifies them to preside over the wives and children sealed to them.

The Mormon patriarchal order, over the century and a half of its existence, has experienced significant changes. Policy decisions by the leading quorums—notably the First Presidency and the Council of the Twelve Apostles—have revised the qualifications for participating in ordinances and the regulations governing covenantal relationships. Nearly all of them have concerned the distribution of power and the pattern of subsumption. Some of the crucial modifications have occurred at important junctures in the internal development of the Mormon group and also in its external relationship to American society. Such changes inevitably have had important consequences for Mormon group cohesion.

Much of the following analysis will focus on how changes in the distribution of power and the pattern of subsumption have affected the relationship between the hierocracy and the individual Mormon family, then discuss the impact of such changes on Mormon group cohesiveness.

NAUVOO DURING JOSEPH SMITH'S LIFE

The Mormons arrived in Illinois as refugees from Missouri during the winter of 1838-39 and were welcomed by the residents. By the spring of 1839, they had purchased land near the existing community of Commerce and had begun building the city of Nauvoo, which flourished for the next five years. During these years, animosity between the Mormons and their Gentile neighbors in Illinois grew in intensity. These tensions centered on the fundamental incompatibility between Mormon group solidarity and the larger society's value of individualism. In June 1844, Joseph Smith and his older brother Hyrum were assassinated while they were being held in prison in nearby Carthage. Despite continued pressure, the Mormons regrouped under Brigham Young, then president of the Quorum of the Twelve, completed the Nauvoo Temple, and evacuated the city in 1846. The first Mormons reached the Salt Lake Valley in July 1847, and colonization began again.

The Nauvoo Charter

In Nauvoo, Joseph Smith and other leading Mormons evidently concluded that the best security against a repetition of the Missouri experience was to increase their political and military control. They envisioned a semiautonomous city-state where they could enact their own laws, maintain their own judiciary, and establish their own military, only nominally subordinate to the state of Illinois. They came to feel that they had received legal authority to do so with the Nauvoo Charter, passed by the state legislature in December 1840.

This charter resembled that granted to Springville the previous year (Flanders 1965:97-98; D. Hill 1977:281). From the Mormon point of view, its most important provisions were Section 2 (which theoretically allowed the city to expand indefinitely), Section 11 (which empowered the city council to enact any law not disallowed by the Constitution of the United States and the state of Illinois), Section 17 (which gave the municipal court power to grant writs of habeas corpus), and Section 25 (which gave Nauvoo the right to organize a military force and establish most of its own regulations, under state auspices) (*HC* 4:239-48).

The Mormons saw in this charter the means to defend their religious community. As Newel Knight (entries of 1841) wrote in his journal shortly after the establishment of the charter: "Prosperity prevailed with the Saints in Nauvoo, they having the last session of the legislature a liberal charter granted them which was attributed to shield them from any invasion and troubles to which they have ever been exposed to the wicked who have ever sought to do us an injury and to bring trouble and death upon the church."

Two and a half years later, Joseph Smith declared in an address before the citizens of Nauvoo on June 1843:

> Relative to our city charter, courts, rights of habeas corpus, etc, I wish you to know and publish that we have all power; and if any man from this time forth says anything to the contrary, cast it into his teeth.
> . . . The United States gave unto Illinois her constitution or charter, and Illinois gave unto Nauvoo her charters, ceding unto us our vested rights, which she has no right or power to take from us. All the

power there was in Illinois she gave to Nauvoo; and any man that says to the contrary is a fool. (*HC* 5:466)

This claim of autonomy did not sit well with the neighbors. Although many citizens of the Bay Colony had felt similarly about the Massachusetts Bay Colony Charter, Parliament was an ocean away. Nauvoo was but a short horseback ride from the county seat at Carthage.

Joseph Smith stated that he had "concocted" the Nauvoo Charter so that "every honest man might dwell secure under its protective influence" (*HC* 4:249). The charter ultimately proved incapable of achieving these ends. Government officials were incensed when the Nauvoo municipal court invalidated legally processed state orders, citizens of surrounding communities became increasingly fearful that the Nauvoo Legion might be unleashed against them, politicians both feared and exploited the Mormon practice of bloc voting, neighboring Christians expressed disdain for Mormon religious beliefs, including rumors of polygamous marriages, and democratic Americans felt exasperation at Mormon exclusiveness.

As early as mid-1842, it must have been apparent to leading Mormons that their position was becoming tenuous. That fall, Joseph Duncan, the unsuccessful Whig candidate for governor ran on a platform that included repealing the Nauvoo Charter. Thomas Ford, the Democratic winner, did not cater to the Mormons either. During the final months of the year, Joseph Smith spent considerable time in hiding to avoid arrest on charges stemming from his still unresolved legal problems in Missouri. Citizens of Nauvoo feared that the governor would place Nauvoo under military occupation until Joseph was apprehended, while Joseph himself felt it might be necessary for him to leave the area "for months and years" (*HC* 5:103-6).

Although Joseph's legal problems were temporarily resolved in January 1843, anti-Mormon sentiment increased. During the fall, "crimes of violence committed against individual Mormons increased alarmingly. Robberies, kidnappings, burnings, shootings, and stabbings, mostly of Mormon farmers in the outlying settlements, spread terror to the whole Mormon community" (Flanders 1965:285).

This external animosity was fueled in part by conflicts within the Mormon community. These internal difficulties largely centered on Joseph Smith's attempt to establish plural marriage as part of Mormonism. When, in April of 1841, he began to involve some of the Nauvoo Saints in this practice, he instructed those with whom he discussed the subject to keep silent and feign ignorance if questioned directly. But some publicly repudiated the practice, generating counter-accusations. The situation was greatly complicated by the activities of John C. Bennett. A trusted confidante of Joseph Smith, a convert, and one-time mayor of Nauvoo, Bennett had taken advantage of the secrecy associated with plural marriage to persuade various citizens in Nauvoo to become involved in "spiritual wifery," a thinly disguised system of adultery that Joseph Smith branded as immoral. After Bennett's excommunication in May 1842 and public exposure the following month, he began a vigorous campaign against Joseph Smith and Mormonism. In doing so, he produced highly sensational and generally inaccurate accounts of Mormon polygamy and other clandestine practices (Bachman 1975:218-60; Flanders 1965:260-67; W. Foster 1981:169-74; D. Hill 1977:297-303).

As the protective wall about the Mormon citadel in Illinois began to crumble, Joseph Smith seemed willing to contemplate almost any plan that might promote Mormon security. During July 1843, he sent Jonathan Dunham to explore areas to the west (*HC* 5:509). In December, the Nauvoo City Council sent a petition to Congress requesting that Nauvoo be granted territorial status and "that the mayor of Nauvoo [Joseph Smith] be . . . empowered . . . to call to his aid a sufficient number of United States forces, in connection with the Nauvoo Legion, to repel the invasion of mobs" (*HC* 6:131). On 29 January 1844, Joseph announced his candidacy for the office of president of the United States (*HC* 6: 187-89). In late February, he "instructed the Twelve Apostles to send out a delegation and investigate the locations of California and Oregon, and hunt out a good location, where we can remove to after the temple is completed, and where we can build a city in a day, and have a government of our own" (*HC* 6:222). On 10 March, he organized "the Council of Fifty," a secret body whom he designated as presiding officers of the newly restored political kingdom of God (Ehat 1980; K. Hansen 1974; Quinn 1980). On 14 March, Joseph Smith and the Council of Fifty sent one of its members, Lucien Woodworth, to open secret negotiations with the government of Texas about Mormon colonization in its western regions (K. Hansen 1974:85-86). And on 26 March, Joseph Smith sent yet a second petition to Congress requesting that "Joseph Smith of the city of Nauvoo [be] authorized and empowered to raise a company of one hundred thousand armed volunteers . . . to open the vast regions of the unpeopled west and south" (*HC* 6:275-77).

At the same time, Mormon eschatological expectations intensified. The year before, in May 1843, Joseph Smith had prophesied

" 'in the name of the Lord God that in a few years this government will be utterly overthrown and wasted so that there will not be a potsherd left' for their wickedness in conniving at the Missouri mobocracy" (Clayton 1982:42). And in May 1844 he stated that "the scripture is ready to be fulfilled when great wars, famines, pestilence, great distress, judgments, &c, are ready to be poured out on the inhabitants of the earth" (*HC* 6:364).

The Patriarchal Order and Group Preservation

The patriarchal order emerged among these fears for survival. In its earliest form, it might be regarded as an attempt to maintain Mormon group identity and provide for Mormon salvation despite any eventuality. Such appears to be a basic premise of Joseph Smith's 21 January 1844 sermon dealing with "the sealing power of the priesthood" in the lee of the half-finished temple (*HC* 6:183-85). He began with a scripture that had become familiar: Malachi's promise that Elijah would come "to turn the hearts of the fathers to the children, and the hearts of the children to their fathers." He specified that *turn* "should be translated *bind* or *seal*," promised his listeners that they could be linked to their relatives by such sealing power once the temple was completed, and warned that his listeners' eternal salvation and protection against imminent eschatological destruction depended on their sealings. He then stated that his only fear was that the membership of the church might somehow be dispersed before these rituals were performed.

Less apocalyptically, he explained in a sermon on 8 April 1844 that once Mormons had received these crucial rituals, they could live scattered in separate communities that would be less threatening to their neighbors, yet still be part of the kingdom of God and have all that is essential to their salvation:

> *The whole of America is Zion itself from north to south.* . . .
> *I have received instructions from the Lord that from henceforth wherever the Elders of Israel shall build up churches and branches unto the Lord throughout the States, there shall be a stake of Zion.* [This] work [of building stakes] shall commence after the washing, anointing and endowments have been performed [in the temple].

Once the temple was completed, a family could come, perform saving rituals for themselves and their dead, and then return to their own homes "to live and wait till they go to receive their reward" (*HC* 6:318-19).

Such statements clearly indicate that shortly before his death, Joseph Smith regarded the temple rituals as a means to maintain Mormon identity while undergoing geographic dispersion. Such a concept was far different from the 1830s understanding that the Saints must gather in the New Jerusalem and there participate in the law of consecration and stewardship to be protected from destruction and to be ultimately saved. Joseph Smith's new formulation held out the possibility of a peaceful solution to the conflicts that accompanied their attempts at territorial control.

The state of insecurity and Joseph Smith's apprehension seem to have motivated his decision to introduce eternal marriage, the endowment, and the second anointing to select followers while the temple was still under construction. There is good evidence that Joseph Smith thought he might be killed or that the Mormons might be expelled from Nauvoo before the temple was finished (J. Smith 1980:116; *TS* 5:651; *HC* 6:184). It is also possible that he saw the creation of an elite group around these rituals as a way to solidify the loyalty of close followers.

Since death interrupted his full implementation of the patriarchal order, we cannot fully know how he intended to organize it nor its consequences for Mormon group identity and solidarity. However, we can examine how he used temple rituals to develop unity among select followers amid the conflict and pressures of Nauvoo.

The Emergence of Sealing Networks

Years after the exodus from Nauvoo, Benjamin F. Johnson related what he could remember of the teachings of his intimate friend Joseph Smith: "The First Command was to *'Multiply'* and the Prophet taught us that Dominion & powr in the great Future would be Commensurate with the no [number] of 'Wives Childin & Friends' that we inherit here and that our great mission to earth was to Organize a *Neculi* of *Heaven* to take with us. To the increase of which there would be no end" (in Zimmerman 1976:47).

These "nuclei of heaven" refer to family kingdoms or sealing networks created though sealing ordinances, by means of which a Mormon male might be linked to wives, children, and other attached individuals over whom he presided as patriarch. This family unit would, as Johnson believed, persist throughout eternity as an entity. Joseph Fielding (1979:154), a British convert, wrote in his journal shortly after the death of Joseph Smith: "I understand that a Man's Dominion will be as God's is, over his own Creatures and the more numerous the greater his Dominion."

When examining sealing practices during the Nauvoo period, it is important to keep five things in mind. First, the concepts and practices were just developing and, hence, were more fluid than they would later become. Second, though not everyone who participated in matrimonial sealing received his or her second anointing, the ideology assumed that either they eventually would, or would be sealed to individuals who had. Third, no adoptive sealings were performed during Joseph Smith's lifetime (Ehat 1982:144, 279, note 414). Fourth, sealing relationships took precedence over those established through civil authority. And fifth, kinship and marital ties created through civil authority could provide the channels for the extension of sealing networks.

Joseph Smith perceived sealing power as having two basic aspects. The first was the promise of personal salvation. This power resided in a patriarch who, by virtue of having received his second anointing, was established as a priest and king over his family kingdom. The second was the power by which this same promise could be extended to others who were linked through sealing ties to this priest and king. Thus, Mary Elizabeth Rollins Lightner (1905, 3) recalled that Joseph Smith promised that being sealed to him would assure her own salvation. She quoted him as saying: "I know that I shall be saved in the Kingdom of God. I have the oath of God upon it and God cannot lie. All that he gives me I shall take with me for I have that authority and that power conferred upon me." In 1844 when William Clayton (1982:2) asked various women to be sealed to him as wives, he recorded in his journal that "Mary Aspen is ready to unite to me as her savior, and sister Booth says that she shall not risk her salvation in Roberts hands & wants me to interfere. . . . Jane Hardman . . . prefers me for a Saviour to any one else, so she says."

Joseph Smith implemented these principles in his own family with his wife, Emma Hale Smith. They had first been married by civil authority in 1827, then were eternally sealed together as husband and wife on 28 May 1843. The following 28 September they jointly received their second anointing (Ehat 1982:102). When Emma became pregnant in the spring of 1844, Joseph was elated. According to Phebe Woodworth, a member of the Holy Order, Joseph "came to her house and said Emma was going to have a son of promise; and if a son of promise was walled in with granite rock when the power of the Holy Ghost fell upon him he would break his way out. He knew the principle upon which a son of promise could be obtained, he had complied with that principle and Emma should have such a son" (in Quinn 1981:16).

Joseph Smith had not instituted adoptive sealing by the time of his death. He consequently remained unlinked by sealing either to his parents or to Emma's previously born children. His patriarchal kingdom, then, consisted of Emma and David Hyrum Smith, the son born five months after his death. However, in addition to these members of his original family were a substantial number of other wives.

Among the various controversial activities of Joseph Smith's controversial life, none has generated more debate than plural marriage or polygamy. Examined from the perspective of active participants, it is intricately associated with Mormon concepts of salvation. The women sealed to Joseph Smith believed that by virtue of that sealing they would participate in his salvation in the celestial kingdom. Mary Elizabeth Rollins Lightner (1902) remembered him saying that "all the Devils in hell should never get me from him." Her patriarchal blessing in 1874 stated, "Great is thy glory and exaltation with thy husband the prophet who is working for thee in the presence of our Father. . . . Thou shalt be a Queen to reign in the kingdom and dominion that are appointed unto him" (Lightner 1874).

A main motive of some plural marriages seems to have been to extend this saving power through the sealed woman to members of her family. (Once the ritual of adoptive sealing had been instituted in January 1846, such a procedure was no longer necessary, for a man could then be sealed as a son to a powerful church leader, by mutual agreement, and share his exaltation.)

For example, on 27 July 1842, Newel K. Whitney, a general bishop of the church, sealed his seventeen-year-old daughter, Sarah Ann, to Joseph Smith (Bachman 1975:334). Just before the sealing, Joseph Smith received a revelation in behalf of Bishop Whitney:

> The thing that my servant Joseph Smith has made known unto you and your family and which you have agreed upon is right in mine eyes and shall be rewarded upon your heads with honor and immortality and eternal life to all your house, both old and young because of the lineage of my Priesthood, saith the Lord, it shall be upon you and upon your children after you from generation to generation, by virtue of the holy promise which I now make unto you. (in Marquardt 1973:23)

Thus, as Whitney sealed his daughter to Joseph Smith, he received a promise of eternal life that extended to all his "house" and to his children "from generation to generation."

Lucy Walker was a similar case. In an autobiographical sketch written after arriving in Utah, she recounts her increasing involvement with Joseph Smith as part of a larger process by which her family gradually became incorporated into Joseph's own. After Lucy's mother had died, Emma Smith had cared for her and her siblings in the Smith home for almost two years. When Joseph Smith asked the seventeen-year-old Lucy to become his plural wife, "he fully explained to me the principle of plural or celestial marriage, said this principle was again to be restored for the benefit of the human family, that it would prove an everlasting blessing to my father's house, and form a chain that could never be broken worlds without end" (L. Kimball, BBS).

They were sealed on 1 May 1843 (Bachman 1975:334). As in Sarah Ann Whitney's case, this sealing bound together eternally two families who were already linked by amity.

Similarly, Apostle Heber C. Kimball offered Helen Mar, his fourteen-year-old daughter, to Joseph as a plural wife so that Heber could become more closely connected with the prophet. In an 1881 autobiography, Helen Mar wrote:

> Just previous to my father's starting upon his last mission but one [10 June 1843] . . . , he taught me the principle of Celestial marriage, & having a great desire to be connected with the Prophet, Joseph, he offered me to him; . . . My father had but one ewe lamb, but willingly laid her upon the altar. . . . I will pass over the temptations which I had during the twenty four hours after my father introduced to me this principle & asked me if I would be sealed to Joseph who came next morning & with my parents I heard him teach & explain the principle of Celestial marriage—after which he said to me, "If you will take this step, it will ensure your eternal salvation & exaltation and that of your father's household & all your kindred." This promise was so great that I willingly gave myself to purchase so glorious a reward. . . .
>
> Pure and exalted was thy father's aim.
> He saw a glory in obeying this high celestial law
> For to thousands who've died without the light
> I will bring eternal joy & make thy crown more bright.
> (Helen Whitney 1881)

Like Sarah Ann Whitney and Lucy Walker, Helen Mar Kimball understood that her matrimonial sealing to Joseph Smith would transmit blessings and salvation from Joseph Smith to her relatives, living and dead.

A number of women who were matrimonially sealed to Joseph Smith during his lifetime were civilly married to other men at the time the ordinance was performed (Bachman 1975:333-36). The premises upon which such sealings were based can be understood in part by examining them within the context of the Mormon concept of law. As already discussed in chapter 4, during the 1830s, the Mormon church promulgated two definitions of marriage: marriage by civil authority and marriage by priesthood authority. The ambiguity that existed between these two forms of marriage is illustrated by the 1835 marriage of Newel Knight and Lydia Goldthwaite (*HC* 2:320; Knight ms a, Fall 1935). Joseph married them by the authority of the priesthood, even though he had no civil authority and even though Lydia was civilly married to another man from whom she had separated at the time the ceremony took place. To examine this situation, in chapter 4 I hypothesized that there are two suborders within the Mormon order of law: the suborder of human law and the suborder of priesthood or divine law. There is an interrelationship between these two forms of law. Since they are based on different premises, however, they are not always consistent. In spheres where both operate, this inconsistency can result in ambiguous rules and regulations.

This perspective is useful in attempting to understand the logic behind the practice of women who were civilly married to one man being matrimonially sealed to another. Like the larger society, the Saints of Nauvoo believed that sexual intercourse should occur only between married individuals. During the Nauvoo years, Mormons tended to regard civil marriage as a human convention that legitimized sexual activity but which could be terminated quite informally (Bachman 1975:129-33). An individual who had been abandoned or wronged by his or her spouse might thus remarry without divorce. Such views were not inconsistent with the thinking of other nineteenth-century Americans living in the less-settled areas of the United States. Where Mormons differed from their fellow Americans was in regard to celestial marriage. Matrimonial sealing was not civilly authorized; but to the Saints, it represented a higher form of authority. Thus, matrimonial sealing could also legitimize sexual relations.

Plural marriage was described by revelation in exclusively polygynous terms: it stated that a man could have more than one wife, not that a woman could have more than one husband (D&C 132:1-2, 34-40, 61-63). Such has evidently been the understanding of the Saints from the time that plural marriage was first introduced. Because of this, the situation of a man being civilly married to one woman while matrimonially sealed to another presents no conceptual difficulties for Mormons who have accepted the revelation on plural marriage to be of divine origin. For such a man to engage in sexual intercourse with both women would place him in violation of civil but not of divine law. For a woman to be civilly married to one living man while matrimonially sealed to another does, however, present conceptual difficulties for Mormons. And for her to engage in sexual intercourse with both men would be regarded by most as a violation of divine law.

It is because of such understandings that the matrimonial sealing of Joseph Smith to civilly married women has presented ideological difficulties for Mormons. All of these incidents, however, can probably be explained within the concept of Mormon ideology if it is understood that while matrimonial sealing could legitimize sexual intercourse, sexual intercourse was not an essential aspect of a matrimonial sealing.

In some cases, the women who were matrimonially sealed to Joseph Smith had experienced matrimonial difficulty and had separated from the men from whom they were civilly married (Bachman 1975:134). Such a practice was not inconsistent with the more general Mormon practice in Nauvoo of allowing women who had separated from their husbands to remarry without a formal divorce; this situation would not have been regarded as a violation of divine law.

More problematic are the cases of women who continued to live with the men to whom they were civilly married while they were also sealed to Joseph Smith. In one case, the civil marriage was a sham to conceal the sealing union. After Sarah Ann Whitney had been matrimonially sealed to Joseph Smith, Joseph C. Kingsbury relates that "I according to President Joseph Smith Couscil & others agreed to Stand by Sarah Ann Whitny as supposed to be her husband & had a pretended marriage for the purpose of Bringing about the purposes of God in these last days" (in Marquardt 1973:13).

There is no good evidence that any of the other women who continued to reside with men to whom they were civilly married had sexual relations with Joseph Smith.[1] As far as I am aware, the same holds

---

[1] A possible exception is suggested in a statement made in 1915 by Josephine Lyon Fisher to Andrew Jenson. According to this statement, while her mother, Sylvia P. Sessions, was on her deathbed in 1882, she told Josephine: that "I [Josephine] was a daughter of the Prophet Joseph Smith, she having been sealed to the Prophet at the time her husband Mr. Lyon

true for all other sealing relationships that were established at Nauvoo. It is thus possible to discuss the instigation of plural marriage without thereby suggesting that the women involved were simultaneously involved in sexual relations with more than one man.

Mormon ideology, as well as statements made by the participants, provides evidence that the basic purpose of such unions was to establish and disseminate salvation. From such a perspective, the sealing of Mary Elizabeth Rollins Lightner makes logical sense.

Adam Lightner was sympathetic to the Mormon people, supportive of the religious activities of his wife, Mary Elizabeth Rollins Lightner, and a personal friend of Joseph Smith's; but he refused to join the church. According to Mormon belief, this situation would jeopardize Mary Elizabeth's position in eternity. As she stated in 1905, "I begged and pled with him to join but he would not. He said he did not believe in it though he thought a great deal of Joseph. . . . After he said this I went forward and was sealed to Joseph for Eternity" (p. 7). Being sealed to Joseph Smith "for eternity," however, did not abrogate her civil marriage. Joseph Smith, indeed, instructed her to continue to live with Adam as his wife. Explaining to Emmeline B. Wells in 1880 why she had continued to live with Lightner, Mary Elizabeth said, "I did just as Joseph told me to do, as he knew what troubles I would have to contend with" (Van Wagoner 1986:39). Despite her husband's disbelief and her matrimonial sealing to Joseph Smith, Mary Elizabeth evidently wanted to maintain some type of eternal relationship with Adam Lightner. Following Adam's death in 1885, he was sealed by proxy as a son to Joseph Smith and Mary Elizabeth as a "representative of the female line" (Rollins p. 35).

Such a situation was allowable by the provisions of the revelation on plural marriage: "If a man receiveth a wife in the new and everlasting covenant, and if she be with another, and I have not appointed unto her by the holy anointing, she hath committed adul-

---

was out of fellowship with the Church" (in Van Wagoner 1986:41). I find the evidence to be less than convincing on three different grounds. First, although the possibility that Josephine was a daughter of Joseph Smith was being discussed as early as 1905, the statement reports a conversation that took place twenty-three years before in 1882. Second, since the statement is transmitted through Andrew Jenson, it is a third-hand account of Sylvia P. Sessions's statement. And third, the statement is unclear about what it meant to be "a daughter of Joseph Smith." For example, because of his mother's matrimonial sealing to Joseph Smith, Heber J. Grant was regarded as a "son of Joseph Smith" even though he was born twelve years after the prophet's death.

tery" (D&C 132:41). It might thus be inferred that Mary Elizabeth was "appointed" to stay with her husband Adam.

Prescinda Huntington Buell appears to have been in a somewhat similar situation. According to her own account, her husband apostatized from the church in 1839 (Bachman 1975:134). Although she continued to live with him until 1846, "he had become a bitter apostate, and I could not speak in favor of the Church in his presence" (in Tullidge 1877:213; Van Wagoner 1986:41).

More problematic are the sealings of such women as Nancy Marinda Johnson Hyde, Patty Bartlett Sessions, and Zina Diantha Huntington Jacobs, whose husbands (Orson Hyde, David Sessions, and Henry B. Jacobs) were all faithful members of the church. These women may simply have preferred to be sealed eternally to Joseph Smith. As Joseph Smith had assured Lucy Walker: "A woman would have her choice, this was a privilege that could not be denied her" (L. Kimball BBS).

Given the conceptual relationship that existed between matrimonial sealing and the extension of salvation, however, it could be hypothesized that such matrimonial sealings were seen as a way to establish a link between Joseph Smith and the men to whom the women were civilly married. If this was so, then the civil union itself might have been regarded as a way to extend the saving power that centered in Joseph Smith through the woman who was matrimonially sealed to him to the husband to whom she was civilly married. This would help explain why the women's husbands apparently were not opposed to the arrangement. Indeed, when Zina Huntington in the Nauvoo was resealed by proxy to the now deceased Joseph Smith, her husband (Henry Jacobs) was a witness. (Tinney 1973:10).

While this hypothesis appears consistent with the way sealing was understood during the Nauvoo period, I have been able to find only three pieces of indirect evidence to support it. First, some women who were matrimonially sealed to Joseph Smith regarded themselves as mediators between him and individuals who were not their blood relatives. Joseph Hovey (4 Mar. 1849) records that after he helped Prescinda Huntington Buell through a period of depression and discouragement, she declared: "Inasmuch as you have comforted me when I was weighted down in the days that are past and now, I also say in the name of Jesus Christ that you shall be blessed. . . . Yea, you shall have your exaltation, for I will see to it for your goodness towards me. Yea, I will tell Joseph Smith of your good works and you shall come on Mount Zion with the hundred and forty four thousand."

Second, some women who were first matrimonially sealed to Joseph Smith and subsequently sealed for time to other men were seen as mediators between the two. After Joseph's death, Lucy Walker was sealed as one of several plural wives to Heber C. Kimball. Shortly before his own death in 1868, Kimball asked her, "What can you tell Joseph when you meet him? Cannot you say that I have been kind to you as it was possible to be under the circumstances? I know you can and am confident you will be as a mediator between me and Joseph and never enjoy any blessing you would not wish Heber to share" (L. Kimball, "statement").

And third, at least after the death of Joseph Smith, some men believed that they could become more closely connected to prominent church leaders by having their wives matrimonially sealed to these leaders. In March of 1847, while addressing a group of men who were linked to him either through actual or potential adoptive sealing ties, Brigham Young remarked:

> If I am able to save one man why cannot [I] save more, and sometimes I wish that I could say unto all the ends of the earth, come and be saved. I have no objection to receiving any man into this organization [i.e., his family kingdom] until he behaves like the very devil as Jos. Woodard did after teasing and whining around me for 3 days to have his wife sealed to me. I told him they were both adopted to me and that was enough, but that would not do. (Lee 1938:135-36)

From the context, it seems clear that Woodard believed he could become more closely linked to Brigham Young by having his wife matrimonially sealed to him than he could through the existent adoption. Although Young denied the petition, he probably would not have allowed Woodard to "tease" him about it for three days if the petition had been completely inappropriate.

Questions of salvation and exaltation aside, it is also appropriate to consider at least some of Joseph Smith's matrimonial sealings as ways of strengthening his personal and religious bonds with other church hierarchs. Through the women that he married, Joseph Smith established ties of affinity with at least ten (living and dead) men with the rank of general authority[2] (Quinn 1973:166-67; 1978:88, note 33;

---

[2] During Joseph Smith's lifetime, general authorities of the Church of Jesus Christ of Latter-day Saints included the First Presidency (a president and two counselors), the Quorum of the Twelve Apostles, the Seven Presidents of the Seventy, the Patriarch to the Church, and the Presiding (or general) Bishops.

Tullidge 1877:422). Since there are only thirty-one well-documented cases of women being matrimonially sealed to Joseph Smith in his lifetime, it is plausible that part of the purpose for about a third of these unions was to fortify such alliances (Bachman 1975:112). There are strong indications that some of the remaining two-thirds provided a basis for relationships with lesser known members. Lucy Walker's narrative suggests that Joseph was also interested in forging a tie of solidarity with her brother Loren. James Henny Rollins, Mary Elizabeth Rollins Lightner's brother, lived in Joseph Smith's household and understood that he would be included in the family kingdom of Joseph Smith (Lightner 1882).

The Beginnings of Other Covenantal Networks

Before his death, Joseph Smith authorized a comparatively small number of his close followers to have wives matrimonially sealed to them. In most cases these involved monogamous unions. In his study on Mormon polygamy, Danel Bachman (1975:189) lists only nineteen men who "are known or thought to have established plural households prior to the martyrdom."

Not all men who were matrimonially sealed were members of the Holy Order. Those who were and who, through their participation received their second anointing, were evidently regarded as centers of salvation to those sealed to them.

In the two years between the Holy Order's organization on 4 May 1842 and Joseph Smith's death in June 1844, it had acquired some features that resembled both the consecration community of the 1830s and the Puritan church covenant group. It was highly select; by the time of the martyrdom, only sixty-five individuals, usually general authorities, and their wives, had joined its ranks. According to Elizabeth Ann Whitney, a member of the order, Joseph Smith said that the endowment ritual should be restricted "to such persons as were pure, full of integrity to the truth, and worthy to be entrusted with divine messages" (*WE* 7:105). They constituted "a religious elite within the church" (Quinn 1978:88).

As with the consecration community, a new member was to be designated by revelation. As in the Puritan church covenant community, he or she also had to be approved by the other members of the order (Ehat 1982:104-6). Their covenants formed the basis of their group solidarity, as in both the covenant community and the consecration community; and membership came with a strong assurance of salvation. In fact, the second anointing, which promised exaltation, was reserved exclusively for members of the Holy Order.

By "common consent . . . and unanimous voice" of the Holy Order, Joseph Smith was chosen as its president (Ehat 1982:94). The group met often, at times more than once a week (Ehat 1982:98-100). Their meetings took place in Joseph Smith's store, in his two residences (the Old Homestead and the Mansion House) and Brigham Young's home. Besides the ritual performance of the endowment and the second anointing, the principal activities were instruction from Joseph Smith and a ritualized form of prayer which gave them special access to God (Ehat 1982:109; Quinn 1978:94). These Saints believed that such prayers protected the Church from its enemies. Thus, in April 1844, Brigham Young told a gathering of Saints that "when John C. Bennett went forth to try to destroy the Saints, a little company of us went before God and asked him to take away his power, and it fell like lightening from Heaven" (Woodruff 9 Apr. 1844). Instructions covered a wide range of issues. A basic concern, however, was the need to remain loyal to the church and its leader.

Summary

In short, during his years at Nauvoo, Joseph Smith initiated an essentially new covenantal system which replaced territoriality and economic cooperation with a kinship-based system. Its two main organizational forms comprised the Holy Order and the sealing networks. The Holy Order symmetrically linked individuals through common participation in covenantally oriented rituals, while sealing networks employed a kinship idiom to asymmetrically unite individuals on the basis of affirmative opposition and hierarchy.

Power in both organizational forms came from Joseph Smith's exclusive priesthood keys and authority. He personally remained the center of both organizations as long as he lived. As president of the Holy Order, he personally conducted the endowment rites for the original inductees; all others admitted to the order received these rituals either from him or from members to whom he had delegated the essential keys.

From matrimonial sealings and the second anointings which Joseph Smith authorized sprang the sealing networks, or family kingdoms, organized around each man who had been anointed a priest and king. Since Joseph Smith, by matrimonial sealings, created bonds between himself and at least some other men, it is possible that he envisioned all the priests and kings within the system eventually being linked to him through some form of sealing network. He certainly wrote about the need for a "whole and perfect union, and the welding together of dispensations, and keys, and powers" (D&C 128:18). And both Brigham Young and Wilford Woodruff, two of his closest followers, would later suggest that one day the entire membership of the church might be linked through sealing ties to Joseph Smith (*Deseret News*, 21 Apr. 1894, p. 543; Lee 1958:80; Woodruff 16 Feb. 1847).

However, as the sealing networks operated in Nauvoo, each family kingdom was semi-autonomous. The kinship-ordered nature of its linkages made such covenantal sealings an effective basis of Mormon group solidarity during the uncertain and crisis-ridden closing months of Joseph Smith's life. The sealing network system was essentially independent of the ecclesiastical organization. It created a new structure of religious organization by fusing the concept of distributed authority with that of kinship association. It did not require its members to be geographically close. Theoretically all contact among them might cease, but the structure itself would remain intact. Despite any externally imposed disruption, a sealed member could be assured of salvation—protection from impending eschatological destruction and a position in the celestial kingdom. As Brigham Young exclaimed, the formulation was "a perfect knock-down to the devil's kingdom" (*HC* 6:321).

The Martyrdom

Joseph Smith's fears that events would outstrip the construction of the temple were accurate. Ironically, the patriarchal order—his mechanism to preserve solidarity and salvation for the church—was also the means of violent dissent and a contributing factor of his death.

From his earliest attempts to instigate plural marriage, Joseph Smith had to deal with Mormons who could not accept it as God-inspired. In April and May of 1844, some of the most prominent dissenters were excommunicated (*HC* 6:341, 398). Experienced leaders, they organized the opposition to Joseph Smith that was forming within the church.

On 28 April the dissenters organized a new church, arguing that Joseph Smith had once been a true prophet but was now fallen and should be replaced as president by someone who would lead the Mormon church correctly. Some 300 members of the Mormon community in Nauvoo joined their ranks and underwrote an opposition newspaper, published to "censure and decry gross moral imperfection wherever found, either in plebeian, patrician or SELF-CONSTITUTED MONARCH" (in D. Hill 1977:392).

Angered at its first issue, Joseph Smith ordered the destruction of the *Nauvoo Expositor* press. He was arrested and imprisoned in Carthage jail a few miles away. There he and his brother Hyrum were murdered by a mob on 27 June 1844.

NAUVOO AFTER THE MARTYRDOM

The Emergence of Apostolic Succession

The death of Joseph Smith was followed by a short hiatus in the Mormon-Gentile conflict. The non-Mormons of Hancock County feared reprisals from the Nauvoo Legion which did not materialize; instead, the inhabitants of Nauvoo turned inward to adjust to their loss.

The most critical issue now facing the Mormons was succession to the presidency of the Church. At different points in his career, Joseph Smith had suggested as many as eight different ways in which succession might occur, and there was no clear consensus at that point (Quinn 1976; 1981). Further compounding the confusion, many of the general authorities were away from Nauvoo as missionaries or "electioneering" for Joseph Smith's presidential campaign.

William Clayton (1982:31-32) soberly recorded in his journal on 6 July 1844: "The greatest danger that now threatens us is dissensions and strifes amongst the church. There are already 4 or 5 men pointed out as successors to the Trustee & President & there is danger of feelings being manifest."

The two strongest contenders were Sidney Rigdon, the only remaining member of the First Presidency, and the Quorum of the Twelve Apostles, headed by Brigham Young. On 8 August, after a forceful address by Brigham Young, the assembled Saints voted "to sustain the Twelve as the first Presidency" (*HC* 7:240).

Although the official church record states that the vote was universal in the affirmative, the inhabitants of Nauvoo were far from unanimous in their unequivocal acceptance of the Twelve. However, the majority was decisive, dissidents tended to leave, and Brigham Young became the effective head of the church, formally sustained as its president in 1847.

As Andrew Ehat (1982) has shown, only the apostles, among the various contenders, wholeheartedly accepted plural marriage and as a group had participated in all the rituals Joseph Smith had secretly introduced. During Joseph Smith's lifetime, most of these men had demonstrated their fierce personal loyalty to their prophet. Now they were determined to carry out his directions to the best of their ability. Completing the temple became the symbol, not only of their determination but of the continuing existence of the church as a corporate entity.

On 15 August, just one week after being sustained as the presidency of the church, the Twelve sent an epistle to the membership of the church throughout the world:

> You are now without a prophet present with you in the flesh to guide you; but you are not without apostles, who hold the keys of power to seal on earth that which shall be sealed in heaven, and to preside over all the affairs of the church in all the world; being still under the direction of the same God, and being dictated by the same spirit. . . .
>
> On the subject of the gathering, let it be distinctly understood that the City of Nauvoo and the Temple of our Lord are to continue to be built up according to the pattern which has been commenced, and which has progressed with such rapidity thus far. (*TS* 5:618-19)

This imperative counteracted the natural caution of many Mormons who wished to move away from the Nauvoo area. Brigham Young preached the need to remain in terms of temple ordinances. For example, on 18 August 1844, he stated:

> I discover a disposition in the sheep to scatter, now the shepherd is taken away. I do not say that it will never be right for this people to go from here . . . ; but I do say wait until . . . you are counseled to do so. . . . *Stay here in Nauvoo,* and build the Temple and get your endowments; do not scatter; 'united we stand, divided we fall.' It has been whispered about that all who go into the wilderness with [Lyman] Wight and [George] Miller will get their endowments, but they cannot give an endowment in the wilderness. If we do not carry out the plan Joseph has laid down and the pattern he has given for us to work by, we cannot get any further endowment. . . . North and South America is Zion and as soon as the Temple is done and you get your endowments you can go and build up stakes, but do not be in haste, wait until the Lord says go. (*HC* 7:254-55, 258)

James Emmett, who as a member of the Council of Fifty believed that he could act independently of the Twelve, had led a company of about 100 Mormons into Iowa (K. Hansen 1974:93-94). The apostles warned these Saints:

[Emmett] has led you forth from our midst and separated you from the body and like a branch severed from a tree you must and will perish together with your posterity and your progenitors unless you are engrafted again thereon before you wither and die. . . .

Do you desire the eternal seal of the priesthood placed upon your head by which your progenitors for ages past and your posterity for endless generations to come shall be secured to you in a covenant that is everlasting? . . .

All of you are ready to answer yes, and respond with a hearty affirmative. But remember there is but one way by which you can realize or partake of these things; it is by hearkening to our counsel in all things. (*HC* 7:378)

Brigham Young was able to ward off large-scale defection, and the population of the city actually continued to grow. In the fall of 1844, anti-Mormon persecution flared up again. In January 1845, the state legislature repealed the Nauvoo Charter in its entirety and did not replace it with an alternative. In response, Brigham Young instigated an extralegal and essentially theocratic form of city government.

By the end of the summer of 1845, civil war seemed imminent. Responding to suggestions from Governor Ford and others that the Mormons leave the state to prevent violence, on 24 September the Twelve Apostles issued a statement that the Mormon people would leave Illinois the following spring (Roberts 1957 2:504-10).

Meanwhile, under the direction of Brigham Young, as work on the temple proceeded apace, so did Joseph Smith's sealing rituals. Plural marriage continued to spread. Between the death of Joseph Smith and the end of 1845, for example, Heber C. Kimball, who had taken probably only one plural wife to that point, was sealed to thirteen more women, three of whom had been sealed to Joseph Smith (S. Kimball 1981:122).

The Holy Order met on 11 August 1844, the first Sunday after the Quorum of the Twelve had been accepted as the First Presidency of the church. It continued to meet until the temple was opened for ordinance work in December of 1845. Throughout the period Holy Order meetings were evidently being held at least biweekly. Members, however, were deeply concerned about their personal safety. As a result, the number of members attending any given meeting was sharply curtailed and their activities were conducted in complete secrecy. On 25 January 1845, the order starting admitting new members. But between then and the opening of the temple in December, perhaps only fifteen additional individuals were admitted to its ranks. Existing records indicate that before the endowment ceremony began to be administered in the temple, only forty individuals in all had become part of the order (Ehat 1982:102-3, 206-8; Quinn 1978:91-92).

During this period, one of the order's most important activities was offering prayers that the Saints might be protected from mob violence until the temple was completed and the Mormons were safely out of Illinois. Thus on 29 May 1845, members of the order prayed "that the Lord would over-rule the mob so that we may dwell in peace until the temple is finished" (Clayton 1982:64). And on 7 December when the order at last assembled as a body in the Nauvoo Temple, Brigham Young told them that "a few of the quorum [of the anointed] had met twice a week ever since Joseph and Hyrum were killed and during the last excitement, every day and in the hotest part of it twice a day, to . . . pray to our heavenly father to deliver his people and this is the cord which has bound this people together" (Clayton 1982:81).

The Nauvoo Temple and Its Ordinances

Baptisms for the dead had been performed in the basement of the unfinished temple as early as November 1841 (*HC* 4:446); but the decision to perform endowments, eternal marriages, and second anointings in the temple's attic story meant that the temple had to be almost completed before these ordinances could begin.

On 30 November 1845 twenty members of the Holy Order met in the attic as Brigham Young dedicated its rooms for the performance of Mormonism's most sacred rituals (H. Kimball 1982, 30 Nov. 1845).

The first endowment was performed in the temple on 10 December. Members of the Holy Order first went through the ritual themselves, essentially following the procedures that Joseph Smith had established (Fielding 1979:158-59), then began administering the same ritual to groups of adult members of the church.

Almost a month later, on 7 January 1846, matrimonial sealings and second anointings began (L. Brown 1979:373; Buerger 1983: 25-26; H. Kimball 1982, 7 Jan. 1846). Again, those who had previously received these rituals were among the first to receive them in the temple.

It was probably on 11 January that, under the direction of Brigham Young, adoptive sealings were added to the Mormon ritual complex. This ordinance was performed both to link children to their biologial parents and to establish an adoptive family relationship between mature individuals and prominent church members with whom they had no kinship ties.

Statements made by recorders at the time these ordinances were performed help us understand their significance. Immediately after the entry regarding the 12 January sealing of Newel and Elizabeth Ann Whitney's children to them, the following statement is recorded: "The children . . . were (at the altar, in Holy Order . . .) sealed up unto their parents for time and all eternity (with the usual reserve in case of mutual agreement) and also unto eternal life . . . with all the blessings there unto which appertain to the fulfillment of the covenant which they mutually entered into at the altar" (BAS:561-62).

An example of nonbiological sealing is recorded in the same book. On 3 February 1846, John Milton Bernhisel "came to the sacred altar in the upper room of the 'House of the Lord' . . . and there upon gave himself to Prest. Joseph Smith (martyred) to become his son by the law of adoption and to become a legal heir to all the blessings bestowed upon Joseph Smith pertaining to exaltation, . . . with a solemn covenant" (BAS, pp. 185-86).

After recording the names of those participating in a ceremony adoptively sealing John and Clarissa Smith's children and their spouses to them, the recorder notes:

> The above mentioned children having all received their endowment were sealed to their parents John and Clarissa Smith at the altar, mutually entering into covenant, the parents and children covenanting together according to the order were all sealed (both natural and adopted) to them for time and all eternity to bear their name and to be numbered with them in their inheritance and kingdom which may be given and also sealed unto eternal life &c on condition of keeping the covenants made on this sacred altar. (BAS, pp. 517-18)

Existing records indicate that by the time the exodus had begun in mid-February 1846, over 5,000 people had received their endowments, approximately 2,500 persons had participated in matrimonial sealings, some 600 individuals had received their second anointing, about 70 children had been sealed to their biological parents, and between 130 and 180 men and women had been sealed as children to individuals who were not their biological parents (BAS, Ehat 1982:240).

Not everyone who desired to do so was able to participate in the various ordinances, and by far the least performed ordinance was adoptive sealing. At least part of the reason for this was the premature closing of the temple for ordinance work on 8 February 1846 and the unexpected departure of the apostles from the city a week later (see *JD* 16:187).

By finishing the construction of the temple and performing the ordinances of the patriarchal order, the Mormons of Nauvoo believed that they had fulfilled the commandment given through Joseph Smith and thus preserved their special relationship with the Lord. As Orson Hyde explained at the temple's public dedication on 3 May 1846, well after the departure of most Mormons from Nauvoo:

> As respecting the finishing of this house I will ask, "Why have we labored to complete it when we were not expecting to stay?" . . . If we moved forward and finished his House we should be received and accepted as a church with our dead. These things have inspired and stimulated us to action. . . . In doing this we have only been saved as it were by the skin of our teeth.

At the same meeting, Wilford Woodruff concurred: "The Saints had labored faithfully and finished the temple and were now received as a church with our dead. This is glory enough for building the temple. And thousands have received their endowments in it and the light will not go out" (Woodruff, 3 May 1846).

They had not overestimated the importance of this mass participation on Mormon group identity and solidarity. It extended to the membership as a whole the sense of exclusiveness previously invested in the Holy Order. The Saints completed the temple and administered the ordinances at a time when they felt their very existence was jeopardized: Would schismatic leaders draw away large numbers of Saints? (Clayton 1982:82; Jacob 1949:17) Would mobs attack the city itself? (*TS* 6:1013) Would state officials disrupt the planned exodus or the federal government prevent their leaving the United States? (*HC* 7:481, 544, 549, 563, 577; Fielding 1979:159; Laud 1978:165).

During January and February 1846, apprehension continued to increase that if the church remained in Nauvoo until spring, it would become impossible to leave (*HC* 7:567). At the same time, the urgency to give as many Mormons temple endowments and sealings as possible increased until, on 20 January, "we determined to continue the administration of the ordinances of endowment night and day" (*HC* 7:570).

At least part of the significance the Saints felt stemmed from the otherworldly nature of the temple itself. As "the house of the Lord" the temple was sacred space, separated from the profane world that surrounded it. Thus Joseph Fielding (1979:158) wrote that when he first entered the temple after it had been dedicated for ordinance work, "I truly felt as though I had gotten out of the World."

Intense sanctity also attached to the rituals. Helen Mar Kimball Smith Whitney was deeply impressed by the seriousness of the covenantal obligations associated with the rituals. Although she and her young second husband, Horace Whitney (son of Bishop Newel K. Whitney), were "gay and highminded in many other things we reverenced the . . . covenants which we had . . . made in that house, so much that we would as soon have thought of committing suicide as to betray them; for in doing either we would have forfeited every right or claim to our eternal salvation" (*WE* 12:11:81). An editorial in the 15 January 1846 issue of the *Times and Seasons* (6:1096) when ordinance work was in full operation rejoices: "O Lord, the true hearted Saints now know that the endowments, and blessing upon the faithful, as far exceeds the earthly glory of Babylon, as the sun outshines a spark from the fire."

Finally Mormons who received their endowments were included in the Holy Order (Quinn 1978:94), thus joining the ranks of a group which was ritually and morally elite. Norton Jacob (1949:14) wrote on 21 December 1845: "I with my wife, first had the exquisite pleasure of meeting with the holy order of the Lord's anointed in his holy House, whose motto is 'Holiness to the Lord.' " Thus the Mormons who followed Brigham Young out of Nauvoo regarded themselves literally as a "Holy Nation."

This sense of ritual separation and moral superiority to the world dovetailed with the plans to evacuate the city to reinforce social and geographic disassociation. Addressing a gathering of Saints in the temple on 1 January 1846, Brigham Young "strongly impressed upon the minds of those present the impropriety of mingling again with the wicked after having come here and taken upon them the covenants which they had. . . . The President invited all those who were willing to covenant that they would keep themselves from mingling with the wicked to rise upon their feet. Where upon all rose up" (H. Kimball 1982, 1 Jan. 1846).

At the time of the exodus and (with varying degrees of intensity) continuing into the final years of the nineteenth century, Mormons believed that the American people generally and their governmental representatives specifically were collectively responsible for Joseph Smith's death and the exile from Nauvoo, that America would be destroyed as a nation, and that the Mormon group would become an independent people in their western stronghold. This belief was given greatest expression during the exodus and early colonization in Utah, during the Civil War, and (to a lesser extent) during the 1880s conflict over polygamy (Campbell 1987; Daniel Davis 8 July 1849; D&C 136:34-37; *HC* 7:575; H. Kimball 1982, 2 Jan. 1846; Spencer 1848:224-31; Woodruff 3 May 1846, 25 Nov. 1860, 30-31 Jan. 1860, 1 Jan. 1861, 5 Jan. 1861, 31 Dec. 1862, 31 Dec. 1863, 1 Jan. 1864, 1 Jan. 1865, 6 Mar. 1865, 22 Dec. 1865, 31 Dec. 1866, 1 Jan. 1867, 3 Mar. 1867, 26 Jan. 1880, 28 Jan. 1880, 31 Dec. 1880, 19 Jan. 1881, 7 Mar. 1898).

The Temple and Apostolic Authority

The temple and its rituals served the additional purpose of consolidating priesthood authority and strengthening the attachment of the Saints to the apostles. Even dissidents recognized that it was Brigham Young and his fellow apostles who had seen to the temple's completion and the administration of the rituals. For instance, George Miller, an original member of the Holy Order who had been active in administering rituals in the temple, broke with Young and the apostles in 1847 over issues of authority. In 1855, describing the events of the last winter in Nauvoo, he did not claim that the temple ordinances were administered under the Holy Order but rather: "At the insistence of Brigham Young, H. C. Kimball and Willard Richards, and others of the quorum of the Twelve, it was agreed upon by them in council that brethren who had been faithful in paying their tithing . . . should receive an endowment of patriarchal priesthood, under the hands of the twelve Apostles so soon as the upper room of the Temple could be fitted therefore" (G. Miller 1916:29).

The Saints saw the Twelve's involvement with the temple and its rituals as carrying out the measures which Joseph Smith had emphasized were necessary for the salvation of the church. The apostles became the gatekeepers of salvation, not only for the church as a corporate body but also for the individual Saints. It was the apostles who decided whether an individual conformed to the basic Mormon code of conduct and was worthy of such an experience. It was the apostles or their direct delegates who issued invitations to participate in the rituals, directed the administration of the rituals, and ordered the reperformance in the temple of endowments, sealings, and second anointings performed prior to its completion. Given Mormon understandings about priesthood keys and delegated authority, most Mormons could not logically view the temple rituals as efficacious while rejecting the apostles' claims to priesthood supremacy.

Matrimonial sealings played a particular role in consolidating the authority of the apostles. Even during Joseph Smith's lifetime, priesthood marriage was established as the only form of marital union that would exist eternally; and he underscored its importance by requiring his closest followers to be remarried (or sealed) by priesthood authority. As the kinship-based system developed, previously existing civil unions were regarded as ultimately irrelevant in the eternal scheme of things.

By the time of the exodus, Mormons felt profoundly alienated from America and its institutions. Civil law was regarded as trivial if not fraudulent, and some regarded civil marriages as virtually nonexistent in the eyes of God—hence the imperative to be married by the power of the priesthood. For example, three weeks after the arrival of the Mormon pioneers at the Salt Lake Valley, Orson Pratt declared that "all the ordinances of the gospel administered by the world since the apostasy of the church was illegal in like manner was the marriage ceremony illegal and all the world who had been begotten through the illegal marriage were bastards" (Woodruff 15 Aug. 1847). In 1853, Orson Spencer (1853:9, 14) impetuously asserted:

> The marriage ties instituted by Christendom are a mere rope of sand. A few years will show that these ties are based merely upon the authority of man, and by no means founded upon the authority of God. When this fact is discovered, society will swing loose from its fastenings and former moorings, a miserable wreck in the swift wake of the dreadful cataract! . . .
> The whole earth is defiled by actual transgression. This general defilement has arisen by . . . changing the *ordinance* of marriage from divine permission to the shallow authority of magistrates and unordained priests.

Mormon authorities did not, however, forbid members from engaging in sexual intercourse with spouses to whom they had been civilly married only, nor have they done so at any point to the present. They seem to have made a pragmatic adjustment to the institution of marriage itself while urging marriage by "proper authority" on members. Thus in a meeting that Heber C. Kimball (1848) held with a group of adult men who had been sealed to him as sons in the Nauvoo Temple, he was asked if "a young woman is justified in marrying without the consent of Brother B[righam]." He answered, "Yes, according to the Gentile custom but bye and by all men and women must be married by the consent of the head."

A logical consequence of assigning the keys of matrimonial sealing to the apostles resulted: the Saints acknowledged the right of the apostles to regulate sexual conduct and establish and dissolve marital relationships. The disaffected Catherine Lewis (1848:19) appears to be completely accurate when she states that within the context of matrimonial sealing, Mormon men were "only allowed to take to themselves wives with the consent of the Twelve." The apostles did not gratuitously prevent such sealings but, in fact, encouraged as many Mormons as possible to be sealed. However, as a function of legitimizing authority, the important point was that the apostles monopolized the priesthood keys by which such marriages were created.

"Family Kingdoms"

The patriarchal order established solidarity among church members through its network of reinforcing kinship and ecclesiastical ties. An example of the "family kingdom" that leading Saints quite consciously developed is that of Heber C. Kimball, then senior ranking apostle after Brigham Young and consistently prominent in all temple rituals. As members of the Holy Order, Heber, his first wife, Vilate Murray Kimball, and daughter Helen Mar Kimball Smith (later Whitney) were among the first to go through the endowment ritual in December 1845. Thereafter, they spent much of their remaining time administering this same ordinance to other members.

Heber and Vilate were matrimonially sealed on 7 January 1846, the first day such ordinances occurred in the temple. The next day, they were the first to receive their second anointings within the temple.

On 12 January, Kimball began the sealings of plural wives and other women who had agreed to marry him. Between January 12 and February 7, he was married in the temple to either thirty-six or thirty-seven women, including probably fifteen wives previously sealed to him. Six of the thirty-seven had formerly been sealed as wives to Joseph Smith while he was still alive. Another four were posthumously sealed to Joseph Smith, then married to Kimball. Another had been sealed to Hyrum Smith and still another had been married but not sealed to Frederick G. Williams before their deaths. These two women were sealed for eternity to Hyrum Smith and Frederick G. Williams respectively, and to Heber C. Kimball for time (BAS; S. Kimball 1981:122).

When Kimball was sealed to women being sealed for eternity for other men, he also acted as proxy, ritually taking the part of the man whose role he would be fulfilling in mortality. Apparently one motive was to fortify his eternal relationship with the men to whom these wives were sealed for eternity, especially in sealings involving Joseph Smith. An important element in such sealings was the understanding that the children born to these women would be covenant children to the deceased husband. Catherine Lewis (1848:19) reported in 1848: "The Apostles said they only took Joseph's wives to raise up children, carry them through to the next world, there deliver them up to him, by so doing they should gain his approbation."

The remaining twenty-six women were sealed to Kimball for time and eternity.

On 11 January Heber's and Vilate's five living children and daughter-in-law Mary Davenport were adoptively sealed to them. Toward the end of January, the same ordinance linked some forty other adult men and women as adoptive children to Heber and Vilate. Most of these were husbands and wives who had themselves been matrimonially sealed in the temple. It is not clear why these particular individuals were sealed as children to the Kimballs. Some were relatives and friends, others were associated with them in ordinance work; none was particularly prominent. Among the men, apparently only Howard Egan had become involved in polygamy during the days of Joseph Smith (see Bachman 1975:189) and most left Nauvoo as monogamists. None had been admitted to the Holy Order before receiving their endowments in the Nauvoo Temple.

Given the ideology associated with adoptive sealing, they probably saw it as a way to share the exaltation of one of the most prominent members of the church and become part of his family in this life. On 14 December 1845, just after the endowments began in the temple, Brigham Young had stated: "To constitute a man responsible he must have the power and ability not only to save himself but to save others; but there are those who are not capable of saving themselves and will have to be saved by others" (*HC* 7:546). To many Mormons of the late Nauvoo period, Heber C. Kimball would have been such a "responsible" man.

The Exodus from Nauvoo

Throughout the early weeks of 1846, conditions in and around Nauvoo were becoming tenser, and preparations for the exodus were speeded up. At a council meeting consisting of "the Twelve, Trustees, and a few others," the decision was made that the best course of action would be for the authorities of the Church to leave for the west as quickly as possible and for "the balance of the Saints [to] follow in the spring as fast as they can get ready" (E. Snow, 1847, entry dealing with early 1846; *HC* 7:578). On 8 February 1846, the administration of endowments ceased (Jacob 1949:18), and on 15 February Brigham Young crossed the Mississippi, traveled nine miles, and camped (*HC* 7:585). Although the Mormons would not fully evacuate Nauvoo until the following September, the exodus had now begun.

The Mormons had had their temple in full operation not quite two months, but it had been long enough for the covenantal ordinances to become the foundation of Mormon group unity. By those rituals, they believed, they had preserved their distinctive relationship with the Lord and were "sealed up," regardless of the mob violence waiting to be unleashed. Helen Mar Kimball Smith Whitney recalled the feelings of the Mormons at the exodus:

> To all earthly appearance we were then to be scattered or wiped out of existence. We were but a little handful and no power to look to but to the Omnipotent, whose hand had thus far kept us together and not the power of man. But He, in his infinite mercy, had endowed them and given them the key by which his faithful servants and handmaidens could approach nearer to His throne, and find greater favor, because of their humble obedience to His laws and requirements. (*WE* 12:3:14)

They left Nauvoo feeling themselves a unified body who could maintain their cohesion despite any obstacle. Orson Spencer (1848: 216, 219, 215) would boast in December 1847 while on a mission in England:

> While the unity of great and powerful nations is undergoing a rapid conversion into fractional weakness, the strength of Israel is accumulating and augmenting beyond all former precedent. . . .
> Driven, and scattered, and robbed in Ohio, Missouri, and Illinois, they have readily re-assembled and re-united. . . . [And] when thousands that now compose the Church, and who have proved before the American people that the cords of their union cannot be sundered by the hottest thunderbolts of persecution, are assembled in the remote, extensive, and fertile valley of the almost unknown mountain, they will be forever invincible.

This unity had been a full fifteen years in the making, despite the acceleration of its development during the Nauvoo period. From the 1830s, the Mormons had accepted the concept of an exclusive priesthood with power to establish divinely sanctioned covenantal relationships. Covenant making separated the religiously qualified from the rest of humankind, and within the church was an even more elite group of the fully religiously qualified.

However, the exile from Missouri had signalled fundamental changes in the Mormon concept of group identity. During the early 1830s, the Mormons regarded themselves essentially as converted Gentiles responsible to take the restoration to the house of Israel and be included with them in the covenant. By 1840 the Mormons instead came to regard themselves as the biological descendants of Israel and literal heirs to the Abrahamic covenant with particularistic ties back to Adam, eternal patriarch of the human race.

For the elite inner group, identity was always linked to covenants that would assure their salvation. That concept provided continuity while the exact nature of the covenant evolved. In the 1830s, it had consisted of participating in the law of consecration and stewardship and receiving an inheritance of the land of Zion. By the end of the Nauvoo period, covenants of sealing had replaced land and economics as basic aspects of salvation.

Thus, in Nauvoo, Mormon covenant organization successfully passed a test of its ability to generate change within a context of continuity. This versatility was central to the Mormon group's survival ability. The gathering of Israel was redefined from physically inheriting a geographical locale to building a temple where sacred ordinances could occur in sacred space. Protection from eschatalogical destruction would come, not from occupying a sacred land, but by becoming a sacred people. As a result, Mormons could see how the spiritually elite could dwell among the wicked while still preserving their religious exclusiveness.

Furthermore, the economic bonds of the 1830s were replaced by kinship-based bonds under priesthood authority. While both systems subsumed individual families to the hierocracy, the Nauvoo development asserted a heavenly pattern for domestic arrangements. Participating in such rituals separated a Latter-day Saint sharply from a Gentile and created an expectation of eternal relationships within the covenant framework.

Participants in patriarchal order rituals became subsumed by the hierocracy in two different ways: by priesthood and by family ties. The hierocracy prescribed the code of conduct which qualified candidates for ordinances as "worthy," administered the ordinances, and could revoke the covenantal promises if candidates violated the code of conduct. Male heads of families were ordained elders and thus became part of the priesthood hierocracy. Second anointings bestowed upon a man power to effect the salvation of all who became part of his family kingdom through the establishment of sealing ties. He presided over them as their priest and king, serving as the link between family and hierocracy and as the critical juncture at which the family system and the priesthood system converged. These concepts were just as true after Joseph Smith's death when the church population at large began to participate in temple ordinances as before when only a handful participated in the Holy Order.

Threatened by attack from without and schism from within, confronted with a forced exodus, and contemplating a future outside the territorial boundaries of the United States, the Mormon people needed a unifying paradigm that would express intense solidarity and operate independently of territorial connotations. The patriarchal order, with sealing ties grounded in kinship, provided such a paradigm.

As the Saints crossed the Mississippi in 1846, the essential elements of the patriarchal order were in place. Many of its details, however, had still to be worked out. Relatively few members of the hierocracy were linked to each other through sealing ties. What, then, was the relationship between patriarchal authority and ecclesiastical jurisdiction? How should conflicts between individualism and the corporate control associated with covenantal organization be resolved? And how could Mormon covenantal organization be reconciled with American institutions?

Each of these questions, dealing with subsumption and the distribution of power, would be dealt with in the coming years as the patriarchal order continued to adjust to the changing nature of the Mormon group.

7

The Patriarchal Order
and Mormon Group Cohesion:
The Post-Nauvoo Period

The president made another speech, showing the way to get along with business where [there are] many hands, namely by the principle of sealing, binding the children to the fathers, laying before them as an example his own family, containing about 200 persons.

—P. Hanson, diary, 24 Apr. 1846

As a system of government, the patriarchal order provides a maximum of opportunity with a minimum of structure and regulation.

—Dean L. Larsen (*Ensign*, Sept. 1982, p. 12)

THE MIGRATION TO WINTER QUARTERS: 1846-47

Leaving Nauvoo

At the October 1845 General Conference of the Church, the assembled Saints covenanted that "we take all the saints with us, to the extent of our ability, this is our influence and property" (*TS* 6:1011). In preparation for the exodus, Mormon leaders had organized the Saints at Nauvoo for the journey and provided detailed lists specifying the provisions required for each individual. The premature departure of the Twelve from Nauvoo and the inability of the Mormons to sell their property at more than rock-bottom prices, however, wrought havoc with such plans.

Brigham Young, Heber C. Kimball, and those who crossed the Mississippi with them in mid-February established a base camp at Sugar Creek, some nine miles from Nauvoo. They remained there for approximately two weeks, waiting for the weather to improve and taking care of last-minute business. In the meantime, Mormons across the river in Nauvoo began flocking to the camp in an ill-prepared and disorganized fashion.

By the first of March, the weather had improved; and the Saints who had congregated at Sugar Creek began to move west. New problems almost immediately developed for the "Camp of Israel," as this initial wave of Mormon migrants was termed: the frozen ground thawed and the wagons and oxen became mired in the mud (Eliza Snow, 2 Mar. 1846). Progress was painfully slow; during the first month, the camp moved an average of only three miles a day (S. Kimball 1981:132). There were few bridges, roads were almost impassable, and sickness was rampant.

Amid such difficulties the basic organizational features of Mormon migration were solidified: the company, the settlement, and the family. All had existed before the exodus; but as the Camp of Israel moved over the soggy plains of Iowa, each became relevant in novel ways.

Antecedents of the company system might be detected in the quasimilitary organization of Zion's Camp. In Nauvoo, the Mormons had been organized into companies presided over by captains, disregarded in the haste to follow the leaders out of Nauvoo. Toward the end of March, Brigham Young reorganized the Camp of Israel hierarchically. At the head was Brigham Young. Under his direct supervision were three "captains of hundreds," each of whom had jurisdiction over two "captains of fifties," who in turn presided over five "captains of tens." A captain of ten was directly responsible for approximately ten nuclear families. Each individual in the camp was thus linked by a formal chain of command to Brigham Young. The company system with its captains of hundreds, fifties, and tens would remain an integral part of Mormon migration (D&C 136:2-3; Roberts 1957 3:52-54; Eliza Snow, 28 Mar. 1846).

The Mormons leaving Nauvoo had already had considerable experience with village organization. Now they built Garden Grove, Mount Pisgah, and other settlements along the route as way stations for those to follow, regulated by a combined ecclesiastical and civil government somewhat like the Nauvoo City government.

The family, under its patriarch's direction, had the primary responsibility to provide for its members and was thus seen as the basic economic and organizational unit. This organization had been contemplated when plans were being made for the exodus. It was hardened, however, after many in the Camp of Israel who had left Nauvoo without sufficient provisions began using the provisions of the more self-sufficient families.

By mid-June the Camp of Israel had reached Council Bluffs, some three hundred miles from Nauvoo. Brigham Young intended to push on, establish other way stations, and perhaps reach the final destination by fall. At Council Bluffs, however, officers of the United States military intercepted them, not, as the Saints initially thought, to prevent their migration but with a request from President James K. Polk that the Saints supply five hundred volunteers for the war with Mexico.

Brigham Young immediately agreed, marking a limit to the separatist ambitions of the Mormons. Jesse C. Little, the presiding church officer in the East and the church agent in Washington, D.C., had fulfilled Brigham Young's instructions in persuading the government to help them migrate. Though church leaders would later use the enlistment to complain about the unreasonable demands of the government on a people it had not helped, they also would use it to demonstrate the high patriotism of the Mormon people. Conflict with the government would persist through the nineteenth century, reaching their peak over polygamy and subsiding only after the Reed Smoot hearings that allowed Utah's senator to keep his seat in 1904. Still, the Mormons would see themselves as superpatriots by the mid-twentieth century.

Among the Mormon Battalion's immediate advantages were: the soldiers would reach the west coast at government expense while their pay would help transport their families west; at discharge, they would retain their arms and supplies; Mormon fears that the government might prevent migration were over; and the Saints received the temporary right to occupy Indian lands.

After filling the quota with his best teamsters and more vigorous men, Brigham Young decided to spend a year at the Missouri River before attempting to "go over the mountains" (Hansen Diary 21 May 1846). He established provisional church headquarters at Winter Quarters, the site of present-day Florence, Nebraska.

From Winter Quarters, Brigham Young and the apostles directed the Mormons congregated along the banks of the Missouri River or still in transit from the now nearly abandoned city of Nauvoo. The pause allowed the Saints a much-need respite and an opportunity to regroup and redirect their efforts. Such efforts were sorely needed.

Centrifugal Tendencies among Mormon Migrants

Records kept by Mormons while en route from Nauvoo and during the early months at Winter Quarters demonstrate three basic conditions working against Mormon unity: (1) abnormally high rates of sickness and death; (2) individualistic economic interests; and (3) forced proximity under difficult circumstances. As Eliza R. Snow (a plural wife of Joseph Smith, at that point sealed for time to Brigham Young) recorded in her journal on 12 August 1846: "It is a growling, grumbling, devilish, sickly time with us now."

Without proper supplies, malnutrition meant lack of resistance to sickness. Journals frequently mention "canker," "black leg," "cholera morbus," and "paroxysm." Based on records of Winter Quarters, Maureen Ursenbach Beecher (1983:16) estimates the overall death rate of migrating Mormons to have been 82.1 per thousand, much higher than the 50 per thousand of poorer third-world nations today and almost four times the rate of 21 per thousand indicated in the 1850 Utah census. Infant mortality at Winter Quarters, she estimates, was 35.5 percent. In personal terms, such statistics translate into debility, emotional stress, and grief.

A second major problem was economic. Requiring families to be self-sufficient was probably the best practical solution to the serious problem of economic survival, but it automatically created more individual economic self-interest and generated great conflict with the Mormon covenant obligation to help the less fortunate and to cooperate with one another. Eliza R. Snow thus recorded in her journal under date of 12 April a sermon in which Heber C. Kimball "strongly impress'd the necessity of union of feelings & action—said his feelings were wounded by reflections made by some respecting sending their teams back for others . . . said that those who were selfish about helping others would find their teams weakening & dying." And later on 1 June when she and other Saints were required to remain temporarily at Mt. Pisgah she wrote: "I prefer stopping behind for the present that every possible means may be appropriated to liberate the Twelve from the oppression of the selfish ones who never have made sacrifices for the truth's sake."

Added to these difficulties were the conflicts resulting from the forced proximity under which the Mormon migrants had to operate. Journals are replete with examples. While many quarrels were petty, they reveal an underlying tension in the companies, settlements, and families. Eliza R. Snow's journal records the growing antagonism between her and the members of a contentious family with whom she was required to travel. "It is my lot to have one about me that is a constant annoyance, one with whom I *cannot* & *will* not hold fellowship" (8 May 1846). "While suffering much in body & lying as it were at the gate of death [I was surrounded] with *family discord* which I think proper to call *hell*'' (Sept entry). "S[ister] M. said [to me], 'Do you think you have been disgrac'd by living in the family? I should not think the Lord would require you to live where you would *disgrace yourself.*' I saw she had a wrong spirit & made no reply'' (29 Nov. 1846).

Antagonistic feelings could at times erupt into violence. Peter O. Hansen (Diary, 9 June 1846), an adopted son of Heber C. Kimball who also kept Kimball's camp journal, records, "Yesterday Br. J. P. being jalious of Br. E. for him being ahead of him with his wagon, struck his oxen to drive them out of the way which made Br. E. angry and he struck br. J. P. After several stricks from both sides, in his eyes so bad that he fell down and still he struck him.''

THE PATRIARCHAL ORDER AND UNITY: 1846-47

Counteracting the centrifugal aspects of the exodus and migration were the ideology, ritual, and covenantal relationships associated with the patriarchal order. While not always successful in preventing specific disruptions and defections, the patriarchal order paradigm provided both a conceptual framework for identity and also the institutional means for adjusting individual desires to group needs.

The Mormons faced an uncertain future but believed that they were establishing a kingdom that would meet with divine approbation. "And this will be the best and greatest kingdom ever known this side of heaven," exulted Orson Spencer (1847:2) in a religious tract composed in September 1847 while serving a mission in England. "Its constitution, laws, and methods of administration will be after the model of the heavenly order.''

The basic unit within this kingdom was the family kingdom, combining nineteenth-century American understandings of kinship amity and domestic order with the Mormon concept of delegated priesthood authority. As Heber C. Kimball had declared while still at Nauvoo: "If we become to be kings & priests unto God we must make our children just as hapy as they can be & we must be rulers over them, to give them their inheritances" (Laud 1978:177).

They believed firmly in the unity that came from such a system. As Orson Spencer (1848:168) wrote in a religious tract dated 30 November 1847: "The strongest tie of government, of union, strength, and happiness in any confederation whatever, either in heaven or on earth, is that which springs from parentage.''

Had apostasy never occurred from the days of Adam, according to Mormon thought, then all marriages would have been performed by priesthood authority and all children would have been born in the covenant. Then everyone by birthright would be part of a family kingdom, and each father would have eternal patriarchal jurisdiction over his own posterity. As Brigham Young explained in February 1847: "Had the keys of the priesthood been retained and handed down from father to son throughout all generations up to the present time then there could have been no necessity of the law of adoption, for we would all have been included in the covenant without it and would have been legal heirs instead of being heirs according to promise" (Lee 1938:81; Woodruff, 16 Feb. 1847).

In the absence of this ideal state of affairs, however, sealing ordinances, particularly adoptive sealings, could link the entire membership of the church to the leading members of the hierocracy, thus merging patriarchal order and ecclesiastical organization. The Mormon church, like its ideal celestial model, could consequently become one vast patriarchal family.

During the winter of 1846-47, while waiting to go west, Brigham Young and other leaders discussed how such a system might organize all the Mormons involved in the exodus into a company system with captains of hundreds, of fifties, and of tens. This superceded the company system that had been worked out the previous spring, and an intense period of organization ensued (see Letter of Heber C. Kimball to John Bernhisel, copied in P. Hansen, diary, 17 Feb. 1847). Upon joining a company, each individual was to "covenant and promise to keep all the commandments and statutes of the Lord our God" (D&C 136:1-10). Those with large families, like Young and Kimball, organized "family companies" that included their own families plus, presumably, enough additional numbers to round out the figures. Apparently these companies were intended to become part of the patriarch's family kingdom, for Wilford Woodruff recorded in his journal on 18 January: "President Young met with his company or family organization of those who had been adopted unto him or were to be, and organized them into a company out of which may grow a people that may yet be called the tribe of Brigham."

Coincidentally, that same week in England, in the 15 January 1847 issue of the *Millennial Star* (9:23-24), Orson Hyde diagrammed "the kingdom of God" and explained:

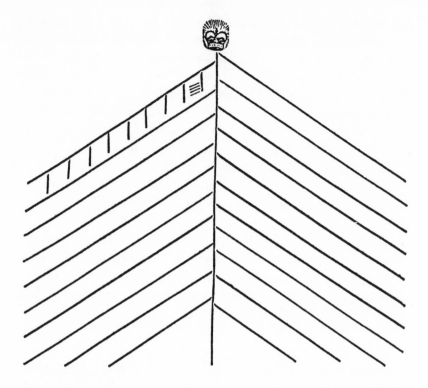

Diagram of the Kingdom of God [*Latter-day Saints' Millenial Star* 9:23 (January 15, 1847]).

> The . . . diagram shows the order and unity of the kingdom of God. The eternal Father sits at the head, crowned King of Kings and Lord of lords. Where the other lines meet, there sits a king and a priest unto God, bearing rule, authority, and dominion under the Father. . . . There are kingdoms of all sizes, an infinite variety to suit all grades of merit and ability. The chosen vessels unto God are the kings and priests that are placed at the heads of these kingdoms. They have . . . been chosen, ordained, and anointed kings and priests to reign as such in the resurrection of the just. . . .
>
> While . . . eternity . . . continue[s], those lines in the foregoing diagram, representing kingdoms, will continue to extend and be lengthened out.

In a February 1847 family meeting with his adopted sons in Winter Quarters, Brigham Young described "the exaltation of the faithful" using himself as an example. "Say that I am ruler over ten sons and soon each one of them will have ten men sealed to them and they would be rulers over them and that would make me ruler over ten presidents (or rather kings), whereas before I was ruler over 10 subjects only. Or in other words I ruled over one kingdom whereas I now rule over 10. Then let each one of those ten get ten more and then I would be ruler of 100 kingdoms and so on continue through all eternity'' (Lee 1938:88; Woodruff, 16 Feb. 1847).

That same month Heber C. Kimball reached what may have been the height of enthusiasm for patriarchal organization when, during a meeting at the home of Daniel Spencer, he ''was led to speak of how a man's kingdom would increase by bringing individuals into the Church and said 'When we get to a settling place I will send off my boys [i.e., his natural and adopted sons], every one of them to preach the gospel to the nations of the earth. And they will bring home their thousands unto Zion and they will say where is thy Father's house, and they will be attached to me; still he who bringest them in will be their king &c &c'' (P. Hansen, diary, 7 Feb. 1847).

In November of the same year, Orson Spencer (1848:170-71) wrote in England:

> The different federative unions of the whole family of heaven and earth, when organized according to the law of adoption, have their own respective patriarch or president to represent them in the grand council of the just, Jesus Christ being head over all things to the church, in all ages. . . .
>
> [This] union of families . . . will form a solid phalanx against the intrusion of discord and the spirit of alienation from God. The righteous will be bound together, by the ties of adoption and kindred, in the ''bundle of eternal life.'' This united confederation of strength and affection will be peculiarly needed, in order to endure the shock which society must receive . . . in the last dispensation; for every tree that the Eternal Father hath not planted shall be hewn down, and the institutions of men shall come to nought.

A practical problem was how to translate a conceptual pattern of delegated authority that included both the living and the dead into a workable hierarchy that included only the living. As early as January of 1845, Brigham Young was teaching that Joseph Smith's right to preside as priest and king over the last dispensation was a function of blood inheritance. ''He was the legal heir to the blood [of Ephraim] that has been on the earth and has come down through a pure lineage. . . . In all the Kingdoms of the World you will find that there will be one king and all will be governed as one family.'' (in Lund 1920:107). Joseph Smith's right to preside in the church as well as to have all members sealed to him could thus be conceptualized as the consequence of an ill-defined principle of primogeniture.

The problem, of course, was that a dead man could not run a church. Brigham Young resolved the problem by pointing out that he, Heber C. Kimball, and a number of other prominent church leaders were related to Joseph Smith by virtue of descent from the same common ancestor and thus he declared, "I am entitled to the keys of the priesthood according to lineage and blood, so is Brother Kimball" (Woodruff, 16 Feb. 1847).

This declaration helped solve the conceptual problem, and Young avoided the practical problems involved by not taking measures to have the entire membership of the church sealed either to Joseph Smith or to himself. The conceptualization of the church as a family, how-ever, gave religious sanctity to individual family units, symbolically interrelated them, and subordinated them to the Quorum of the Twelve. In fact, Brigham Young did not authorize endowments, adop-tive sealings, or second anointings until the Saints were in the Salt Lake Valley. One live endowment would be given in 1849; it was not until endowments began to be administered in the Council House in 1851 that the general membership of the church would again be able to participate in this ordinance. Second anointings would wait until 1866, while cross-generational adoptive sealings would not recom-mence until after the St. George Temple (the first Mormon temple completed after Nauvoo) had been dedicated for that purpose in Janu-ary 1877 (Buerger 1983:27-29; Irving 1974:297, 306, Woodruff 1 Jan. 1877, 28 March 1877).

Matrimonial sealings were an exception. Although there is some evidence that authorized hierocrats continued to perform matrimonial sealings in the Nauvoo Temple as late as April, it is impossible to determine how many people or who might have been sealed between February and April. By mid-December 1846, Brigham Young was personally approving, performing, and authorizing others to perform matrimonial sealings at Winter Quarters (Lee, 1938:43).

This pattern restricted the development of family kingdoms in important ways. Adoptive sealings had been the least-performed ritual sealing in the Nauvoo Temple. "The Book of Adoptions and Seal-ings" lists only twenty-five men who had either their biological off-spring or non-biologically related adults sealed to them as children. Ten of these had only their biological offspring sealed to them. Three of the remaining fifteen (Joseph Smith, Hyrum Smith, and Robert Thompson) were dead at the time the ordinance was performed. Most of the others were members of the hierarchy. Five (Brigham Young, Heber C. Kimball, Willard Richards, John Taylor, and Amasa Lyman) were apostles. Two (Newel K. Whitney and George Miller) were the general bishops of the church. Another (John Smith) was an uncle to Joseph Smith and would shortly be appointed patriarch to the church. The remaining four (Alpheus Cutler, Samuel Bent, Winslow Farr, and Isaac Morley) were less prominent, although Cutler and Morley had both been members of the Holy Order during Joseph Smith's lifetime (Ehat 1982:102-3). Although not recorded in "The Book of Adoptions and Sealings," John D. Lee, an adult adoptively sealed to Brigham Young, also had adult individuals linked to him through adoptive sealing, and it is possible that the record likewise fails to mention a few others. The total number, therefore, was small and could not grow at this time.

Thus, the development of family kingdoms was restricted in two ways. Because no second anointings were being performed, a sealed husband and wife lacked full religious qualification to preside as king and queen over their posterity. And second, without adoptive sealings, family kingdoms could not rapidly expand by drawing in non-biological members. As a result, power concentrated more in the head of the church and less within individual family kingdoms. It is possible to argue that Joseph Smith prepared the church to endure despite dispersion by introducing the family kingdom concept while Brigham Young prepared it for an even more tightly organized group life by limiting the concept's expansiveness.

However, the momentum of Nauvoo meant that people behaved as if second anointings and adoptive sealings had been performed or shortly would be. Each Mormon elder was expected to preside over his wife (or wives) and children as patriarch whether an actual sealing had taken place or not, and a covenant relationship similar to an adoptive sealing could exist between a given man and other men and women who were willing to accept him as their patriarch and leader. Although Brigham Young and other church leaders were sometimes consulted regarding the establishment of such ties, there is no evidence that they tried to regulate their creation or establish who could or could not become involved. Either "parent" or "child" could initiate the request; if both agreed, they would behave as if the sealing had occurred. To vigorously " 'lectioneer'' for such associations, however, was not considered proper (Lee 1938:94). As Heber C. Kimball explained: "To urge anyone to be adopted or sealed to you is like damming water to make it run up hill" (Lee 1938:91).

If the individuals involved desired that at some point the covenant tie be formalized through an adoptive sealing ordinance, then they sought Brigham Young's official approval. For example, Brigham Young's journal records on 6 January 1847: "Thomas Alvord had made covenant to be sealed to bro Sam'l Bent and attached to his kingdom. Advised him, when a Temple should be built, to have himself sealed to Bent" (Young 1971:493). Lists of applicants were made. For example, under the heading of "A list of those to be adopted in B. Young's family," John D. Lee's journal contains the names of twelve individuals who had "petitioned" to become his adopted children (Lee 1938:198). And "The Book of Adoptions and Sealings" contains the names of 275 individuals who had made the same petition (Irving 1974:297, note 17).

Applicants could be intense in their desires. For example, George Dykes (1846), shortly after leaving with the Mormon Battalion, wrote to Brigham Young asking to someday become his adopted son. He explained his reasons: "I am now an orphan wandering through a wicked world without a Father of promise. Shall my days be numbered and my pilgrimage ended I go to the silent tomb without a Father to call me forth from the deep sleep? or shall I enjoy in common with other citizens of the commonwealth of Israel the legal rights of adoption?"

Furthermore, once an individual was sealed to a "father of promise," it was logical to extend the potential sealing relationship to the adoptee's kin. Thus, on 16 February 1847 John D. Lee (1938:76) recorded in his diary that Chester Loveland, an adult adoptively sealed to him in Nauvoo but whom he had not seen since leaving Nauvoo, found him and reported that he "had been prospered and that he, his father and family, Brother-in-law, and Bros. wife were all ready to be disposed of according to my council as they claimed me to be their counsellor." A few days later, discussing "the law of adoption" with "quite a No. of families of my house," he reported that one of these adoptees, R. Allen "proffered to go as a pioneer and take my team and that likely his father and connection would be attached to my family by the law of adoption" (Lee 1938:104).

The flexibility accepted in such adoptive unions frequently makes it difficult to tell from existing sources whether two particular individuals have been adoptively sealed, have formally agreed to be so joined at a later date, or are considering the possibility of doing so.

The obligations of such ties, real or potential, were a significant factor in internal solidarity for the 1846-48 period. Those involved commonly addressed each other by terms of kinship ("father," "son," etc.). Adopted sons often used their father's last name as their own

(Irving 1974:296). They were free to ask each other for assistance; and an individual who did not aid an adopted father, child, or sibling was considered undutiful. Finally, the patriarch of each family kingdom had jurisdiction over its various members, could make decisions about one individual's behavior based on the well-being of the group, and expected to counsel with family members who were either in difficulties or in transgression (Lee 1938:31-32, 58-59).

The adoptive children were expected to obey these patriarchal instructions. In recalling the experiences that he had had during this period as an adopted son of Heber C. Kimball, Peter Hansen (autobiography) later wrote that "I . . . subjected myself to his will & wishes & prided myself in obedience & often attained to a good understanding of the power & authority of the priesthood." In a comment that reveals much about American individualism, even among the hierarchically minded Mormons, Danish-born Hansen added: "I have felt thankful for being brought up under a monarchical government."

The family unit, whether a single couple or the large family kingdom of Heber C. Kimball or Brigham Young, thus provided a point of mediation between individual interests and group good. While the family remained the basic unit of economic maintenance, individual family members were expected to cooperate. If a particular family lacked essential resources, it could become attached to a more prosperous family; or various families could pool their resources and engage in intensive economic cooperation. As the entire Mormon group was conceptualized as a group of interlocking family kingdoms, the needs of a particular family were considered basically those of the group as a whole.

The general organizational pattern provided a flexible way in which authority, order, and group cohesion could be maintained amid the unsettled conditions of the migration.

Heber C. Kimball's Family Kingdom

Heber C. Kimball's family and its migration illustrates several aspects of how this family-centered organization worked. It is unclear how many individuals were part of the Kimball family kingdom at any point. No known document lists the various individuals who covenanted to be sealed as children, and Kimball theoretically made no distinction among biological offspring, adoptive sealings in the

Nauvoo Temple, and those who had agreed to such sealings in a new temple (Hovey, 24 Mar. 1847).

During preparations in Nauvoo for the migration, Kimball selected the individuals who would accompany him as part of the Camp of Israel. The others were to follow as circumstances permitted. About thirty of them left Sugar Creek on 1 March, including his first wife, Vilate, all of their children, eleven to thirteen additional wives, and various adopted children (S. Kimball 1981:129). It was Kimball's responsibility to provide for the spiritual and temporal needs of this group as well as for other family members that would be joining them.

In addition, the family of Bishop Newel K. Whitney was closely aligned to Kimball's, and they acted in concert on many matters throughout the migration.

When the Camp of Israel was divided into companies, Kimball was appointed a captain of fifty and extended the familial ties established by adoptive sealings in a more tentative way to the rest of the company; some members began referring to him as "Father Kimball" (Eliza Snow, 7 Apr. 1846). While it is not known how effective such kinship ideology was in reducing conflict, it did provide a model for social interaction that was easy to understand.

Evidence that Kimball still maintained a distinction between his family kingdom and the company came when provisions in the company began to run low. On 19 April 1846 just before reaching Garden Grove, Eliza R. Snow recorded in her journal: "Father K[imball] spoke of the lavish manner in which prov[isions] had been used by many, that to pursue that course would bring destruction upon the Camp & we should be scatter'd to the four winds. Said . . . that each one must help himself—he should divide no longer—the com[pany] voted to sustain him."

At Garden Grove, which they reached on 24 April, Kimball effected a more efficient organization among the members of his family. Daughter Helen Mar writes: "Father's and Bishop Whitney's families were divided up into messes, each ten having one or two women to cook for the teamsters, and wagons were provided for all the women and their little children to ride and to sleep in at night" (*WE* 14:66). At Mount Pisgah, thirty-five miles further on, Kimball split his family, one group to stay and one to go, assigning some of the men to build houses while others made trips into Missouri for supplies (P. Hansen, diary, 12 May-1 June 1846). The party going on made the trip from Mount Pisgah to the Missouri River with little difficulty, as the various members cooperated in driving teams, standing watch, going on trading missions to nearby settlements, and cooking meals.

After the Camp of Israel reached the Missouri River in mid-June, Kimball took direct steps to increase the cohesiveness of his family kingdom. On 28 June 1846, he called his family together and preached to them, revealing much about Mormon understandings of patriarchal family organization at that point:

> I have called my family together as many as are here for I want to have my family in an organized state &c. I want that you should have good feelings one toward the other and every one to have common interest for the good of the whole family &c. . . . I have become your father, and I am your priest, your head, your prophet, your apostle, and your revelator, and from none other man can you receive revelation, neither now nor in eternity. And I want your prayers that I may have wisdom. (Hansen, diary, 28 June 1846)

Kimball's authority seems to have been real. He designated who would or would not join the Mormon Battalion, which sons would be involved in various economic activities in the Winter Quarters area, and who might marry. For example, seven months after adopted son Joseph Hovey's only wife died at Winter Quarters, Heber told him he "should have me a wife later for truly I do feel as though I need some one to help me" (Hovey 1 April 1847). The following December, after Hovey found a woman whom he felt would make a good wife, "Br. Heber spoke to me concerning my intended Sarah Baily, that he thought it was all right. He would see her, and he would speak to Br. Brigham and, he would get leave and would seal us in the evening. Sarah was sealed to me for time" (Hovey Dec. 1847).

Kimball also acted as a mediating link between the hierocracy and his family kingdom. When the Quorum of the Twelve, to which he belonged, made a decision, he presented it to his family group and did what he could to have them comply. Just prior to the selection of the site of Winter Quarters, church leaders decided to locate the Saints at a place called Cutler's Park. Daniel Davis records that Kimball called his adopted sons together and "said that he wanted to lay before the brethren that the twelve had considered to leave this place and go to a place near the head of the Elk Horn and near the Missouri and there cut hay and prepare for the winter and it came to pass that he said how that he would like to know how it suited the feelings of the brethern. . . . And he said that all that was in favor of it might rise the right hand. It was unanimous or satisfactory to

all present" (Daniel Davis 3 Aug. 1846). Kimball endeavored to in-
still in his adoptive sons' minds that it was a religious imperative to
follow the advice and direction of church leaders. For example, when
family members became upset because some church members had
been whipped "for improper conduct," Heber explained "that the
men who executed justice on the offenders were appointed and commanded to do it by the counsel and authority we had made a solemn
covenant to uphold and sustain, consequently we were in a state of
rebellion against God when we resisted such things" (Horace Whitney 8 Sept. 1846).

Vilate Kimball demonstrated motherly concern for the members
of the family. They in turn tended to reciprocate with respect and
esteem. Peter Hansen (autobiography), for example, relates that in
the fall of 1846 "I woke up one morning shaking with the ague and
I became very sick. Mother Kimball tried all in her power to rid me
of the fever." In the fall of 1848, when returning to Winter Quarters
from the Salt Lake Valley he acquired a half-pound of coffee, which
he kept "for Mother Kimball as a precious thing."

It would be natural for at least some of Kimball's adopted children to harbor resentments at having to subordinate their own wills
so completely, but they also understood both the material and spiritual
advantages of belonging to such an organization. Peter Hansen points
out, "I was a poor chap, without means. How could I have undertaken such a journey on my own hook? I could not have done it. I
would have had no other alternative than to go to St. Louis as many
did, staying there for years laboring hard for a fitout" (Hansen, autobiography, entry dealing with Feb. 1846). Furthermore, Kimball
promised family members in August 1846 that "if they were faithful
& obedient, they should be greater kings & queens than Victoria"
(Daniel Davis 9 Aug. 1846).

This extended family genuinely appears to have interacted with
one another essentially as brothers and sisters. Journals kept by Daniel
Davis, Peter Hansen, Joseph Hovey, and Horace Whitney during
the Winter Quarters period record almost daily social interaction
among members of the Kimball family kingdom. To cite one example,
adopted son Daniel Davis, then managing the family farm at a site
some ten miles away, recorded his activities on 11 August 1847 during a brief visit to Winter Quarters. At the time, Heber was with
the pioneer company in the Salt Lake Valley:

> Went to Bishop [Newel K.] Whitney's and borrowed his carriage
> and & Wm [Kimball, Heber and Vilate's oldest son] helped me to har-

ness the horses. I then went and invited Sister Frances* to ride with me. She did. Sarah Lawrence*, Helen [Heber and Vilate's daughter], Harriet* and Sarah Noon* went also. We went to the mount where Sister Frances's* babe was buried. . . . Br. Wm. Brown with several of the sisters went to the school house and had a meeting. I opened with prayer. Sang a hymn, several of the sisters spoke in tongues. Sister Frances* interpreted. Sister Lorey & Frances* blessed me. Sister Jennet did also bless me [Her name appears repeatedly as part of the Kimball family organization, but her exact position is unclear]. . . . At sundown we did close the meeting. I then went with Sister Frances* to Sister Christeen's* and took supper. Went home with Sister Frances*. Stopped a short time. Sister Randel gave me some dried apples for Lucy*. Stayed at Father's [the home of Heber and Vilate in Winter Quarters] all night.

---

* A wife of Heber C. Kimball. For a list of his wives, see S. Kimball 1981:307-16.

As part of the Camp of Israel, Heber and those members of his family kingdom then travelling with him reached the Missouri River in mid-June 1846. In September they helped establish the Mormon base camp across the river at Winter Quarters. Between August and December 1846 most of the remaining family members who either had not left Nauvoo with the Camp of Israel or who were left behind at Mount Pisgah joined the main group. A few others, however, arrived even later. For example, David Candland (journal), who left for a mission to England shortly after being adopted to Heber in January of 1846, did not arrive until August 1847.

Like most of the other Mormon migrants, the Kimball family's main economic resource was its livestock. Soon after the family arrived at Cutler's Park and just before the establishment of Winter Quarters, the individual members of the Kimball-Whitney family organization decided to merge their individual animals into a larger herd, which Horace Whitney (10 August 1846) estimated to be "350 head of cattle, 31 horses and mules, and 48 sheep." Thereafter one of the chief activities of the male members of the family organization was caring for this livestock. During the next few weeks, the diaries of Daniel Davis, Peter Hansen, Joseph Hovey, and Horace Whitney refer frequently to teams of Kimball family members making hay frames, and mowing and stacking the hay, while others herd and search for lost cattle. Throughout the winter, family members continue to care for the livestock.

Kimball work teams, cooperating with the Whitney family, during the fall and early winter of 1846 also worked hard building log

and sod houses for the "different divisions of [the] family" (Horace
Whitney 9 Nov. 1846). This work continued on into December.

Still other family members were trading in the region for needed
provisions. Daniel Davis, for example, records on 29 June 1846 that
"Father came to me and asked me if I would take a team and go
down into Missouri for some provisions." By noon, Daniel and John
Davenport, the son of Kimball's adopted son James Davenport, and
Henry Forsyth (who was part of the Kimball organization although
no record of his actual adoption to Kimball has been found) were on
their way with "seven yokes of oxen and one horse and wagon."

Following Brigham Young's 14 January revelation on company
organization and migration procedures, Heber C. Kimball organized
a family company on 19 January 1847 of about 200 individuals, with
more being added later (Horace Whitney 19 Jan., 29 Jan. 1847;
Woodruff 19 Jan. 1847). Some of the nonrelated individuals were
wives of men in the Mormon Battalion and others who would find
it difficult to migrate.

Like the trek across Iowa where Kimball had combined his family and his company, he seems to have been attempting, perhaps as
part of a larger effort, to unite smaller family kingdoms into a larger
organization. He gave Alpheus Cutler and Winslow Farr, two of the
few nonapostles who had had adult men adopted to them in the Nauvoo Temple, important leadership positions in his company and instructed his subcaptains to "act as fathers in Israel; and he wished
them to treat the people as children, and nurse them, and be careful
of their feelings" (Horace Whitney 29 Jan. 1847).

After this organizational meeting, the journals of Peter Hansen,
Joseph Hovey, Daniel Davis, and Horace Whitney at times refer to
Kimball's family kingdom as a "company" or "little company," while
the larger company that was organized on 19 January is sometimes
called his "family." For the sake of clarity, I will call the smaller entity his "family" and the larger his "company."

According to the provisions of the 14 January revelation, Brigham
Young planned for able-bodied men to be selected from the newly
organized companies and to set out early in the spring "as pioneers"
to establish a new Mormon gathering place and "prepare for put-
ting in spring crops." The bulk of the Mormon people, however, were
to remain temporarily in the Winter Quarters area. It was the responsibility of the companies to provide for their needs and help them prepare to migrate the following spring (D&C 136:1-10, Horace Whitney
22 Mar. 1847).

Following this plan, Heber C. Kimball's company selected a farm site about ten miles north of Winter Quarters (Daniel Davis 27 Mar. 1847). Members of Kimball's family together with others in his company began farming it.

In mid-April, the pioneer company left. It included Kimball and most of his fellow apostles, his plural wife Ellen Sanders Kimball, and fourteen men who were part of his family. He was with Brigham Young when the church leader entered the Salt Lake Valley on 24 July. On 25 July, Kimball instructed the members of his family to be harmonious and united, and assigned them to plant crops, build houses, and prepare for the arrival of the rest of the family. After a month of hard work, Kimball and a number of his sons along with others of the pioneer company started back to Winter Quarters. Kimball left some of his family in the Salt Lake Valley to continue preparations for the general arrival of the family the following summer (Egan 1917:103-31; H. Kimball, journal 24 July-16 Aug. 1847; Horace Whitney 24 July-16 Aug. 1847).

While Heber was gone, Vilate and most of his plural wives had remained at Winter Quarters proper, with William Kimball, the oldest son, managing family concerns there. Many of the adopted children lived on the farm where Daniel Davis was in charge. The produce was cooperatively shared between the two groups. On 31 October, when the advance party returned, Kimball promptly called a meeting of his family and, according to Daniel Davis's journal, "spoke concerning the managing of his family in his absence. Approved of the same."

Now everyone focused on the coming migration in the spring of 1848. At a conference in December 1847, the Saints voted to sustain a First Presidency separate from the Quorum of the Twelve, consisting of Brigham Young and the counselors he appointed, Heber C. Kimball and Willard Richards. Each man took responsibility for a main division of the Mormons who in the spring were to migrate with them to the Salt Lake Valley.

Kimball's division, consisting of some 662 individuals, left Winter Quarters in the latter part of May (S. Kimball 1981:180). Sixty-one Kimball family members made up a "little company" within this division, with Joseph Hovey as their captain or "father" (Hovey 6 May, 13 May, 16 July 1848). This count does not seem to have included the offspring of Kimball's adopted children and probably does not represent all the members of the Kimball family who were migrating at this time. After various difficulties the group reached the Salt Lake Valley on 26 September 1848.

Although the David Candland family and perhaps others in the Kimball family organization did not leave Winter Quarters until later, Heber had found the means to move his large family kingdom to the Mormons' new headquarter's. In the process, he had employed the ideology and organization forms associated with the temple sealing rituals to fulfill the covenant that he and other Mormons had made at the October 1845 conference—that to the extent of their ability, they would use their influence and property to help the Saints migrate (*TS* 6:1011). In so doing, he had proved himself to be a "responsible" man indeed (*HC* 7:564).

Difficulties with Family Kingdoms

Many of the predictable difficulties involved in the creating of family kingdoms involved conflicts between individual desires and group allegiance. For example, some individuals were entering into covenants without the sanction of the church hierocracy and for purposes that were not consistent with those of the church. Apostle Orson Hyde, who presided over the Pottowattamie High Council on the east bank of Missouri, for example, tried to break up a counterfeiting and theft ring based on covenants. The high council minutes record on 3 July 1847 Hyde's statement that "all who were honest and had been drawn into any thing relative to counterfeit money or stolen property, he would absolve them from all covenants, and any person knowing anything of the kind and will not reveal it to him, the curse of God shall rest upon that house or person."

Second, many were reluctant to become subordinate children in another man's family kingdom, feeling that their own exaltation might somehow be diminished. Thus, when talking about adoption on 17 February 1847, Heber C. Kimball stated that he was "aware that many have had trials for fear that they had given away their birthright when in fact they had none, not having been adopted" (Lee 1938:91). And the following month he told his adopted sons that "some say that it is clipping a man's privilege to be sealed to the twelve. It does not" (Hovey 24 March 1847).

Third, once they were part of a prominent elder's family kingdom, some Mormons felt that they had acquired a special status that allowed them to act independent of general church regulations. When in 1877 John D. Lee (1877:198) was recalling his life at Winter Quarters, he stated that Andrew Little was "an adopted son of Brigham Young, and consequently did about as he pleased." In December 1847, a church court was held on Heber C. Kimball's adopted son Milo Andrews "for Abusing his wife, turning her away & marrying another." At the trial, Heber C. Kimball "said the day had come when iniquity could not be harboured in the church and men because they belong to my family or Br. Brigham Young's family will not be screened in wickedness. . . . Br. Andrews has been adopted into my family, but let the laws of God have its demand upon him if it takes his head off" (Woodruff 21 Dec. 1847). And at a family meeting held a few weeks later, Kimball (1848) told his adopted sons: "I do not calculate to screen you from the law and its officers. If you are guilty you must bear the lash. Remember the Lord spoke through Samuel to Eli and how he was blotted out because he did not restrain his family. There are families in this Israel that do the same thing and bring this trespass upon them."

Fourth, personal disagreements within family kingdoms could disrupt covenantal organization. George Laud, adopted to John D. Lee in the Nauvoo Temple, shifted from near-hero worship of the older man to disillusionment a little more than a year later, broke with Lee, and left Winter Quarters for Missouri in the spring of 1847. He confided in his journal: "It seems this Council of Lee seeks its own interest and none else" (Laud, journal, p. 64).

At this time, Lee was managing Brigham Young's family farm thirteen miles outside Winter Quarters while Young was en route to the Salt Lake Valley with the pioneer company. During this time, several conflicts broke out between Lee and others of Brigham's family company at the farm. After Brigham Young's return in October 1847, he held a church court to evaluate the complaints and ordered that all who had been sealed to Lee could, if they chose, dissolve their covenants (Irving 1974:300-301; Lee 1938:132-97; Stout 1:277-78, 290; Woodruff 9 Dec. 1847).

And fifth, even when relationships were fairly harmonious, managing large family kingdoms was strenuous. At a family meeting held on 9 August 1846, Heber C. Kimball "spoke of some tattling and bringing trouble and sorrow upon him. He said that he had so much of it that he was all wore rare as a piece of beef" (Daniel Davis 9 Aug. 1846). In an 1848 family meeting held sometime before the migration to the Salt Lake Valley, he told the male members of his family about a dream of watching fish swarming around him from all directions. He asked family members not to "proselyte" others to join the organization. Rather than promising salvation to individuals sealed to him, he stressed independence: "You being mine by adoption will not save you neither will obeying Christ's commands unless you continue faithful. I cannot save you nor can Brigham unless you adhere to our council. You must be saved by harking to the council of the 12 . . . anyhow. You must act independently, have more courage, nor follow my base example, but stand on your own ground. You must save yourself." He also told them to "call me Br. Heber or Br. Kimball. . . . I am only a guide to act as a father" (H. Kimball 1848).

This sermon is a marked shift from his attitude a year earlier. While it did not signal the end of the Kimball family kingdom as an organization, it signaled an important shift from a complete theological concept to a practical organization for mutual assistance and cooperation.

GREAT BASIN ISOLATION

Like the Puritans in their geographical isolation and religious homogeneity, the Mormons in Utah also had a period of relative isolation in which to consolidate the social manifestations of their covenant theology. Neither society completely excluded those of different religious persuasions, but the existing pluralism usually consisted of variants in religious beliefs, and could be accommodated in a way that maintained order and minimized dissension.

As a result, both Massachusetts and Utah had very cohesive societies, whose members were oriented to a localized center with its own elite, values, and institutions. Covenantal organization provided the institutional framework for ordering the comprehensive meanings for both societies (Berger and Luckmann 1966:73). It was this organization that the local elite sought most diligently to preserve and enhance.

Historical Context

When the pioneer company entered the Salt Lake Valley in July 1847, Utah was in Mexican territory. By the time each member of the First Presidency arrived in the fall of 1848 with their three large divisions, the region had been ceded to the United States as part of the treaty of Guadalupe Hidalgo; and the discovery of gold in California would place the Mormons directly in the path of a massive rush the next year. However, the gold rush did not hinder their creation of a society saturated with religious values and effectively under the control of the Mormon hierocracy.

Mormon political history from 1848 through the end of the century is extremely complex. It may be interpreted as an uneasy balance, shifting to accommodate the federal government when necessary but striving to maintain as much autonomy as possible. At least until the end of the Civil War, many Mormons assumed that the federal government would dissolve in anarchy or become subordinate to the kingdom of God at the imminent return of Christ.

Although their 1849 petition to be admitted directly as a state was shunted aside—statehood would not come until 1896—Utah was made a territory in 1850 with Brigham Young as its first governor (Arrington and Bitton 1979:161-63; Larson 1961:77-83; Roberts 1957 3:414-502). Quite logically, the Mormons applied many of their assumptions about government in Nauvoo to this new setting, making little effort to separate religious and political authority and equally little effort to maintain political pluralism.

As a territory, Utah had to accept federal appointees for judges but bypassed them in February 1852 when the legislature authorized itself to appoint a probate judge in each county with "power to exercise original jurisdiction both civil and criminal, and as well in Chancery as at Common law" (Utah Territory Legislative Assembly 1852:43). This act gave probate judges concurrent jurisdiction with the federally appointed district court judges. Not surprisingly, virtually all probate judges were Mormons, and most were either bishops or stake presidents within the hierocracy (Allen 1968:133-34).

Responding to hyperbolic reports from disgruntled federal judges that the residents of Utah were in revolt against the federal government, U.S. President James Buchanan ordered an army under Colonel Albert Sidney Johnston into the territory in 1857. Although the Mormons prepared to defend themselves by force, the action was confined mostly to guerilla raids that harassed the army and bogged it down for the winter at Camp Scott, near Fort Bridger, Wyoming. A peaceful compromise resulted. A federal appointee replaced Young as governor, and federal troops established Camp Floyd some twenty miles southwest of the Salt Lake Valley.

While the federal government was occupied with fighting the Civil War, Mormons were able to ignore more regulatory legislation and maintain local autonomy through its Mormon-elected legislature and legislature-selected probate courts. The passage of the Poland Act of 1874, aimed directly at stamping out polygamy and reducing Mormon political control changed that.

The years between the arrival in the valley and the Poland Act leave an interesting record of Mormon success in maintaining their society by bringing as many Saints as possible to the new Zion, by settling as much territory as possible, and by placing virtually all institutions under the control of the hierocracy.

Territorial Control

Between 1847 and 1850, about 11,000 Mormons migrated to Utah (Roberts 1957 3:487-8, note 34). After 1850, the church sponsored migration through the Perpetual Emigration Fund, which loaned funds and organized companies from Europe with the understanding that the immigrants would repay these loans when they were financially stable in the valley. By the time the transcontinental railroad was completed in 1869, this fund had assisted about 51,000 Mormon migrants from Great Britain and Europe; and before it was dissolved by the Edmunds-Tucker Act in 1887, this number had risen to at least 85,000 (Allen and Leonard 1976:282-87; Arrington 1958:97-108; Larson 1961:101-17).

Incoming immigrants were distributed among the Mormon settlements that began to spring up immediately, most of them founded under official direction. The first decade saw close to a hundred; by the end of the century, the Mormons had founded over five hundred settlements in the West between Canada and Mexico, through Utah, Idaho, Arizona, with ventures into Nevada, Wyoming, Colorado, and California (Allen and Leonard 1976:263-70; Arrington 1958:88-95).

Indian threats occasionally caused the temporary evacuation or sometimes the relocation of a community, and outlying settlements were abandoned at the approach of Johnston's army. With these exceptions, most Mormon settlements were permanent; and territoriality became the basis for ecclesiastical organization. Ecclesiastical wards were organized in each settlement, with several wards in larger towns and cities. The hierocracy appointed a bishop for each ward who selected two counselors; the bishopric was responsible for the temporal and spiritual affairs of the members under his jurisdiction. Groups of wards were organized into "stakes of Zion," each presided over by a stake president with two counselors and a high council of twelve men. The stake presidents reported directly to the First Presidency and the Quorum of the Twelve.

The bishop's court at the ward level and the high council court at the stake level adjudicated conflicts among members and had the power to disfellowship (suspend) or excommunicate individuals who violated the LDS code of conduct or rebelled against the leaders. In nineteenth-century Utah, there was little territorial organization independent of the church's ecclesiastical system. These ecclesiastical-territorial units remained stable over time even though individual families came and went within an area.

These ecclesiastical units also organized many of the large-scale economic enterprises like transportation, industrial production, and irrigation canals that required cooperative effort or centralized control (Arrington 1958; Raber 1978; 1980).

An important part of dominating the area was not only the settlements but also economic self-sufficiency. Brigham Young actively discouraged trade with Gentile merchants and enthusiastically encouraged home production and local industries. Although neither prong of this program was completely successful, the concept of an economically independent Mormon commonwealth permeated Mormon thinking until well into the 1880s (Arrington 1958:96-349).

Family Organization

However, the basic unit of production and also of theological identification remained the family. Although territory was highly significant, the theology remained family centered and the celestial kingdom continued to be defined as a vast family order, not as a "place." This pattern indicates the strength of the kinship-based covenantal system that Joseph Smith had instituted and his followers had developed.

On 28 July 1847, only four days after Brigham Young's entry into the Salt Lake Valley, he selected the site for a new temple. Construction lasted from 1853 to 1893, and temples were completed in the Utah cities of St. George (1877), Logan (1884), and Manti (1888) first. However, marital sealings were performed in a variety of locations in several settlements starting from the 1848 arrival of Brigham Young.

When a small building called the Endowment House was constructed on the block where the temple was being built, most of the church's temple rituals were performed there. Immediately after its dedication in 1855, baptisms for the dead, live endowments, and matrimonial sealings for the living and dead began to be performed within its walls. Beginning in 1866, second anointings were added. But no adoptive sealings were performed; these Brigham Young maintained could only be performed within a temple, and they perforce waited until the St. George temple was completed in 1877.

The lack of adoptive sealings and second anointings continued the process, begun at the abandonment of Nauvoo, of checking the development of large family kingdoms. Such mega-units were not compatible with the socioeconomic conditions of the frontier and the need to settle a broad expanse of territory. For example, Brigham Young and his associates frequently called men on colonizing missions to establish or reinforce Mormon settlements. They expected these men to comply promptly. If a man were embedded in a large family kingdom, his family ties would have worked against such mobility.

As another example, agricultural land was always distributed by individual household unit. It would have been theoretically possible to allocate land on the basis of larger family kingdoms, but this system was never tried; and Raber's work suggests that small-scale household production was probably the most efficient and effective basis for agricultural output in early Utah.

Some members continued to covenant that they would be adoptively sealed to each other. For example "between 1849 and 1854 the 'waiting list' of those desiring to join Brigham Young's family increased by 175 names" (Irving 1974:304). However, the fact that no temple would be ready for many years and the lack of active encouragement from church leaders meant that the practice gradually dwindled.

The journals of Daniel Davis, Peter Hansen, and Joseph Hovey demonstrate that, during the first years in Utah, they and others of Heber C. Kimball's adopted sons continued to assist his economic enterprises. By the late 1850s, however, Daniel Davis was apparently the only one still in Kimball's service (Cooper 1985:460-67). Furthermore, he was the only adopted son who received part of Kimball's property after his death in 1868 (S. Kimball 1981:317-20).

By 1857 even Heber C. Kimball was stating that:

> He did not believe in this custom of adoption that had been practiced in the Church. No man should give his birthright to another but should keep it in the lineage of his Fathers. . . . Now unless a man is a poor cuss he should keep his priesthood and unite it with his fathers and not give it to another. The Lord will save our Fathers. Every man that got his patriarchal blessing and Priesthood, he becomes the patriarch of his own family and should bless his own family (Woodruff 3 Jan. 1857).

Despite these reservations, however, a vignette ten years later shows that Kimball attached value to these bonds of adoption. Sarah M. Granger Kimball (her husband was a Nauvoo merchant but no relation to Heber C. Kimball) had been adopted as a daughter to Heber C. and Vilate Kimball in Nauvoo. She visited the Kimball home in 1867, sixteen months before Heber C. Kimball's death, and sent this account to one of Heber C.'s biological sons:

> About a week ago I called on Mother Kimball. . . . She was just preparing dinner, she said for her children that were around her. . . . She claimed me as one of the number of which I have ever been proud. . . . Father Kimball had been all day in the Endowment house. He came in while we were at table. He took me down by saying that I had always been too haughty to acknowledge my adoption. I thought I was misunderstood but did not indicate my cause. I have always felt proud to say Father Kimball. I have smarted and withered under his fatherly admonitions, but I hope and believe that I have never rebelled against them.

While the disintegration of family kingdoms can be linked to economic issues in pioneer Utah, earlier ideological changes had prepared the way. During the Nauvoo period, sealing was associated with a concept of corporate salvation based on family association. Such a perception persisted among Church leaders at least until February of 1847 (Lee 1938:87-88, Woodruff 16 Feb. 1847). By the spring of 1848, however, Heber C. Kimball was telling his adopted sons that their salvation depended not on their sealing to him, but on being obedient to the hierocracy. Since second anointings were no longer being performed, there was no clear ritual advantage to being part of one family kingdom as opposed to another.

Instead, matrimonial sealing became the dominant sealing ritual in the covenant complex. By controlling these sealings, the hierocracy regulated most of the important ways the patriarchal order contributed to Mormon group solidarity during this period.

Matrimonial Sealings

An interesting development that demonstrates the control of the hierocracy over matrimonial arrangements lay in the relationship between civil marriage and matrimonial sealing. The legislature, in creating the county probate courts in 1852, also gave them "jurisdiction in all cases of divorce and alimony, and of guardianship, and distribution of property connected therewith." It further specified situations that might warrant a divorce, including the elastic clause, "when it shall be made to appear to the satisfaction and conviction of the Court, that the parties cannot live in peace and union together, and that their welfare requires a separation" (Utah Territory Legislative Assembly 1852:82-84).

Allowed these broad parameters, the patriarchal order operated within the context of Utah civil law. The offspring of polygamous wives could inherit property even though their parents were not united in a civil union. Mormon women could easily be divorced from non-believers and be free to remarry. There was no longer any need for women like Lydia Goldthwaite and Prescinda Huntington Buell to remain civilly married to one man and sealed to another by priesthood authority.

For a number of years many Mormons continued to regard civil marriage and civil divorce as of little significance; and some women who had left husbands behind in Gentile society felt little need to obtain civil divorces in the territorial probate courts before being matrimonially sealed to other men (S. Pratt 1975:233 note 26).

The patriarchal order thus adapted well to socioeconomic conditions in early Utah. The individual family kingdom became even more completely subsumed by the hierocracy than previously because salvation became increasingly identified with the church as an institution rather than with individuals. In Weber's terms, charisma had shifted from personal to office. There was no need for secrecy about plural marriages as during the life of Joseph Smith, nor were there the time pressures associated with the night-and-day temple ceremonies conducted in the Nauvoo Temple. This public order meant more consistent control by the hierocracy. Furthermore, excommunication suspended sealings, the basis of family association. All these factors worked together to reinforce a social code of conformity with the hierarchy.

The smaller family kingdoms of early Utah were much more consistent with the American concept of individualism than were the large family kingdoms. From the perspective of the individual male, religious progress could be identified with establishing and developing his own family kingdom.

First, he had to conform sufficiently to the Mormon code of conduct to be ordained to the Melchizedek Priesthood. While such ordination came as a matter of course to any minimally qualified young Mormon male, it was denied to any who were antagonistic to the hierocracy or indifferent to the Mormon gospel.

Next, he had to persuade a Mormon woman to become his wife. While this might not have posed a problem for the energetic, ambitious, and religiously inclined, the fact that it was possible for Mormon women to obtain social status and religious security by becoming the plural wives of prominent Mormon elders meant that a prospective suitor also needed to have something to offer a wife.

Third, to be married, both he and his prospective wife had to receive recommends from their local ecclesiastical leaders certifying their worthiness.

Then they could be married. Although bishops all over the territory performed marriages, matrimonial sealings (with a few specially authorized exceptions) could occur only in the Endowment House after 1855 or, later, a temple. The endowment, a prerequisite for sealing, presented a pattern of patriarchal organization that identified the husband as presiding patriarch within the family with wife and children expected to obey him.

This newly established family kingdom could increase in two ways: by the births of children or by taking additional wives. At least in theory, men had to comply with the full Mormon code. Although it is clear that the majority of Mormon families remained monogamous, considerable research remains to be done before we have an accurate understanding of the rates of polygamous living at different periods during the nineteenth century. Arrington and Bitton (1979: 199) estimate that between 1850 and 1890 "no more than 5 percent of married Mormon men had more than one wife, [that] about 12 percent of Mormon women were involved in the principle, [and that] no higher than 10 percent of Mormon children were born into polygamist families." Restricting his examination to 1880 "when 'plurality' probably reached its maximum extent," Lowell "Ben" Bennion comes up with a considerably higher rate. He concludes "that *at least* one-fifth of all Mormons lived in plural homes in 1880" (Bennion 1984:28, 38).

Most patriarchs who did become polygamists tended to have a comparatively small number of additional wives. Using a sample of 1,784 Mormon polygamists drawn from the entire period in which polygamy was being practiced in Utah, Stanley Ivins (1967:313) found that of those who were polygamists, "66.3 percent married only one extra wife. Another 21.2 percent were three-wife men, and 6.7 percent went as far as to take four wives. This left a small group of less than 6 percent who married five or more women." As a consequence, most family kingdoms in Utah began, within the first generation, to look more like variants of the standard American extended family than like innovative social units.

While the male head was regarded as the presiding authority within his family unit, there were clear limitations to his power. First, his wives had to obey him only to the degree that what he asked was consistent with the commandments of God. Second, he had to manage his family according to the Mormon code of conduct if he hoped to remain sealed to them in the next life. Third, if he failed to make his wives sufficiently happy, they could separate from him with little difficulty (Campbell and Campbell 1978). And fourth, if he grossly violated the Mormon code or unduly antagonized his presiding ecclesiastical authorities, he might find himself excommunicated from the church with all sealing relationships to members of his family terminated. At an 1857 public meeting in which John Hyde was excommunicated, Heber C. Kimball stated: "He has taken a course by which he has lost his family and forfeited his Priesthood. . . . His wife is not cut from this Church, but she is . . . just as free from him as though she never had belonged to him. The limb she was connected to is cut off, and she must again be grafted into the tree, if she wishes to be saved" (*JD* 4:165).

Except for plural marriage, Mormons' domestic relations did not differ greatly from those of their fellow Americans. What was distinctive was how such relationships were linked with concepts of Mormon identity and solidarity, with the regulation of conduct within the Mormon group, and with Mormon theology about salvation and the cosmic order.

REINTEGRATION: 1869-1904

The Mormon period of isolation ended in 1869 with the completion of the transcontinental railroad at Promontory Point, Utah. Like the Puritans, the Mormons' isolation was followed by reintegration into a broader social system. But while Puritan reintegration eroded its covenant organization as a unified system, the Mormon patriarchal order basically survived intact.

Unlike the Puritans, however, the contest between society and religion was a hostile confrontation that did not stop short of violence. Much of the accommodation on the Mormon side was forced and grudging. But in the end, after Utah was sufficiently "Americanized," it was granted statehood in 1896 (Lamar 1971; Larson 1971; Lyman 1986; Wolfinger 1971).

While the conflict was fought out along the lines of federal control versus local autonomy, the central issue was American individualism and pluralism versus Mormon solidarity. In the popular mind, Mormonism became a monolithic, anti-American, and sinister force whose leaders were exercising despotic control through theocratic domination, secret oaths, and economic monopolization (David Davis 1960). The Mormons, for their part, regarded American pluralism as a threat to their group integrity, and opposition to their institutions as the devil's continuing effort to destroy the kingdom of God.

The first federally enacted law against Mormon activities was the Morrill Anti-Bigamy Act of 1862. It outlawed the practice of polygamy in United States territories, annulled acts passed by the Utah legislature incorporating the LDS church and empowering it to regulate and perform marriages, and stipulated that no religious organization in U.S. territories could hold property in excess of $50,000 (Bancroft 1964:606-7).

Preoccupied with the Civil War, the federal government made no efforts to have the law enforced. The First Presidency discreetly transferred church property to the names of individuals. Church officials continued to perform marriages and sealings as before. And since grand juries were composed almost exclusively of Mormons and the Mormon-run probate courts had jurisdiction to try such cases, no one was convicted of bigamy.

The United Order and the St. George Temple

A more serious immediate threat was the changing economy after the Civil War. Brigham Young and other LDS leaders regarded private merchandising and mining as inimical to Mormon group solidarity. As a result, these activities rapidly acquired "Gentile" labels, perpetuating a dual economic-religious polarization. Furthermore, since most civilian Gentiles in early Utah were usually associated either with merchandising or mining, the Saints naturally saw them not only as religious outsiders, but as economically disruptive (Arrington 1958:81-84, 201-5, 293-94; Peterson 1977:60-61, 72-73; Roberts 1957 5:61-69).

While Brigham Young welcomed the railroad as a way to bring more Saints to Utah, he was apprehensive that it would radically altar the merchandising channels within the territory, cause the Mormons to become economically dependent upon Gentiles, greatly expand the mining industry, and result in a large influx of antagonistic outsiders. Therefore, shortly before the arrival of the railroad, he began to implement a series of measures to increase Mormon economic exclusiveness, self-sufficiency, and solidarity (Arrington 1958:235-56; Roberts 1957 5:216-25, 239-49).

At first, such measures focused on attempting to limit Mormon interaction with Gentile merchants. In 1874, however, church leaders ambitiously attempted to organize the members into an economically based covenantal order known as the "United Order of Enoch." The system flourished between 1874 and Brigham Young's death in the summer of 1877 with at least 221 separate groups being organized during this period. While such local groups had considerable leeway in determining exact procedures, they were all under the general management of the church hierocracy and each took the 1830s law of consecration and stewardship as its basic operating model (Arrington 1958:323-49; Arrington, Fox, and May 1976:135-310, 394-419).

Simultaneously, Brigham Young ordered the construction of a temple at St. George in southern Utah. He selected the site in 1871 and dedicated it in 1877. Baptisms for the dead, endowments, and matrimonial sealings had been routinely performed in the Endowment House at Salt Lake City since 1855 with second anointings following in 1866. Now all of these ordinances were performed in the temple, plus adoptive sealings for the first time since Nauvoo, and endowments for the dead for the first time in church history.

Many more second anointings were also performed within the temple. Between 1877 and the end of 1893, this ordinance was performed for some 3,415 living individuals and by proxy administration for 2,439 deceased persons. Only matrimonially sealed couples who were considered persons of exemplary worthiness were qualified for this ritual, and each person receiving his or her second anointing had to be individually approved by the president of the church, even though local stake presidents could and routinely did make recommendations (Buerger 1983:29-36).

Perhaps the ordinance that became most important to the membership at large was adoptive sealings, so that individuals not born in the covenant could be sealed as children to parents. From 28 March 1877 until the close of 1893, about 19,000 living persons were adoptively sealed to their biological parents, approximately 1,200 living persons were sealed to nonbiological parents, 16,000 deceased individuals were adopted to their biological parents, and another 13,000 deceased individuals were sealed to nonbiological parents (Irving 1974:308-9).

The policy governing such sealings was quite explicit (Irving 1974:306-10). An individual was to be adopted to his or her biological parents if they had joined the church, whether they were living or dead. If the parents had not joined the church while living, he or she was sealed to another Mormon couple (living or dead) who had been matrimonially sealed. This policy represented the lingering understanding that one's salvation was influenced by the patriarch to whom one was sealed. A faithful member should, therefore, not risk being sealed to someone who might not accept the gospel in the spirit world.

Nonbiological adoptive sealings did not produce social and economic cooperation at this period among father-son pairs or "brothers" sealed to the same adoptive father. It was not uncommon for an individual to travel some distance to a temple, there be adoptively sealed to a temple official that he or she had never seen before, then have no more contact with the man whom he or she believed would now act as his or her father throughout eternity. General authorities were the most popular adoptive parents, with temple officials coming in second. Dead general authorities were particularly popular. "Of those adopted to general authorities, 60 percent of the living and 68 percent of the dead were adopted to deceased general authorities." Part of the reason for this was the popularity of these deceased persons. Probably as significant, however, was the fact that (unlike living general authorities), they did not have to be present when the ordinance was performed (Irving 1974:309-10).

Conceptually, the United Order of Enoch might have become a competing covenantal pattern to that based on kinship. In point of fact, it did not. Internal conflicts, legal difficulties, a lack of support from Young's successor, John Taylor (Young died 29 August 1877), and social disruption caused by federal pressures on the church were serious hindrances (Arrington, Fox, and May 1976:311-35). Furthermore, even if these problems had not existed, the fact remained that the United Order operated on different principles from kinship sealings. A United Order involved only temporary mortal relationships, had primarily economic objectives, and established a boundary between Mormons and Gentiles by involving order members in intense economic cooperation and by cutting them off from economic contact with non-Mormons.

The sealing collectivity, on the other hand, was based upon eternally enduring kinship ties. Beyond the individual family unit, however, such relationships had few consequences for actual social interaction. Believed to involve relationships in a future existence, the significance of suprafamilial sealing ties for the here and now were largely conceptual in nature. Conceptual solidarity essentially won over economic solidarity, and the patriarchal order would remain the predominant basis for Mormon group identity and solidarity.

Increased Federal Pressure

John Taylor's administration (1880-87) was characterized by a deepening conflict between the federal government and the Mormon church. In 1874, at the height of the attempt to establish the United Order, Congress passed the Poland Act to provide legal "teeth" for the Morrill Act. It granted district courts exclusive jurisdiction in criminal and civil cases. It abolished the offices of territorial marshal and territorial attorney general and merged their responsibilities with those of the federally appointed United States marshal and district attorney general (Larson 1971:77). Basically, it put Gentiles in control of the courts and the territorial law enforcement agencies.

The Edmunds Act, passed in 1882, was designed to strengthen the Morrill Act. It outlawed not only the contracting of polygamous marriages, but also the act of polygamous living ("unlawful cohabitation"). It disfranchised polygamists and barred them from public office. Both polygamists and monogamists who believed polygamy to be right could be disqualified from jury duty (Larson 1971:95; Lyman 1986:22-23; Roberts 1957 6:43-44).

Thus began the period of Mormon history commonly referred to as "the raid." To avoid arrest, both men and women practicing plural marriage "went on the underground," where they assumed different identities and moved frequently from hiding place to hiding place. The Mormon community as a whole usually closed ranks, hiding individuals on the run and giving the "feds" no information. Since most prominent Mormon hierocrats ended up either in prison or on the underground, many of the normal operations of the church were disrupted.

In July 1887, John Taylor died after two and a half years in hiding. In March of that year Congress had passed the Edmunds-Tucker Act. Among other things, this law made voting, holding office, and serving on juries contingent upon taking an antipolygamy test oath that many Mormons regarded as offensive, abolished woman suffrage within the territory, disinherited illegitimate children, disincorporated the church; and escheated church property in excess of $50,000 to the attorney general (Larson 1961:213-14; Lyman 1986:42-44).

During the ensuing months, over 1,300 Mormons were convicted of polygamy and over 12,000 were disfranchised (Larson 1961:214). In May 1889, the U.S. Supreme Court upheld the constitutionality of the Edmunds-Tucker Act.

The Manifesto of 1890

Congress was planning even stricter legislation when, on 25 September 1890, the fourth president of the church, Wilford Woodruff, issued what has become known as the Manifesto. In this document he publicly affirmed his intention to submit to laws "enacted by Congress forbidding plural marriage" and to use his influence to have members of the church do the same (D&C Official Declaration 1; Lyman 1986:124-49).

The best evidence to date indicates that a number of general authorities felt that this Manifesto was a public gesture that still allowed Mormon men to live with their plural wives and even contract new marriages; they also interpreted the declaration to apply only to the United States, encouraging polygamists to move to Canada or Mexico (Cannon 1978; Quinn 1985). Unrelenting public pressure, however, continued; long hearings in the U.S. Senate, ostensibly over whether Apostle Reed Smoot, Utah's senator, could keep his seat, put even Mormon church president Joseph F. Smith, a son of Hyrum Smith, on the witness stand. A "second manifesto" in 1904 made the prohibition against polygamy more explicit than the first and established excommunication for members who made new plural marriages.

In retrospect, the Manifesto not only led to the abandonment of plural marriage but signaled a fundamental change in how LDS leadership would orient the Mormon group to secular society (Arrington 1958:378-79). At its deepest level, the church acknowledged its submission to human law.

For the first time in the history of the church, members were encouraged to become politically diversified. The People's Party (the church's political arm) disbanded, and members of the church affiliated with national political parties. In 1893 President Benjamin Harrison granted amnesty to Mormon polygamists who agreed to obey the law. In 1894, the government returned the church's escheated property. LDS leaders became staunch advocates of capitalism, discouraged "gathering" to Utah, and stopped formal colonizing attempts.

In February 1907, the First Presidency issued an "Address to the World" which was unanimously adopted by the Saints attending the 1907 April conference of the church. This address affirmed: "The Church of Jesus Christ of Latter-day Saints holds to the doctrine of the separation of church and state; the non-interference of church authority in political matters; and the absolute independence of the individual in the performance of his political duties" (Roberts 1957 6:436).

While the Manifesto was accompanied by far-reaching changes in church-society relationships and tried the faith of a number of members, the official abandonment of plural marriage had little immediate impact on the patriarchal order. The church no longer permitted a male member in good standing to be simultaneously married to more than one living woman. Theologically, it abandoned the claim that a man could not be fully exalted unless he established polygamous unions. However, the rituals sealing parents and children and wives and husbands remained unchanged. Thus the Manifesto had profound consequences for the development of the Mormon group but not for the conceptual bases of Mormon group identity and solidarity.

The 1894 Revelation on Lineal Sealing

On 6 April 1893, two and one half years after Wilford Woodruff issued the Manifesto, he dedicated the Salt Lake Temple and, a year later, announced a revelation on lineal sealing:

> Let every man be adopted to his father. When a man receives the endowments, adopt him to his father; not to Wilford Woodruff, nor to any other man outside the lineage of his fathers. . . . We want the Latter-day Saints from this time to trace their genealogies as far as they can, and to be sealed to their fathers and mothers. Have children sealed to their parents, and run this chain through as far as you can get it. When you get to the end, let the last man be adopted to Joseph Smith, who stands at the head of the dispensation. This is the will of the Lord to this people. (*Deseret News Weekly*, 21 Apr. 1894, p. 543)

The policy both refined and expanded the sealing procedures established in the St. George Temple. Sealings were now to occur strictly between biological parents and children (or between parents and their formally adopted children). Woodruff's instructions about sealing the most remote ancestor to Joseph Smith were soon set aside, perhaps because of the practical problem that an individual could almost never be certain when the genealogical line had been extended back as far as possible.

Such a procedure seems to have been well suited for the type of solidarity that the church was attempting to achieve in the days following the Manifesto. By these sealing practices, the committed members of the church would become involved in a unified covenantal order that was instigated and regulated by the church and which would theoretically link them all back to Adam. By having each individual lineally linked to his or her deceased ancestors, however, the various family units would effectively be independent of one another. Heads of households would receive direction from the hierocracy regarding the management of their personal family units and at the same time be free to seek individual secular objectives. Individual families within the Mormon kingdom were thus freed to make their own way in pluralistic American society while at the same time conceptually remaining part of the patriarchal Mormon kingdom.

8

The Patriarchal Order
in the Twentieth Century

The principle on which the government of heaven is conducted
[is by] revelation adapted to the circumstances in which the
children of the kingdom are placed.
                                        —Joseph Smith (*HC* 5:135)

The patriarchal order has continued to be a vital force in twentieth-
century Mormonism. An adequate treatment of its impact on contemporary Mormon identity and solidarity would require a much more
extended treatment than is here possible, but a few general observations regarding its current significance seem in order.

As the church has survived and thrived in the twentieth century,
it has done so by giving up aspects of its belief and practice which
have, in retrospect, turned out to be nonessential. The various regulations and operations associated with Mormon covenantal organization in general and with sealing practices in particular have remained
intact. But the relationship between the localized Mormon center and
the national center has changed. America has subsumed Mormonism.

As the church abandoned polygamy, economic cooperation, and
political solidarity, these changes—though bitter at the time—removed
obstacles to the full participation of Latter-day Saints in American
life while still permitting them to retain their distinctive identity. The
Mormon hierocracy remained free to regulate Mormon covenant organization and group life, but such regulations had to be consistent
with American law and legal procedures.

CONTEMPORARY MORMON MARRIAGE

For example, the twentieth century has seen a reconciliation of
civil and priesthood-performed marriages. Although for long periods
in the nineteenth century, civil marriage was unnecessary or even
irrelevant to a proper priesthood-sanctified marriage, the twentieth
century saw the church's official policy change. For two individuals

to be matrimonially sealed, they must first be legally married from the perspective of state law. Eternal marriage remained crucial to salvation, but the sealing power operated within the constraints of state regulation.

Writing in the early 1930s, Apostle Joseph Fielding Smith, (1958:241), son of Joseph F. Smith and future president of the church, explained:

> Marriages among Latter-day Saints are eternal marriages, if they are properly performed, because the Eternal Father gave the covenant of marriage which is received by couples who go to the temple to receive this blessing there.
>
> It is necessary that marriages be regulated by civil law. Under the present world conditions the state must have power to form the laws governing marriages because of their close connection with the social structure of the state. . . . When the kingdom of God is set up on the earth in all its fulness, and Christ comes to reign, marriage, like all other ordinances, will be controlled by the law of God. . . . Under present conditions when "the powers that be" have jurisdiction in the earth, all men, no matter what their religious beliefs or lack of them may be, must be subject to the governments which exist. When Christ comes he will bring the "perfect law of liberty" and in it all the faithful will be made free and happy.

CONTEMPORARY MORMON IDENTITY

The patriarchal order has continued to have important consequences for Mormon group identity and solidarity. The concept of Abrahamic descent has provided members of the church with a basis for perceiving themselves as distinctive. On-going programs of genealogy and temple work fortify this concept by linking members of the church to deceased ancestors from generation to generation in sealing networks. The Mormon church is conceptualized as a vast association stretching far into the distant past. Outside of individual nuclear families, however, such networks have little consequence for existent relationships. Thus, while being embedded in a sealing network, individual Mormons remain free to pursue their own economic and political objectives within the context of pluralistic secular society.

Because Mormon covenant organization resides in individual families, the church has been able to abandon probably foredoomed attempts to regulate economic and political activities but can still maintain its control by supervising sexuality and family life. Mormons express their Mormonism primarily in familial terms.

WORLDWIDE TEMPLES

Temple rituals continue to play an important role in Mormon belief and practice. Mormons still cannot enter a temple without a recommend, issued for no longer than a year, requiring an interview from their local bishop and a member of the stake presidency. A number of questions associated with the granting of such a recommend center upon proper familial conduct. Believers still feel that a sealed family unit will be perpetuated after death only if its members abide by the ethical rules established by the church. This belief naturally motivates a high level of conformity with the church's established code of conduct.

As the Mormon church has expanded worldwide, the rituals of the patriarchal order have been made available to members of the church. As of January 1989, forty-one temples were functioning in twenty-one countries and eleven states of the United States with four additional temples announced for the United States and two more for foreign countries. Church leaders regard available temples as sufficient reason to discourage gathering to particular geographic locations.

Accompanying the expansion of temple building has been an accelerated genealogical program in which volunteers extract names from church-microfilmed public documents, and other volunteers perform temple ordinances for these individuals, whether or not their descendants are members of the church. The emphasis is now more on the church as a body redeeming all the dead than on individual members of the church redeeming their individual deceased ancestors. However, sealing ordinances must link the living and dead into familial associations, and believers hold that eventually such sealing ties will link all the righteous posterity of Adam into one great family.

CHANGES IN THE PATRIARCHAL ORDER

Two important changes have occurred within the patriarchal order during the twentieth century. First, the number of people receiving second anointings has dropped sharply. During his administration, Wilford Woodruff (1889-98) authorized about 300 second anointings a year, Lorenzo Snow (1898-1901) about 600 a year, Joseph F. Smith (1901-18) about 300, and Heber G. Grant (1918-45) fewer than thirty a year, most of them in the early years of his administration. ''In the Salt Lake Temple the frequency of second anointings . . . fell sharply in 1922 to a mere trickle by 1929. After 1928, the average was less then two per year for at least the next decade and a half.

Data after 1941 are not presently available to historians'' (Buerger 1983:40-41). Furthermore, a strict policy of secrecy forbids any couple receiving their second anointing to tell anyone else that this has happened. As a result, a visible elite within the patriarchal order has disappeared; all endowed and sealed individuals are, for all practical purposes, on an equal ritual footing.

The second modification was a revelation announced in June 1978 which annulled the policy of excluding Black males from the priesthood. Blacks can now be ordained, receive their endowments, be sealed, and thus achieve a condition of formal equality with other male members of the church. This development permits the church to become universal, at least in concept. It can now proselyte all races and allow them to enter the church as equals.

Preceding this event but conceptually associated with it has been a deemphasis of nineteenth-century Mormon teachings linking behavioral and spiritual conditions with racial distinctions. Mormons still regard themselves as the literal descendants of Abraham and believe that preexistent spirits were foreordained to come to earth under varying conditions. They are much less likely, however, to understand these issues in racial terms than were their ancestors a century ago.

THE MORMON CODE OF CONDUCT

Throughout the history of the church the understanding has persisted that to be fully Mormon one must adhere to Mormonism's code of conduct. This code has always included basic Christian and ethical principles and loyalty to the leaders of the church. Beyond this, the aspects of the code have changed according to differing circumstances. Historically, it has included the economic provisions of the law of consecration and stewardship, polygamy, "gathering," and settling the western frontier. Now it includes having on hand a year's supply of food, making home teaching visits, and following church-provided lesson outlines when teaching Sunday School lessons.

For the most part, Mormons routinely accept such variations and developments in the Mormon code of conduct as manifestations of how God deals with human beings. Joseph Smith observed: "The principle on which the government of heaven is conducted [is by] revelation adapted to the circumstances in which the children of the kingdom are placed" (*HC* 5:135). Sociological observers in the tradition of Peter Berger and Thomas Luckmann (1966:73) would regard the same phenomena as manifestations of the ability of Mormonism's "institutional ordering of comprehensive meanings for everyday life" to adapt to the changing circumstances in which its members find themselves.

CHANGE AND THE CHURCH

The Mormon church has changed in various directions at different points in its development. Changes in Mormon covenant organization in the late 1880s and early 1900s might be seen as adjustments to secularization within the Mormon church as an institution, among the Mormon people as a community, and within general American society. Berger and Luckmann (1966:74) define secularization as the "progressive autonomization of societal sectors from the domination of religious meanings and institutions."

Among the Puritans, secularization centered on the process by which visible saints ceased to monopolize state power. In a somewhat analogous fashion, the Mormon church stopped trying to regulate immigration, colonization, and political, economic, and educational institutions. Instead, these social sectors acquired secular meanings.

This process in the Mormon church mirrors in small what Berger and Luckmann see happening more broadly in Western religion: that since the Reformation, religion has progressively retreated from involvement with such primary institutions as the polity and the economy to the "private sphere" (Berger 1969:105-71; Berger and Luckmann 1969:79-86; Luckmann 1967:77-114). A primary purpose of religion, they point out, is to provide individuals with meanings and patterns of action in aspects of life over which they have some direct control. At present, individuals fundamentally control only their private lives; thus, when involved with activities within the private sphere, they seek for religious meaning and direction.

Berger and Luckmann maintain that "the most important institution in [the private] sphere is the family. It is in the complex of social conduct surrounding that institution, including sexuality in its extra- or pre-familial expression, that most individuals seek personal meaning and identity in contemporary society" (Berger and Luckmann 1966:80). If we accept their premises, then it would appear that the Mormon church's retreat from involvement in the public sphere and its current emphasis on the family and sexuality are rational and appropriate pragmatic adjustments to the current social milieu.

MORMONISM AND THE FUTURE

From the perspective of Mormon covenant organization, the church faces some significant strains that are distinctive to its contemporary situation: (1) maintaining solidarity as diversity increases; (2) dealing with increases in fundamentalist radicalism, (3) reversing the marginalization of nonnormative families, and (4) managing the contradiction between the social value of egalitarianism and the formal subordination of Mormon women. These four conditions are interrelated and their existence suggests limitations to the current ability of the patriarchal order paradigm to provide members with an adequate framework for the "ordering of comprehensive meanings for everyday life."

As the church expands worldwide, its members are increasingly involved in a public sphere which the church can neither regulate nor modify in any significant manner. Furthermore, because of the increasing geographic dispersion of church members, they have increasingly fewer contacts with fellow Mormons outside of such formalized contexts as Sunday meetings. This is a unique situation in Mormonism. Throughout the nineteenth century, "gathering" was an important Mormon value, and so was the resulting church organization and supervision of both their public and their private activities. For the church to maintain group identity and solidarity, it cannot rely on the propinquity and contact frequency that served it in the past.

In the social model of center and periphery I have used, dissent stems from the refusal of individuals to submit to the elite at the center. In Mormonism this takes the form of members refusing to "follow the brethren."

Dissent is not, of course, a new problem in Mormon history. During the nineteenth century, most serious dissension came from what might be termed the "Mormon left"—individuals and groups who in various ways and over various issues—maintained that the church was too monolithic, too far out of step with the pluralism and secularism of general American society.

Dissension from the left remains endemic to Mormonism. While an unusually high percentage of college-educated Mormons remains active and highly committed to the church, a number of political liberals are concerned with church leaders' essentially conservative political orientation. Intellectuals resist the official view on organic evolution and contextual history, among other elements, and feminists voice reservations about general authorities' essentially traditional view of the role of women in society and in the church. However, unlike the nineteenth century, dissension from the left has not generally become schism.

Beginning with the Manifesto and continuing to the present, however, significant dissension has arisen from the fundamentalist "right" which has, in contrast, typically manifest itself by forming a number of relatively small schismatic groups. Fundamentalists hold that the church has compromised too much with the world, praise nineteenth-century Mormonism as a model, deplore modern secularism, and—at the far right, beyond the boundaries of the church—experiment with both polygamy and communalism. In a manner reminiscent of early New England radicals, such individuals stress the primacy of personal religious experience over the public policies of a hierocracy.

In recent years, a few radicals at the fringe of the fundamentalist right like the Lafferty brothers and Ervil LeBaron and his followers have not stopped short of murder to eliminate "the unrighteous" and rivals. The best way to understand such extreme phenomena is to see the tensions created when a pervasive institution like the church contracts its field of operation, requiring members who historically were guided by a comprehensive sacred pattern for social action to cope as individuals with a secular world. Fear, withdrawal, and defensiveness are predictable reactions to such stresses.

The church has always emphasized familial connections. The individual family as an isolate is probably more prominent in Mormon belief and practice now than at any other time. As the church withdrew from economic, political, and community institutions within which the family interacts, the relationships between the church and the family lost important external contexts. The minimal Mormon institutional structure therefore became the church and the family, rather than the composite of church and the family within the community, the polity, and the economy. The attention once spread over a broad base has contracted to a single relationship. Sometimes that attention is seen as nourishing and supporting, but sometimes it can also be perceived as intrusive and managing.

Mormon covenant organization supplies a model of the ideal family as consisting of an endowed and sealed couple with their children, all of them active in the church and conforming to its code of conduct. This model can be termed the normative Mormon family. In the nineteenth century, the church had considerable flexibility in organizing individuals into normative families. For example, a single woman who migrated to Utah could readily attach herself to a normative family as a polygamous wife. With some exceptions, essentially the only people who were not part of normative families were individuals who did not wish to be.

Today, of course, the church lacks this power, and an increasingly higher proportion of Mormons live in families that are not normative by Mormon definitions. These include single adults, women-headed families, part-member families, and families where only some of the members are active. Because of the dynamics of Mormon covenant organization and because of how the church regulates and orders Mormon relationships through the family, it increasingly marginalizes such individuals within the Mormon community.

Throughout the history of the church, women have been formally subordinate to men. There is little indication that this situation has ever resulted in Mormon women being less assertive in their households and within the society than women elsewhere. And except for the practice of plural marriage, nineteenth-century Mormon understandings regarding female subordination were essentially consistent with those in general American culture. This situation, however, has changed in the twentieth century. The mid-twentieth century has seen the emergence of such values as individualism, egalitarianism, the movement of women from the private sphere of the home to the public sphere of work, with a parallel male revaluing of home and family values, and feminism as a political as well as a social movement. Patterns of female subordination have become increasingly distasteful to Americans in general.

As a result of these trends, many Mormon women experience what Robert Merton (1976) has termed "sociological ambivalence"—being simultaneously drawn in opposing directions by conflicting social forces. As Americans they accept the premise of sexual equality and participate in institutions that foster this understanding. As Mormons they belong to an organization whose ideology includes formal female subordination, whose public institutions in varying degrees embody that ideology, and whose pattern of domestic relationships preserve the same premises.

The church attempts to overcome this ambivalence by stressing that men and women are of equal worth, that sex role distinctions are divinely ordained, and that while men and women have separate roles to perform, these roles are of equal importance. Furthermore, in terms of actual functioning, church leaders encourage partnership rather than subordination/superordination between husband and wife.

Even so, the church continues to maintain that men are formally to preside both within the church and within their homes and that women are not to seek employment outside the household. Because of this position, female subordination in a fundamental sense remains unresolved within the minds of some members.

None of these four conditions is currently significant enough to threaten either the corporate existence of the church or its worldwide expansion. They do indicate, however, that Mormonism continues to be confronted with situations to which it must pragmatically adjust. Nor is it clear what adjustments to these particular problems the rules of the patriarchal order paradigm can generate. Given the adaptive capacity that the church has manifested in the past, however, there is good reason to anticipate satisfactory resolutions.

CONCLUSION

The history of the church can be seen as a record of developments that have facilitated the worldwide development of the Mormon church and permitted members from increasingly diverse backgrounds to be integrated into the Mormon group through the patriarchal order.

Covenant organization remains as significant to Mormon solidarity now as at any point in its history, despite the vast changes that have occurred since Joseph Smith and a few close associates organized the church in 1830. Much of this continuity can be explained by the power of Mormon covenant organization to create an institutionalized pattern of comprehensive meanings, to provide for orderly transformations in understandings, and to enable the organization to meet and master changing circumstances.

Bibliography

Note: Historical Archives refers to those of the Church of Jesus Christ of Latter-day Saints, Salt Lake City, Utah.

AHLSTROM, SYDNEY E. 1972. *A Religious History of the American People*. New Haven, Conn.: Yale University Press.

ALLEN, JAMES B. 1968. "The Unusual Jurisdiction of County Probate Courts in the Territory of Utah." *Utah Historical Quarterly* 36:132-42.

_____. 1979. "One Man's Nauvoo: William Clayton's Experience in Mormon Illinois." *Journal of Mormon History* 6:37-59.

ALLEN, JAMES B., and LEONARD, GLEN M. 1976. *The Story of the Latter-day Saints*. Salt Lake City, Utah: Deseret Book Co.

ANDERSON, RICHARD LLOYD. 1971. *Joseph Smith's New England Heritage: Influences of Grandfathers Solomon Mack and Asael Smith*. Salt Lake City, Utah: Deseret Book Co.

ANDRUS, GEORGE B. 1959. March 15. Patriarchal blessing given in Holladay Stake, Utah. Typescript in possession of the author.

ARRINGTON, LEONARD J. 1958. *Great Basin Kingdom: An Economic History of the Latter-day Saints, 1830-1900*. Cambridge: Harvard University Press.

ARRINGTON, LEONARD J., and BITTON, DAVIS. 1979. *The Mormon Experience: A History of the Latter-day Saints*. New York: Alfred A. Knopf.

ARRINGTON, LEONARD J.; FOX, FERAMORZ Y.; and MAY, DEAN L. 1976. *Building the City of God: Community and Cooperation among the Mormons*. Salt Lake City, Utah: Deseret Book Co.

BACHMAN, DANEL W. 1975. "A Study of the Mormon Practice of Plural Marriage Before the Death of Joseph Smith." M.A. thesis, Purdue University.

BACKMAN, MILTON V., JR. 1969. "Awakenings in the Burned-over District: New Light on the Historical Setting of the First Vision." *Brigham Young University Studies* 9:301-20.

_____. 1980. *Joseph Smith's First Vision: Confirming Evidences and Contemporary Accounts*. 2d ed. Salt Lake City, Utah: Bookcraft. First published in 1971. (Neibaur account written 1844.)

BANCROFT, HUBERT HOWE. 1964. *History of Utah*. Bookcraft: Salt Lake City, Utah. First published in 1890.

BARRON, HOWARD. 1977. *Orson Hyde: Missionary, Apostle, Colonizer*. Bountiful, Utah: Horizon.

BAS. "Book of Adoptions & Sealings." 1847-1857. Typescript and photocopy in possession of author.

BBS. N.d. "A Brief Biographical Sketch of the Life and Labors of Lucy Walker Kimball Smith." Historical Archives.

BEATTIE, JOHN. 1964. *Other Cultures: Aims, Methods, and Achievements in Social Anthropology*. New York: Free Press.

BEECHER, MAUREEN URSENBACH. 1983. "Women at Winter Quarters."
    Sunstone 8:4:11-19.
BELLAH, ROBERT N. 1978. "American Society and the Mormon Community."
    In Madsen 1978: 1-12.
BENNION, LOWELL "BEN". 1984. "The Incidence of Mormon Polygamy in
    1880: 'Dixie versus Davis Stake'." *Journal of Mormon History* 11:27-42.
BERCOVITCH, SACVAN. 1975. *The Puritan Origins of the American Self.* New Ha-
    ven, Conn.: Yale University Press.
_____. 1978. *The American Jeremiad.* Madison: University of Wisconsin Press.
BERGER, PETER L. 1969. *The Sacred Canopy: Elements of a Sociological Theory of Re-
    ligion.* Anchor Books edition. Garden City, N.Y.: Anchor Books. First pub-
    lished in 1967.
BERGER, PETER L., and LUCKMANN, THOMAS. 1966. "Secularization and
    Pluralism." *International Yearbook for the Sociology of Religion* 2:73-84.
_____. 1967. *The Social Construction of Reality: A Treatise in the Sociology of Knowl-
    edge.* Anchor Books edition. Garden City, N.Y.: Anchor Books. First pub-
    lished in 1966.
BERTHOFF, ROWLAND. 1971. *An Unsettled People: Social Order and Disorder in Ameri-
    can History.* New York: Harper & Row.
BLUMIN, STUART M. 1976. *The Urban Threshold: Growth and Change in a Nine-
    teenth Century American Community.* Chicago: University of Chicago Press.
BM. [THE BOOK OF MORMON]. 1981. *The Book of Mormon: An Account Written
    by the Hand of Mormon upon Plates Taken from the Plates of Nephi.* Salt Lake
    City, Utah: Church of Jesus Christ of Latter-day Saints.
BOAS, FRANZ. 1974. *The Shaping of American Anthropology, 1883-1911: A Franz Boas
    Reader.* Edited by George W. Stocking, Jr. New York: Basic Books.
[BOOK OF COMMANDMENTS]. 1833. *A Book of Commandments for the Govern-
    ment of the Church of Christ, Organized According to Law, on the 6th of April, 1830.*
    Zion [Independence, Mo.]: W. W. Phelps & Co.
BREEN, TIMOTHY H. 1980. *Puritans and Adventurers: Change and Persistence in Early
    America.* New York: Oxford University Press.
BREEN, TIMOTHY H., and FOSTER, STEPHEN. 1977. "The Puritans'
    Greatest Achievement: A Study of Social Cohesion in Seventeenth-Century
    Massachusetts." In *Puritan New England: Essays on Religion, Society, and Cul-
    ture,* pp. 110-27. Edited by Alden Vaughan and Francis J. Bremer. New
    York: St. Martin's Press.
BRODIE, FAWN M. 1977. *No Man Knows My History: The Life of Joseph Smith, the
    Mormon Prophet.* 2d ed. New York: Alfred A. Knopf. First published in 1945.
BRONFENBRENNER, URIE. 1979. *The Ecology of Human Development: Experiments
    by Nature and by Design.* Cambridge: Harvard University Press.
BROOKS, CLEANTH; LEWIS, R. W. B.; and WARREN, ROBERT PENN,
    eds. 1973. *American Literature: The Makers and the Making.* 2 vols. New York:
    St. Martin's Press. ("Deacon's Masterpiece" written 1858.)
BROWN, LISLE G. 1979. "The Sacred Departments for Temple Work in Nau-
    voo: The Assembly Room and the Council Chamber." *Brigham Young
    University Studies* 19:361-74.
BROWN, W. ADAMS. 1914. "Covenant Theology." In *Encyclopaedia of Religion
    and Ethics,* 12 vols. Edited by James Hastings. New York: Charles Scrib-
    ner's Sons, 1913-22. Vol. 4, pp. 216-24.
BUERGER, DAVID JOHN. 1983. " 'The Fulness of the Priesthood': The Sec-
    ond Anointing in Latter-day Saint Theology and Practice." *Dialogue: A
    Journal of Mormon Thought* 16:1:10-44.

BUNYAN, JOHN. 1909. "The Pilgrim's Progress." In *Harvard Classics*. 50 vols. Edited by Charles W. Eliot. New York: P. F. Collier & Sons. Vol. 15, pp. 5-324. First published in 1678.

BURRAGE, CHAMPLIN. 1967. *The Early English Dissenters in the Light of Recent Research (1550-1641)*. 2 vols. Vol. 1: *History and Criticism*. New York: Russell & Russell. First published in 1912.

BURROW, J. W. 1970. *Evolution and Society: A Study in Victorian Social Theory*. Cambridge: Syndics of the Cambridge University Press.

BUSH, LESTER E., JR. 1973. "Mormonism's Negro Doctrine: An Historical Overview." *Dialogue: A Journal of Mormon Thought* 8:1:11-68.

————. 1979. "Mormon Medical Ethical Guidelines." *Dialogue: A Journal of Mormon Thought* 12:3:97-106.

BUSHMAN, RICHARD L. 1955. "New Jerusalem, U.S.A.: The Early Development of the Latter-day Saint Zion Concept on the American Frontier." Honor's thesis, Harvard University.

————. 1960. "Mormon Persecutions in Missouri, 1833." *Brigham Young University Studies* 3:11-20.

————. 1967. *From Puritan to Yankee: Character and the Social Order in Connecticut, 1690-1765*. Cambridge: Harvard University Press.

————. 1984. *Joseph Smith and the Beginnings of Mormonism*. Chicago: University of Illinois Press.

CAHOON, REYNOLDS. 1831-32. Journal. Microfilm. Historical Archives.

CALVIN, JOHN. 1957. *Institutes of the Christian Religion*. 2 vols. Translated from Latin by Henry Beveridge. Grand Rapids, Mich.: William B. Eerdmans Publishing Co. (based on 1559 edition.)

CAMPBELL, EUGENE E. 1987. "Pioneers and Patriotism: Conflicting Loyalties." In *New Views of Mormon History: A Collection of Essays in Honor of Leonard J. Arrington*, pp. 307-22. Edited by Davis Bitton and Maureen Ursenbach Beecher. Salt Lake City: University of Utah Press.

CAMPBELL, EUGENE E., and CAMPBELL, BRUCE L. 1978. "Divorce among Mormon Polygamists: Extent and Explanations." *Utah Historical Quarterly* 46:4-23.

CANDLAND, DAVID. 1841-1901. Journal. Photocopy of typescript. Historical Archives.

CANNON, DONALD Q., and COOK, LYNDON W. 1983. *Far West Record: Minutes of the Church of Jesus Christ of Latter-day Saints, 1830-1844*. Salt Lake City, Utah: Deseret Book.

CANNON, KENNETH L., II. 1978. "Beyond the Manifesto: Polygamous Cohabitation Among LDS General Authorities After 1890." *Utah Historical Quarterly* 46:1:24-36.

CLAYTON, WILLIAM. 1982. *Clayton's Secret Writings Uncovered: Extracts from the Diaries of Joseph Smith's Secretary William Clayton*. Introduction by Jerald and Sandra Tanner. Salt Lake City, Utah: Modern Microfilm Co. (Journal entries, 22 Jan. 1843 to 28 Jan. 1846.)

COHEN, CHARLES LLOYD. 1986. *God's Caress: The Psychology of Puritan Religious Experience*. New York: Oxford University Press.

COOPER, REX EUGENE. 1985. "The Promises Made to the Fathers: A Diachronic Analysis of Mormon Covenant Organization with Reference to Puritan Federal Theology." Ph.D. dissertation, University of Chicago.

CORRILL, JOHN. 1839. *Brief History of the Church of Christ of Latter Day Saints. (Commonly Called Mormons;) Including an Account of Their Doctrine and Discipline; with the Reasons of the Author for Leaving the Church*. St. Louis, Mo.: Printed for the Author.

CROSBY, CAROLINE BARNES. 1851-83. "Memoirs, begun at Tubuai, Society Islands, 1851." Microfilm. Historical Archives.

CROSS, WHITNEY R. 1965. *The Burned-over District: The Social and Intellectual History of Enthusiastic Religion in Western New York, 1800-1850.* New York: Harper & Row.

DAVIS, DANIEL. 1846-92. Journal. Microfilm. Historical Archives.

DAVIS, DAVID BRION. 1960. "Some Themes of Counter-Subversion: An Analysis of Anti-Masonic, Anti-Catholic, and Anti-Mormon Literature." *Mississippi Valley Historical Review* 47:205-24.

————. 1972. "The New England Origins of Mormonism." In *Mormonism and American Culture,* pp. 13-28. Edited by M. Hill and J. Allen. New York: Harper & Row. First published in 1953.

DAVIS, THOMAS M. 1972. "The Traditions of Puritan Typology." In *Typology and Early American Literature*, pp. 11-45. Edited by Sacvan Bercovitch. N.p.: University of Massachusetts Press.

D&C. [DOCTRINE AND COVENANTS]. 1835. *Doctrine and Covenants of the Church of the Latter Day Saints, Carefully Selected from the Revelations of God.* Kirtland, Ohio: F. G. Williams & Co.

————. 1981. *Doctrine and Covenants of the Church of Jesus Christ of Latter-day Saints. Containing Revelations Given to Joseph Smith, the Prophet, with Some Additions by His Successors in the Presidency of the Church.* Salt Lake City, Utah: Church of Jesus Christ of Latter-day Saints.

DEPILLIS, MARIO S. 1966. "The Quest for Religious Authority and the Rise of Mormonism." *Dialogue: A Journal of Mormon Thought* 1:68-88.

Deseret News Weekly. 1850–1898. Vol. 1, no. 1 (June 1850)–Vol. 57, no. 26 (December 1898), Salt Lake City, Utah.

DE TOCQUEVILLE, ALEXIS. 1969. *Democracy in America.* Edited by J. P. Mayer. Translated from French by George Lawrence. Garden City, N. Y.: Doubleday & Co. First published in 1835, 1840.

DILLENBERGER, JOHN. 1978. "Grace and Works in Martin Luther and Joseph Smith." *In* Madsen 1978:175-86. Edited by T. Madsen. Provo, Utah: Religious Studies Center, Brigham Young University.

DIXON, WILLIAM HEPWORTH. 1973. "A Humanitarian Looks at the 'Mormon Question'." In Mulder and Mortensen 1973:364-68.

DURANT, WILL, and DURANT, ARIEL. 1968. *The Lessons of History.* New York: Simon & Schuster.

DURKHEIM, EMILE. 1964. *The Division of Labor in Society.* Translated from French by George Simpson. New York: Free Press. First published in 1893.

DYKES, GEORGE P. 1846. Letter to Brigham Young, 17 August 1846. Typescript of original in possession of the author.

EGAN, HOWARD. 1917. *Pioneering the West, 1846 to 1878: Major Egan's Diary; Also Thrilling Experiences of Pre-Frontier Life among Indians; Their Traits, Civil and Savage; and Part of Autobiography, Inter-Related to His Father's, by Howard R. Egan.* Edited by W. Egan. Richmond, Utah: Howard R. Egan Estate.

EHAT, ANDREW F. 1980. " 'It Seems Like Heaven Began on Earth': Joseph Smith and the Constitution of the Kingdom of God." *Brigham Young University Studies* 20:253-79.

————. 1982. "Joseph Smith's Introduction of Temple Ordinances and the 1844 Mormon Succession Question." Master's thesis, Brigham Young University.

EJ. *Elders' Journal.* 1837–1838. Vol. 1, no. 1 (October 1837), Kirtland, Ohio. Vol. 1, no. 2 (November 1837)–Vol. 1, no. 4 (August 1838), Far West, Mo.

ELLSWORTH, SAMUEL GEORGE. 1951. "A History of Mormon Missions in the United States and Canada, 1830-1860." Ph.D. dissertation, University of California at Berkeley.

ELY, RICHARD T. 1903. "Economic Aspects of Mormonism." *Harper's Monthly Magazine* 106:667-78.

EMS. *The Evening and Morning Star.* 1832–1834. Vol. 1, no. 1 (June 1832)-Vol. 2, no. 14 (September 1833), Independence, Mo. Vol. 2, no. 15 (December 1833)-Vol. 2, no. 24 (September 1834), Kirtland, Ohio.

Ensign of the Church of Jesus Christ of Latter-day Saints. 1971– . Vol. 1, no. 1 (January 1971)-present.

EVANS-PRITCHARD, E. E. 1962. *Social Anthropology and Other Essays.* New York: Free Press.

ESPLIN, RONALD K. 1979. "Brigham Young and Priesthood Denial to the Blacks: An Alternative View." *Brigham Young University Studies* 19:394-402.

Excerpts from the Weekly Council Meetings of the Council of the Quorum of the Twelve Apostles Dealing with the Rights of Negroes in the Church. 1849–1940. George Albert Smith Collection, Manuscripts Division. Special Collections Department, University of Utah Libraries, Salt Lake City, Utah.

FIELDING, JOSEPH. 1979. " 'They Might Have Known That He Was Not a Fallen Prophet': The Nauvoo Journal of Joseph Fielding." (Transcribed and edited by Andrew F. Ehat.) *Brigham Young University Studies* 19:133-66. (Journal entries December 1843 to October 1846.)

FIRTH, RAYMOND. 1961. *Elements of Social Organization.* Boston: Beacon Press.

FISH, CARL RUSSELL. 1927. *The Rise of the Common Man.* New York: Macmillan.

FLANDERS, ROBERT BRUCE. 1965. *Nauvoo: Kingdom on the Mississippi.* Urbana, Ill.: University of Illinois Press.

FORELL, GEORGE W. 1975. *The Protestant Faith.* Fortress Press ed. Philadelphia: Fortress Press. First published in 1960.

FORTES, MEYER. 1969. *Kinship and the Social Order: The Legacy of Lewis Henry Morgan.* Chicago: Aldine Publishing Co.

————. 1970. *Time and Social Structure, and Other Essays.* London School of Economics Monographs on Social Anthropology, no. 40. London: Athlone Press.

FOSTER, STEPHEN. 1984. "English Puritanism and the Progress of New England Institutions, 1630-1660." In *Saints and Revolutionaries: Essays on Early American History,* pp. 3-37. Edited by David D. Hall, John W. Murrin, and Thad W. Tate. New York: W. W. Norton & Co.

FOSTER, W. LAWRENCE. 1981. *Religion and Sexuality: Three American Communal Experiments of the Nineteenth Century.* New York: Oxford University Press.

GATES, SUSA YOUNG. 1977. "From Impulsive Girl to Patient Wife: Lucy Bigelow Young." Edited by Miriam B. Murphy. *Utah Historical Quarterly* 45:270-88. (Written between 1880 and 1933.)

GEERTZ, CLIFFORD. 1973. *The Interpretation of Cultures.* New York: Basic Books.

GENTRY, LELAND HOMER. 1965. "A History of the Latter-day Saints in Northern Missouri from 1836 to 1839." Ph.D. dissertation, Brigham Young University.

————. 1974. "The Danite Band of 1838." *Brigham Young University Studies* 14:421-50.

GORDON, MICHAEL, ed. 1973. *The American Family in Socio-Historical Perspective.* New York: St. Martin's.

GREW, RAYMOND. 1980. "The Case for Comparing Histories." *The American Historical Review* 85:763-78.

GURA, PHILIP F. 1984. *A Glimpse of Sion's Glory: Puritan Radicalism in New England, 1620-1660*. Middletown, Conn.: Wesleyan University Press.

HAIGHT, DAVID B. 1979. "Woman as Mother." In *Woman* [no editor or compiler], pp. 13-20. Salt Lake City, Utah: Deseret Book Co.

HANSEN, KLAUS J. 1974. *Quest for Empire: The Political Kingdom of God and the Council of Fifty in Mormon History*. Bison Book ed. Lincoln: University of Nebraska Press. First published in 1967.

_____. 1981. *Mormonism and the American Experience*. Foreword by Martin E. Marty. Chicago History of American Religion Series. Chicago: University of Chicago Press.

HANSEN, PETER OLSEN. 1846–1847. Diary, 12 May 1846-23 February 1847. (Contained in Heber C. Kimball's journal, Book # 90, 1837-38, 1840, 1846-23 February 1847). Microfilm. Historical Archives.

_____. Ca. 1850–1879. Autobiography and journal ms. Microfilm. Historical Archives.

HC. *History of the Church of Jesus Christ of Latter-day Saints*. 1978. 7 vols. 2d ed. Introduction and notes by B. H. Roberts, ed. Vols.1-6: *Period I. History of Joseph Smith, the Prophet, by Himself.* Vol 7: *Period II. Apostolic Interregnum, From the Manuscript History of Brigham Young and Other Original Documents*. Salt Lake City, Utah: Deseret Book Co.

HILL, DONNA. 1977. *Joseph Smith: The First Mormon*. Garden City, New York: Doubleday & Co.

HILL, MARVIN. 1968. "The Role of Christian Primitivism in the Origin and Development of the Mormon Kingdom, 1830-1844." Ph.D. dissertation, University of Chicago.

_____. 1969. "The Shaping of the Mormon Mind in New England and New York." *Brigham Young University Studies* 9:351-72.

_____. 1975. "Quest for Refuge: An Hypothesis as to the Social Origins and Nature of the Mormon Political Kingdom." *Journal of Mormon History* 2:3-20.

_____. 1980. "The Rise of Mormonism in the Burned-over District: Another View." *New York History* 61:411-30.

HOLIFIELD, E. BROOKS. 1974. *The Covenant Sealed: The Development of Puritan Sacramental Theology in Old and New England, 1570-1720*. New Haven, Conn.: Yale University Press.

HOVEY, JOSEPH GRAFTON. 1845–1856. Journal. Microfilm. Historical Archives.

HOWE, Eber D. 1834. *Mormonism Unveiled: Or a Faithful Account of That Singular Imposition and Delusion, from Its Rise to the Present Time, with Sketches of the Characters of Its Propagators, and a Full Detail of the Manner in Which the Famous Golden Bible Was Brought before the World, To Which Are Added Inquiries into the Probability That the Historical Part of the Said Bible Was Written by One Solomon Spalding More Than Twenty Years Ago, and by Him Intended to Have Been Published as a Romance*. Plainsville, Ohio: E. D. Howe.

HYDE, JOSEPH SMITH, comp. 1933. *Orson Hyde: One of the First Council of the Twelve Apostles of the Church of Jesus Christ of Latter-day Saints—Jerusalem, Nauvoo, Salt Lake City*. [Salt Lake City, Utah?]: N.p.

IRVING, GORDON. 1974. "The Law of Adoption: One Phase of the Development of the Mormon Concept of Salvation, 1830-1900." *Brigham Young University Studies* 14:291-314.

IVINS, STANLEY S. 1967. "Notes on Mormon Polygamy." *Utah Historical Quarterly* 35:309-21. First published in 1956.

JACOB, NORTON. 1949. *The Record of Norton Jacob*. Edited by C. Edward Jacob and Ruth B. Jacob. Salt Lake City, Utah: Norton Jacob Family Association.

JAMISON, A. LELAND. 1961. "Religions on the Christian Perimeter." In *Religion in American Life*. 4 vols. Princeton Studies in American Civilization, no. 5. Edited by James Ward Smith and A. Leland Jamison. Princeton, N. J.: Princeton University Press. Vol. 1: *The Shaping of American Religion*, pp. 162-231.

JAMES, JANE ELIZABETH MANNING. 1893. "Biography of Jane E. Manning James written from her own verbal statement and by her request, she also wishes it read at her funeral by E J D Roundy." Ms. Historical Archives.

JD. *Journal of Discourses*. 1855-1886. Vol. 1 (1855)-Vol. 26 (1886), Liverpool.

JENNINGS, WARREN A. 1962. "Zion is Fled: The Expulsion of the Mormons from Jackson County, Missouri." Ph.D. dissertation, University of Florida.

_____. 1973. "The City in the Garden: Social Conflict in Jackson County, Missouri." In McKiernan, Blair, and Edwards 1973:99-119.

JH. "Journal History of the Church." Historical Archives.

JOHNSON, RICHARD R. 1981. *Adjustment to Empire: The New England Colonies 1675-1715*. New Brunswick, N.J.: Rutgers University Press.

KETT, JOSEPH F. 1977. *Rites of Passage: Adolescence in America, 1700 to the Present*. New York: Basic Books.

KIMBALL, HEBER C. 1982. *Heber C. Kimball's Journal: November 21, 1845 to January 7, 1846*. Introduction by Jerald and Sandra Tanner. Salt Lake City, Utah: Modern Microfilm.

_____. 1847. Journal 5 April-30 October 1847 (Book # 94). Microfilm. Historical Archives.

_____. 1848. Family Meeting Discourse, Spring 1848. Microfilm. Historical Archives.

KIMBALL, LUCY WALKER. 1858. "Statement of Mrs. L. W. Kimball." Historical Archives.

KIMBALL, SARAH MELISSA GRANGER. 1867. Letter to Brigham Willard Kimball, 17 February 1867. Kimball Family Correspondence Collection. Ms. Microfilm. Historical Archives.

KIMBALL, STANLEY B. 1981. *Heber C. Kimball: Mormon Patriarch and Pioneer*. Urbana, Ill.: University of Illinois Press.

KLUCKHOHN, CLYDE. 1956. "Toward a Comparison of Value-Emphasis in Different Cultures." In *The State of Social Sciences: Papers Presented at the 35th Anniversary of the Social Science Research Building, November 10-12, 1956*, pp. 116-32. Edited by Leonard White. Chicago: University of Chicago Press.

_____. 1961. "The Study of Values." In *Values in America*, pp. 17-45. Edited by Donald Barrett. Notre Dame, Ind.: University of Notre Dame Press.

KLUCKHOHN, FLORENCE, and STRODTBECK, FRED L. 1961. *Variations in Value Orientations*. Evanston, Ill.: Row, Peterson & Co.

KNAPPEN, MARSHALL MASON. 1966. *Tudor Puritanism: A Chapter in the History of Idealism*. Chicago: University of Chicago Press.

KUPER, ADAM. 1983. *Anthropology and Anthropologists: The Modern British School*. London: Routledge & Kegan Paul.

KNIGHT, NEWEL. Ca. 1846-1847. Autobiography and Journal. Microfilm. Historical Archives.

KROEBER, A. L. 1917. "The Superorganic." *American Anthropologist* 19:163-213.

LAMAR, HOWARD R. 1971. "Statehood for Utah: A Different Path." *Utah Historical Quarterly* 39:307-27.

LARSEN, HERBERT RAY. 1954. " 'Familism' in Mormon Social Structure." Ph.D. dissertation, University of Utah.

LARSON, GUSTAVE O. 1961. *Outline History of Utah and the Mormons.* 2d ed. Salt Lake City, Utah: Deseret Book. First published in 1958.

————. 1971. *The "Americanization" of Utah for Statehood.* San Marino, Calif.: Huntington Library.

LATOURETTE, KENNETH SCOTT. 1937-1945. *History of the Expansion of Christianity.* 7 vols. New York: Harper & Brothers. Vol. 4: *The Great Century, A.D. 1800-A.D. 1914,* 1941.

LAUD, GEORGE. 1978. "George Laud's Nauvoo Journal." Edited by Eugene England. *Brigham Young University Studies.* 18:151-78. (Entries 1 Jan. 1845-6 June 1846.)

————. 1845-1877. Journal ms. Typescript. Utah Historical Society Archives and Library, Salt Lake City, Utah.

LEACH, EDMUND R. 1971. *Rethinking Anthropology.* London School of Economics Monographs on Social Anthropology, no. 22. London: Athlone Press.

LEE, JOHN DOYLE. 1877. *Mormonism Unveiled, or the Life and Confessions of the Late Mormon Bishop, John D. Lee (Written by Himself), Embracing a History of Mormonism from Its Inception Down to the Present Time, with an Exposition of the Secret History, Signs, Symbols, and Crimes of the Mormon Church. Also the True History of the Horrible Butchery Known as the Mountain Meadows Massacre.* St. Louis, Mo.: Bryan, Brant & Co.

————. 1938. *Journals of John D. Lee, 1846-47 and 1859.* Edited by C. Kelly. Salt Lake City, Utah: Western Printing Co. Reprint ed. 1984. Salt Lake City: University of Utah Press.

LEONE, MARK P. 1979. *Roots of Modern Mormonism.* Cambridge: Harvard University Press.

LEVI-STRAUSS, CLAUDE. 1960. "On Manipulated Sociological Models." *Bijdragen Tot de Taal- Land- en Volkenkunde* 116:45-54.

LEWIS, CATHERINE. 1848. *Narrative of Some of the Proceedings of the Mormons: Giving an Account of Their Iniquities, with Particulars Concerning the Training of the Indians by Them, Descriptions of the Mode of Endowment, Plurality of Wives, &c., &c.* Lynn: Published by the Author.

LIENHARDT, GODFREY. 1964. *Social Anthropology.* The Home University Library of Modern Knowledge, No. 253. Oxford: University of Oxford Press.

LIGHTNER, MARY ELIZABETH ROLLINS. 1874. Patriarchal blessing dated 5 July 1874. Photocopy. Mary Elizabeth Rollins Collection. Historical Archives.

————. 1882. Letter of Mary Elizabeth Rollins Lightner, James H. Rollins and John D. T. McAllister to John Taylor, 22 May 1882. Photocopy of original in possession of the author.

————. 1902. Sworn statement dated 8 Feb. 1902. Photocopy. Mary Elizabeth Rollins Collection. Historical Archives.

————. 1905. "Remarks by Sister Mary E. Lightner, Who Was Sealed to Joseph Smith in 1842. B.Y.U., April 14, 1905, She is 87 Years Old." Historical Archives.

LITTELL, FRANKLIN. 1962. *From State Church to Pluralism: A Protestant Interpretation of Religion in American History.* Garden City, N.Y.: Anchor Books.

LOWIE, ROBERT. 1937. *The History of Ethnographic Theory.* New York: Holt, Rinehart & Winston.

LUCKMANN, THOMAS. 1967. *The Invisible Religion: The Problem of Religion in Modern Society.* New York: Macmillan Publishing Co. First published in 1963.

LUND, ANTHON H., ed. 1920. "A Family Meeting in Nauvoo." *The Utah Genea-logical and Historical Magazine* 11:104-17. (Meeting held 8 Jan. 1845.)

LYMAN, EDWARD LEO. 1986. *Political Deliverance: The Mormon Quest for Utah State-hood.* Foreword by Leonard J. Arrington. Urbana: University of Illinois Press.

MA. *Latter Day Saints' Messenger and Advocate.* 1834-1837. Vol. 1, no. 1 (October 1834)-Vol. 3, no. 12 (September 1837), Kirtland, Ohio.

MACK, SOLOMON. 1811. *A Narrative of the Life of Solomon Mack, Containing an Ac-count of the Many Severe Accidents He Met with during a Long Series of Years, To-gether with the Extraordinary Manner in Which He Was Converted to the Christian Faith. To Which Is Added a Number of Hymns Composed on the Death of Several of His Relations.* Windsor, [Vt.]: [Solomon Mack].

MCCONKIE, BRUCE R. 1966. *Mormon Doctrine.* 2d ed. Salt Lake City, Utah: Bookcraft. First published in 1958.

MCKIERNAN, F. MARK. 1973. "Mormonism on the Defensive: Far West." In McKiernan, A. Blair, and Edwards, 1973:121-40.

MCKIERNAN, F. MARK, BLAIR, ALMA, and EDWARDS, PAUL M., eds. 1973. *The Restoration Movement: Essays in Mormon History.* Lawrence, Kans.: Coronado Press.

MACLEAR, JAMES FULTON. 1975. "New England and the Fifth Monarchy: The Quest for the Millennium in Early American Puritanism." *William and Mary Quarterly,* 3d Ser. 32:223-60.

MCLOUGHLIN, WILLIAM GERALD. 1974. "Revivalism." In *The Rise of Ad-ventism: Religion and Society in Mid-Nineteenth Century America,* pp. 119-53. Edited by Edwin G. Gaustad. New York: Harper & Row.

————. 1978. *Revivals, Awakenings and Reforms: An Essay on Religion and Social Change in America, 1607-1977.* Chicago History of American Religion Series. Chicago: University of Chicago Press.

MADSEN, TRUMAN G., ed. 1978. *Reflections on Mormonism: Judeo-Christian Parallels. Papers Delivered at the Religious Studies Center Symposium. Brigham Young Univer-sity. March 10-11, 1978.* Provo, Utah: Religious Studies Center, Brigham Young University.

MAIR, LUCY. 1965. *An Introduction to Social Anthropology.* Oxford: Clarendon Press.

MALINOWSKI, BRONISLAW. 1926. *Myth in Primitive Psychology.* London: Ke-gan Paul.

————. 1944. *A Scientific Theory of Culture and Other Essays.* Chapel Hill: Univer-sity of North Carolina Press.

MARTY, MARTIN E. 1970. *Righteous Empire: The Protestant Experience in America.* New York: Dial Press.

MARQUARDT, H. MICHAEL. 1973. *The Strange Marriages of Sarah Ann Whitney to Joseph Smith the Mormon Prophet, Joseph C. Kingsbury and Heber C. Kimball.* Salt Lake City, Utah: Modern Microfilm.

[MATHER, COTTON]. 1705. *Baptistes. A Conference about the Subject and Manner of Baptism: Moderately But Successfully Managed between a Minister Who Maintan'd Infant Baptism, and a Gentleman Who Scrupled It.* Boston: N.p. (Early Ameri-can Imprints: 1639-1800. Evans number 1172).

MEAD, SIDNEY E. 1954. "Denominationalism: The Shape of Protestantism in America." *Church History* 23:291-320.

————. 1956. "From Coercion to Persuasion: Another Look at the Rise of Reli-gious Liberty and the Emergence of Denominationalism." *Church History* 25:317-37.

MERTON, ROBERT K. 1976. *Sociological Ambivalence and Other Essays.* New York: The Free Press.

MILLER, GEORGE. 1916. *Correspondence of Bishop George Miller with the Northern Islander from His First Acquaintance with Mormonism up to Near the Close of His Life, 1855.* Burlington, Wis.: [Wingfield Watson].

MILLER, PERRY. 1961. *The New England Mind: The Seventeenth Century.* Boston: Beacon Press. First published in 1939.

————. 1964. *Errand into the Wilderness.* New York: Harper & Row. First published in 1956.

————. 1965. *The Life and Mind in America from the Revolution to the Civil War.* New York: Harcourt, Brace & World.

MILLER, PERRY, and JOHNSON, THOMAS H., eds. 1963. *The Puritans: A Sourcebook of Their Writings.* 2 vols. Rev. ed. New York: Harper & Row. First published in 1938.

MILLER, ROBERTA BALSTAD. 1979. *City and Hinterland: A Case Study of Urban Growth and Regional Development.* Westport, Conn.: Greenwood Press.

MILLS, H. W. 1917. "De Tal Palo Tal Astilla." *Annual Publications. Historical Society of Southern California* 10:3:86-172.

MORAN, GERALD FRANCIS. 1974. "The Puritan Saint: Religious Experience, Church Membership, and Piety in Connecticut, 1636-1776." Ph.D. dissertation, Rutgers University.

MORGAN, EDMUND S. 1958. *The Puritan Dilemma: The Story of John Winthrop.* Edited with a preface by Oscar Handlin. Boston: Little, Brown & Co.

————. 1965. *Visible Saints: The History of a Puritan Idea.* Ithaca, New York: Cornell University Press. First published in 1963.

————. 1966. *The Puritan Family: Religion and Domestic Relations in Seventeenth Century New England.* Rev. ed. New York: Harper & Row. First published in 1944.

The Mormon. 1855–1857. Vol. 1, no. 1 (17 February 1855)–Vol. 3, no. 31 (19 September 1857), New York City.

MS. *The Latter-day Saints' Millennial Star.* 1840–1970. Vol. 1, no. 1 (May 1840) - Vol. 2, no. 11 (March 1842), Manchester. Vol. 2, no. 12 (April 1842) - Vol. 95, no. 9 (March 2, 1933), Liverpool. Vol. 95, no. 10 (March 9, 1933) - Vol. 130, no. 12 (December 1970), London.

MULDER, WILLIAM, and MORTENSEN, A. RUSSELL, eds. 1953. *Among the Mormons: Historic Accounts by Contemporary Observers.* New York: Alfred A. Knopf. Reprint 1973. Bison Book ed. Lincoln: University of Nebraska Press.

MURCH, JAMES DEFOREST. 1962. *Christians Only: A History of the Restoration Movement.* Cincinnati, Ohio: Standard Publishing.

MYRDAL, GUNNAR. 1944. *An American Dilemma: The Negro Problem and Modern Democracy.* New York: Harper & Brothers.

NADEL, S. F. 1951. *Foundations of Social Anthropology.* London: Cohen & West.

NEWELL, LINDA KING, and AVERY, VALEEN TIPPETS. 1984. *Mormon Enigma: Emma Hale Smith.* Garden City, N.Y.: Doubleday & Company.

NYE, RUSSEL BLAINE. 1960. *The Cultural Life of the New Nation, 1776-1830.* New York: Harper & Row.

O'DEA, THOMAS F. 1954. "Mormonism and the Avoidance of Sectarian Stagnation: A Study of Church, Sect, and Incipient Nationality." *American Journal of Sociology* 60:285-93.

————. 1957. *The Mormons.* Chicago: University of Chicago Press.

————. 1966a. Foreword to *Deseret Saints,* by Nels Anderson. Chicago: University of Chicago Press.

————. 1966b. *The Sociology of Religion.* Foundation of Modern Sociology Series. Englewood Cliffs, N.J.: Prentice-Hall.

_____. 1968. "Sects and Cults." In *International Encyclopedia of the Social Sciences*. Vol. 14, pp. 130-36. Edited by David L. Sills. New York: Macmillan Co./Free Press.

_____. 1972. "The Mormons: Church and People." In *Plural Society in the Southwest*, pp. 115-65. Edited by Edward M. Spicer and Raymond H. Thompson. Albuquerque: University of New Mexico Press.

ONG, WALTER J. 1967. "Peter Ramus." In *The Encyclopedia of Philosophy*, vol. 7:66-68. Edited by Paul Edwards. New York: Macmillan Publishing Co.

ORR, JAMES. 1913. "Calvinism." In *Encyclopaedia of Religion and Ethics*, 12 vols. Edited by James Hastings. New York: Charles Scribner's Sons. 1913-22. Vol. 2, pp. 146-55.

PAGDEN, ANTHONY. 1982. *The Fall of Natural Man: The American Indian and the Origins of Comparative Ethnology*. Cambridge Iberian and Latin American Studies. Cambridge: Cambridge University Press.

PARK, ROBERT E., and BURGESS, ERNEST W. 1924. *Introduction to the Science of Sociology*. 2d ed. Chicago: University of Chicago Press.

PARKIN, MAX H. 1966. "The Nature and Causes of Internal and External Conflict of the Mormons in Ohio between 1830 and 1838." Master's thesis, Brigham Young University.

PARSONS, TALCOTT. 1961. "Introduction, Part Two: Differentiation and Variation in Social Structures." In *Theories of Society: Foundations of Modern Sociological Theory*, pp. 239-64. Edited by Talcott Parsons, Edward Shils, Kaspar D. Naegele, and Jesse R. Pitts. New York: Free Press of Glencoe.

PARTRIDGE, SCOTT H. 1972. "The Failure of the Kirtland Safety Society." *Brigham Young University Studies* 12:437-54.

PESSEN, EDWARD. 1969. *Jacksonian America: Society, Personality, and Politics*. Homewood, Ill.: Dosey Press.

_____. 1971. "The Egalitarian Myth and the American Social Reality: Wealth, Mobility, and Equality in the 'Era of the Common Man'." *American Historical Review* 76:989-1034.

PETERSON, CHARLES. 1977. *Utah: A Bicentennial History*. New York: W. W. Norton & Co.

PGP. [PEARL OF GREAT PRICE.] 1981. *Pearl of Great Price: A Selection from the Revelations, Translations, and Narrations of Joseph Smith, First Prophet, Seer, and Revelator of the Church of Jesus Christ of Latter-day Saints*. Salt Lake City, Utah: Church of Jesus Christ of Latter-day Saints.

PIXLEY, B. 1958. "New Jerusalem: Letter from Independence." In *Among the Mormons: Historic Accounts by Contemporary Observers*, pp. 72-75. Edited by W. Mulder and A. R. Mortensen. New York: Alfred A. Knopf.

PLATT, FREDERIC. 1913. "Arminianism." In *Encyclopaedia of Religion and Ethics*. 12 vols. Edited by James Hastings. New York: Charles Scribner's Sons, 1913-22. Vol. 1, pp. 807-16.

POPE, ROBERT G. 1969. *The Half-Way Covenant: Church Membership in Puritan New England*. Princeton, N.J.: Princeton University Press.

Pottowattamie High Council Minutes Book. 1846-1852. Microfilm. Historical Archives.

PRATT, PARLEY P. 1837. *A Voice of Warning and Instruction to All People, Containing a Declaration of the Faith and Doctrine of the Church of Latter-day Saints, Commonly Called Mormons*. New York: W. Sanford.

_____. 1855. *Key to the Science of Theology: Designed as an Introduction to the First Principles of Spiritual Philosophy; Religion; Law and Government; as Delivered by the Ancients, and as Restored in This Age, for the Final Development of Universal Peace, Truth, and Knowledge*. Liverpool: F. D. Richards.

PRATT, STEVEN. 1975. "Eleanor McClean and the Murder of Parley P. Pratt." *Brigham Young University Studies* 15:225-56.

Prepare Ye the Way of the Lord: Melchizedek Priesthood Personal Study Guide 1978-79. Salt Lake City, Utah: Church of Jesus Christ of Latter-day Saints.

QUINN, D. MICHAEL. 1973. "Organizational Development and Social Origins of the Mormon Hierarchy, 1832-1932: A Prosopographical Study." Master's thesis, University of Utah.

————. 1976. "The Mormon Succession Crisis of 1844." *Brigham Young University Studies* 16:187-233.

————. 1978. "Latter-day Saint Prayer Circles." *Brigham Young University Studies* 19:79-105.

————. 1980. "The Council of Fifty and Its Members, 1844 to 1845." *Brigham Young University Studies* 20:163-97.

————. 1981. "Joseph Smith III's Blessings and the Mormons of Utah." *John Whitmer Historical Association Journal* 1:12-27. (Woodworth statement made in 1861.)

————. 1985. "LDS Church Authority and the New Plural Marriage, 1890-1904." *Dialogue: A Journal of Mormon Thought* 18:1:9-105.

RABER, MICHAEL S. 1978. "Religious Polity and Local Production: The Origins of a Mormon Town." Ph.D. dissertation, Yale University.

————. 1980. "Production and Distribution in Early Mormon Utah: The Limits to Regional Autonomy." Paper presented at the 15th annual meeting, Mormon History Association, Canandaigua, New York, 1-4 May 1980.

RADCLIFFE-BROWN, ALFRED R. 1965. *Structure and Function in Primitive Society: Essays and Addresses*. Foreword by E. E. Evans-Pritchard and Fred Eggan. New York: Free Press.

REMINI, ROBERT V. 1976. *The Revolutionary Age of Andrew Jackson*. New York: Harper & Row.

RICHARDSON, ALEXANDER. 1629. *The Logician's School-Master: Or a Comment Vpon Ramvs Logicke*. London: Printer for Iohn Bellamsie, at the Three Golden Lyons in Cornhill.

RIGDON, SIDNEY. 1838. *Oration Delivered by Mr. S. Rigdon on the 4th of July, 1838. At Far West, Caldwell County, Missouri*. Far West, Mo.: Journal Office.

ROBERTS, BRIGHAM HENRY. 1957. *A Comprehensive History of the Church of Jesus Christ of Latter-day Saints*. 6 vols. Provo, Utah: Brigham Young University Press. First published in 1930.

ROCKWOOD, ALBERT PERRY. 1988. "The Last Months of Mormonism in Missouri: The Albert Perry Rockwood Journal." Edited by Dean C. Jessee and David J. Whittaker. *Brigham Young University Studies* 28:5-41. (Journal entries 6 Oct. 1838-30 January 1839).

ROLLINS, MARY LIGHTNER ROLLINS CARTER. N.d. "Family Record Book of Mary Lightner Rollins Carter Rollins." Photocopy of original ms. Historical Archives.

ROSENBERG, CARROLL SMITH. 1971. "Beauty, the Beast, and the Militant Woman: A Case Study of Sex Roles and Social Stress in Jacksonian America." *American Quarterly* 23:563-84.

————. 1972. "The Hysterical Woman: Sex Roles and Role Conflict in 19th Century America." *Social Research* 39:652-78.

RUPP, I. DANIEL, comp. 1844. *An Original History of the Religious Denominations at the Present in the United States. Containing Authentic Accounts of Their Rise, Progress, Statistics and Doctrine. Written Expressly for the Present Work by Eminent Theological Professors, Ministers, and Lay-Members of the Respective Denominations*. Philadelphia: J. Y. Humphreys.

RUTMAN, DARRETT B. 1970. *American Puritanism: Faith and Practice*. New York: J. B. Lippincott Co.

_____. 1972. *Winthrop's Boston: A Portrait of a Puritan Town, 1630-1649*. New York: W. W. Norton. First published in 1965.

SAMPSON, D. PAUL, and WIMMER, LARRY T. 1972. "The Kirtland Safety Society: The Stock Ledger Book and the Bank Failure." *Brigham Young University Studies* 12:427-36.

SCHLESINGER, ARTHUR M., JR. 1945. *The Age of Jackson*. Boston: Little, Brown, & Co.

SCHNEIDER, DAVID M. 1968. *American Kinship: A Cultural Account*. Englewood Cliffs, N.J.: Prentice-Hall.

_____. 1969. "Kinship, Nationality, and Religion in American Culture: Toward a Definition of Kinship." In American Ethnological Society. *Forms of Symbolic Action: Proceedings of the 1969 Spring Meeting*, pp. 116-25. Edited by Robert F. Spencer. Seattle: University of Seattle Press for American Ethnological Society. Distributed.

_____. 1972. "What is Kinship All About?" In *Kinship Studies in the Morgan Centennial Year*, pp. 32-63. Edited by Priscilla C. Reining. Washington, D.C.: Anthropological Society of Washington.

_____. 1976. "Notes toward a Theory of Culture." In *Meaning in Anthropology*, pp. 197-220. Edited by Keith H. Basso and Henry A. Selby. Albuquerque: University of New Mexico Press.

_____. 1979. "Kinship, Community, and Locality in American Culture." In *Kin and Communities: Families in America*, pp. 155-74. Edited by Allan J. Lichtman and Joan R. Challinor. Washington, D.C.: Smithsonian Institution Press.

SCHNEIDER, HERBERT W. 1958. *The Puritan Mind*. Ann Arbor Paperback ed. N.p.: University of Michigan Press. First published in 1930.

SCOTT, W. RICHARD. 1981. *Organizations: Rational, Natural and Open System*. Englewood Cliffs, N.J.:Prentice-Hall.

The Seer. 1853-1854. Vol. 1, no. 1 (January 1853)-Vol. 2, no. 6 (June 1854), Washington, D.C. Vol. 2, no. 8 (August 1854), Liverpool.

SHAPIRO, R. GARY, comp. 1977. *An Exhaustive Concordance of The Book of Mormon, Doctrine and Covenants, and Pearl of Great Price*. Salt Lake City, Utah: Hawkes.

SHILS, EDWARD. 1975. *Center and Periphery: Essays in Macrosociology*. Chicago: University of Chicago Press.

SHIPPS, JAN. 1974. "The Prophet Puzzle: Suggestions Leading Toward a More Comprehensive Interpretation of Joseph Smith." *Journal of Mormon History* 1:3-20.

_____. 1985. *Mormonism: The Story of a New Religious Tradition*. Urbana: University of Illinois Press.

SKLAR, KATHRYN. 1973. *Catherine Beecher: A Study in Domesticity*. New Haven: Yale University Press.

SMITH, H. SHELTON. 1955. *Changing Conceptions of Original Sin: A Study in American Theology Since 1750*. New York: Charles Scribner's Sons.

SMITH, HYRUM MACK, and SJODAHL, JANNE M., eds. 1965. *The Doctrine and Covenants: Containing Revelations Given to Joseph Smith Jr., the Prophet, with an Introduction and Historical and Exegetical Notes by Hyrum M. Smith of the Council of the Twelve Apostles and Janne M. Sjodahl*. Rev. ed. Salt Lake City, Utah: Deseret Book Co. First published in 1919.

SMITH, JOSEPH, JR. 1839. Letter of Sidney Rigdon, Joseph Smith and Hyrum Smith to H. C. Kimball and B. Young, 16 January 1839. Microfilm. Kimball Family Correspondence Collection. Historical Archives.

_____. 1970. *Joseph Smith's "New Translation" of the Bible*. Introduction by F. Henry Evans. Independence, Mo.: Herald Publishing House.

_____. 1980. *The Words of Joseph Smith: The Contemporary Accounts of the Nauvoo Discourses of the Prophet Joseph*. Religious Studies Monograph # 6. Compiled and edited by Andrew F. Ehat and Lyndon W. Cook. Foreword by Truman G. Madsen. Provo, Utah: Religious Studies Center, Brigham Young University.

_____. 1984. *The Personal Writings of Joseph Smith*. Compiled and edited by Dean C. Jessee. Salt Lake City, Utah: Deseret Book Co.

SMITH, JOSEPH FIELDING. 1942. *Essentials in Church History*. 9th ed. Salt Lake City, Utah: Deseret News Press. First published in 1922.

_____. 1958. *The Way to Perfection: Short Discourses on Gospel Themes*. 11th ed. Salt Lake City, Utah: Genealogical Society of the Church of Jesus Christ of Latter-day Saints. First published in 1931-32.

SMITH, LUCY MACK. ca. 1910. "A Gospel Letter, Written by Sister Lucy Mack Smith, the Mother of the Prophet Joseph Smith." In *Scrap Book of Mormon Literature, Religious Tracts*, Vol. 2:543-45. Edited by Ben E. Rich. Chicago: Ben E. Rich. (Letter written 6 Jan. 1831.)

_____. 1958. *History of Joseph Smith by His Mother, Lucy Mack Smith*. With notes and comments by Preston Nibley. Salt Lake City, Utah: Bookcraft. First published in 1853.

SMITH, RUBY K. 1954. *Mary Bailey*. Salt Lake City, Utah: Deseret Book Co.

SMITH, WILLIAM ROBERTSON. 1882. *The Prophets of Israel and Their Place in History to the Close of the Eighth Century B.C.* Edinburgh: A. and C. Black.

_____. 1885. *Kinship and Marriage in Early Arabia*. Cambridge: Cambridge University Press.

SNOW, ELIZA R. 1846-1849. Journal. Microfilm. Historical Archives.

SNOW, ERASTUS. 1818–1837. "E. Snows Sketch Book No. 1." 1818-Dec. 1837. Microfilm. Erastus Snow Collection. Historical Archives.

_____. 1847. "E Snow's Journal continued from last Page of Book 2d." Diary, 22 June to ca. February 1847. Microfilm. Erastus Snow Collection. Historical Archives.

SOMKIN, FRED. 1967. *Unquiet Eagle: Memory and Desire in the Idea of American Freedom, 1815-1860*. Ithaca, New York: Cornell University Press.

SPENCER, ORSON. 1847. *Letters by Orson Spencer, A.B., In Reply to the Rev. William Crowel, A.M. Editor of the Christian Watchman, Boston, Massachusetts, U.S.A. Letter IX: The Priesthood*. Liverpool: R. James, Printer.

_____. 1848. *Letters Exhibiting the Most Prominent Doctrines of the Church of Jesus Christ of Latter-day Saints. By Orson Spencer, A.B., President of the Church of L.D.S., in Europe. In Reply to the Rev. William Crowel, A.M., Boston, Massachusetts, U.S.A. "The Wise Shall Understand." Daniel*. Liverpool: Orson Spencer. First published in 1842-47.

_____. 1853. *Patriarchal Order, or Plurality of Wives! By Elder Orson Spencer, A.B., Chancellor of the University of Deseret, Utah Territory, U.S.A., and President of the Prussian Mission of the Church of Jesus Christ of Latter-day Saints. Being His Fifteenth Letter in Correspondence with the Rev. William Crowel, A.M. , Editor of the "Western Watchman," St. Louis, U.S.A. (Late Editor of the "Christian Watchman," Boston, Massachusetts*. Liverpool: S. W. Richards.

STAVELY, KEITH W. F. 1987. *Puritan Legacies: "Paradise Lost" and the New England Tradition, 1630-1890*. Ithaca, N.Y.: Cornell University Press.

STOCKING, GEORGE W., JR. 1968. *Race, Culture, and Evolution: Essays in the History of Anthropology*. New York: Free Press.

————. 1984. Ed. *Functionalism Historicized: Essays on British Social Anthropology*. History of Anthropology Vol. 2. Madison, Wis.: University of Wisconsin Press.

————. 1986. Ed. *Malinowski, Rivers, Benedict, and Others: Essays on Culture and Personality*. History of Anthropology Vol. 4. Madison, Wis.: University of Wisconsin Press.

————. 1987. *Victorian Anthropology*. New York: Free Press.

————. Ed. 1988. *Bones, Bodies, Behavior: Essays on Biological Anthropology*. History of Anthropology Vol. 5. Madison, Wis.: University of Wisconsin Press.

STOUT, HOSEA. 1969. *On the Mormon Frontier: The Diary of Hosea Stout 1844-1861*. 2 vols. Edited by Juanita Brooks. Salt Lake City, Utah: University of Utah Press, Utah State Historical Society.

SWEET, WILLIAM WARREN. 1952. *Religion in the Development of American Culture, 1765-1840*. New York: Charles Scribner's Sons.

TANNER, N. ELDON. 1979. "No Greater Honor: The Woman's Role." In *Woman* [no editor or compiler], pp. 4-12. Salt Lake City, Utah: Deseret Book Co.

[THAYER, JAMES B.] 1953. "An After-Clap of Puritanism." In Mulder and Mortensen 1953:382-84.

TINNEY, THOMAS MILTON. 1973. *The Royal Family of the Prophet Joseph Smith, Jr.* N.p.: Thomas Milton Tinney.

TOON, PETER, ed. 1970. *Puritans, The Millennium and the Future of Israel: Puritan Eschatology 1600 to 1660*. Cambridge, England: J. Clarke and Co.

TS. *Times and Seasons*. 1839-1846. Vol. 1, no. 1 (November 1839)–Vol. 6, no. 3 (February 1846), Nauvoo, Ill.

TULLIDGE, EDWARD W., ed. 1877. *The Women of Mormondom*. New York: Tullidge & Crandall.

TURNER, VICTOR. 1974. *Dramas, Fields, and Metaphors: Symbolic Action in Human Society*. Ithaca, N.Y.: Cornell University Press.

TYLER, ALICE FELT. 1962. *Freedom's Ferment: Phases of American Social History from the Colonial Period to the Outbreak of the Civil War*. New York: Harper & Row. First published in 1944.

[UTAH TERRITORY LEGISLATIVE ASSEMBLY.] 1852. *Acts, Resolutions, and Memorials, Passed by the First Annual, and Special Sessions, of the Legislative Assembly, of the Territory of Utah, Begun and Held at Great Salt Lake City, on the 22nd Day of September, A.D., 1851. Also the Constitution of the United States, and the Act Organizing the Territory of Utah*. G[reat] S[alt] L[ake] C[ity], U[tah] T[erritory]: [Utah] Legislative Assembly.

VAN WAGONER, RICHARD. 1986. *Mormon Polygamy: A History*. Salt Lake City, Utah: Signature Books.

VOGT, EVON Z., and ALBERT, ETHEL M., eds. 1966. *Peoples of Rimrock: A Study of Values in Five Cultures*. Cambridge: Harvard University Press.

VOGT, EVON Z., and O'DEA, THOMAS F. 1953. "A Comparative Study of the Role of Values in Social Action in Two Southwestern Communities." *American Sociological Review* 18:645-54.

WA. [WESTMINSTER ASSEMBLY OF DIVINES.] 1967. *The Confession of Faith, The Larger and Shorter Catechism, with the Scripture Proofs at Large, Together with the Sum of Saving Knowledge (Contained in the Holy Scripture, and Held Forth in the Said Confession and Catechisms,) and Practical Use Thereof; Covenants, National and Solemn League; Acknowledgment of Sins, and Engagement to Duties; Directories for Publick and Family Worship; Form of Church Government, Etc. Of Publick Authority in the Church of Scotland; With Acts of Assembly and Parliament, Relative to, and Approbative of, the Same; With Special Words of the Proof-Passages*

Printed in Italic Type. Edinburgh: Publication Committee of the Free Presbyterian Church of Scotland. Westminster Confession first issued in 1645-47.

WALKER, WILLISTON. 1960. *The Creeds and Platforms of Congregationalism*. Introduction by Douglas Horton. Philadelphia: Pilgrim Press. First published in 1893.

WE. *Woman's Exponent*. 1872–1914. Vol. 1, no. 1 (June 1872)–Vol. 41, no. 14 (February 1914), Salt Lake City, Utah.

WEBER, MAX. 1958. *From Max Weber: Essays in Sociology*. Translated, edited and with an introduction by Hans H. Gerth and C. Wright Mills. New York: Oxford University Press.

_____. 1968. *Economy and Society: An Outline of Interpretive Sociology*. 3 vols. Edited by Guenther Roth and Claus Wittich. Translated from German by Ephraim Fischoff, Hans Gerth, A. M. Henderson, Ferdinand Kolegar, C. Wright Mills, Talcott Parsons, Max Rheinstein, Guenther Roth, Edward Shils, and Claus Wittich. New York: Bedminster Press. Written 1910-20.

WHITNEY, HELEN MAR KIMBALL. 1881. "Helen Mar Kimball Whitney, Autobiography 1881." Historical Archives.

WHITNEY, HORACE KIMBALL. 1846-1847. Journal. Microfilm. Historical Archives.

WHITNEY, ORSON F. 1884. "The Aaronic Priesthood." *Contributor* 6:1-9.

_____. 1927. *Saturday Night Thoughts: A Series of Dissertations on Scriptural, Historical and Philosophical Themes*. Rev. ed. Salt Lake City, Utah: Deseret Book Co. First published in 1921.

WILCOX, LINDA. 1980. "The Mormon Concept of a Mother in Heaven." *Sunstone* 5:5:9-15.

WILSON BRYAN R. 1959. "An Analysis of Sect Development." *American Sociological Review* 24:3-15.

WINTHROP, JOHN. 1964. "A Modell of Christian Charity." In *The Founding of Massachusetts: Historians and the Sources*, pp. 190-204. Edited by Edmund S. Morgan. Indianapolis: Bobbs-Merrill Co.

WOLF, ERIC R. 1959. "Specific Aspects of Plantation Systems in the New World: Community Sub-Cultures and Social Classes." In *Plantation Systems of the New World: Papers and Discussion Summaries of the Seminar Held in San Juan, Puerto Rico*. Social Science Monograph no. 7, pp. 136-47. Washington, D.C.: Pan American Union.

WOLFINGER, HENRY J. 1971. "A Reexamination of the Woodruff Manifesto in the Light of Utah Constitutional History." *Utah Historical Quarterly* 39:328-49.

WOOD, GORDON S. 1980. "Evangelical America and Early Mormonism." *New York History: Quarterly Journal of New York State Historical Association* 61:359-86.

WOODRUFF, WILFORD. 1833-1898. Journal. Microfilm. Special Collections, Harold B. Lee Library, Brigham Young University, Provo, Utah.

WOTTON, ANTHONY. 1626. *The Art of Logick. Gathered Out of Aristotle and Set in Due Forme, According to His Instructions, by Peter Ramus, Professor of Philosophy and Rheterick in Paris and There Martyred for the Gospell of the Lord Iesus. With a Short Exposition of the Praecepts by Which Any One of Indifferent Capacitie May with a Little Paines Attaine to Some Competent Knowledge and Use of that Noble and Necessary Science. Published for the Instruction of the Unlearned by Anthony Wotton*. London: I. D. for Nicholas Bourne.

YORGASON, LAURENCE M. 1974. "Some Demographic Aspects of One Hundred Early Mormon Converts, 1830-37." Master's thesis, Brigham Young University.

YOUNG, BRIGHAM. 1971. *Manuscript History of Brigham Young, 1846-1847.* Edited by Elden J. Watson. Salt Lake City, Utah: Elden J. Watson.

ZARET, DAVID. 1985. *The Heavenly Contract: Ideology and Organization in Pre-Revolutionary Puritanism.* Chicago: University of Chicago Press.

ZIFF, LARZER. 1973. *Puritanism in America: New Culture in a New World.* New York: Viking Press.

ZIMMERMAN, DEAN R. 1976. *I Knew the Prophets: An Analysis of the Letter of Benjamin F. Johnson to George F. Gibbs, Reporting Doctrinal Views of Joseph Smith and Brigham Young.* Bountiful, Utah: Horizon. (Letter written 1903.)

Index